"Offering historical investigation and myriad facts, and complementing that research with personal experiences and stories of human beings, *Incarceration Nations* captures the reader into more inquiry about this vast and critical subject. This is a great read for students of criminal justice, as well as citizens of the world."

—**DEBBIE MUKAMAL**, Executive Director,
Stanford Criminal Justice Center, Stanford Law School

"[*Incarceration Nations*] is a vital work—part memoir, part scholarly excavation—that manages to inspire even as it chronicles some of the world's most horrific places. Dreisinger's long history of work with the currently and formerly incarcerated is the perfect background and material for weaving an account that asks all of the right questions, setting us on a path while acknowledging that answers are really just the ground for asking anew."

—**GINA DENT**, Associate Professor, Feminist Studies,
University of California, Santa Cruz

"Through trenchant and deeply arresting prose, Professor Dreisinger places a microscope on the now global phenomenon of American-style incarceration, forcing us to confront the collectively authored catastrophes we'd rather look away from. Through it all, Dreisinger places unflinching emphasis on prison's greatest offense: the destruction of human life."

—**GLENN E. MARTIN**, Founder and President, JustLeadershipUSA

"If you are asking yourself, How do we end the dehumanizing impact of prisons? How do we abolish, reform, or educate our way out of this twenty-first-century barbarism deceptively dubbed 'criminal justice'? We definitely can't do it without listening to those who continue to be kidnapped from our communities around the country and caged. But what if we take it a step further and give a critical look and listen to folks behind bars the world over? What can we learn about our own humanity—or lack thereof—from a global dialogue with *Incarceration Nations*? Just turn the page..."

—**BRYONN BAIN**, artist and Assistant Professor in Residence, UCLA,
Founder of International Day of Action and Dialogue on Prison Activism

Also by Baz Dreisinger

Near Black: White-to-Black Passing in American Culture

INCARCERATION NATIONS

A Journey to Justice
in Prisons Around the World

Baz Dreisinger

Other Press
New York

Production editor: Yvonne E. Cárdenas
Text designer: Julie Fry
This book was set in Quiosco and Serifa by
Alpha Design & Composition of Pittsfield, NH.

10 9 8 7 6 5 4 3 2 1

Library of Congress Cataloging-in-Publication Data

Dreisinger, Baz, 1976- author.
    Incarceration nations : a journey to justice in prisons around the
world / Baz Dreisinger.
        pages cm
    ISBN 978-1-59051-727-7 (hardcover) — ISBN 978-1-59051-
728-4 (e-book)   1. Imprisonment.   2. Corrections.
3. Discrimination in criminal justice administration.
4. Criminal justice, Administration of.   I. Title.
    HV8705.D74 2016
    365—dc23
                                                2015018691

Disclaimer: The names of many individuals mentioned in this
book have been changed to protect their privacy.

For my Prison-to-College Pipeline students—
my teachers, my inspirations, my family

*Anthony, Carl B, Carl L, Craig, Dale,
Devon, Domingo, Gerrard, Johnny, Joseph C,
Joseph L, Joseph T, Juan, Justin, Kenneth,
Kevin, Korey, Lenny, Lumumba, Marcus,
Matthew, Melvin, Rasheen, Richard, Robert,
Robert T, Rory, Rowland, Sean, Shawnon,
Theron, Tomas, Vinicio, Will*

Sometimes I think this whole world is one big prison yard.
Some of us are prisoners, some of us are guards. —Bob Dylan

Contents

Introduction

Here there is a world apart, unlike everything else, with laws of its own, its own dress, its own manners and customs, and here is the house of the living dead—life as nowhere else and a people apart. —Fyodor Dostoyevsky

"*Mzungu!*" The prison guard growls, beckoning me with the Swahili term for "white person."

Shit.

I'd been trying to blend in, though that's an absurd aspiration for a white girl in a Kampala slum. I'm poised outside the side gate of Luzira Maximum Security Prison, a rambling complex built to accommodate six hundred but currently home to an estimated five thousand men, women, children, and death-row prisoners. Strapping on my inner bulletproof vest, I approach the Uzi.

"What do you want here?" comes the growl again.

With a plastered-on smile, I string together a sentence involving the words "volunteer," "please," "sir," and "thank you." The growling guard flicks my words away with his wrist, shooing me off as if I'm a stubborn mosquito.

Five minutes later I am back, prostrated before him with my fellow volunteer. Having worked here for four months now, she, unlike me, actually saw her paperwork properly processed by the prison powers-that-be and was thus legal to enter Luzira. I'd been mostly slipping in on the sly, having been given unofficial permission to be here—in the form of a "you may enter and you may teach" from the head officer on duty last week—but granted no papers to prove it.

Two grovelers work better than one. With enough kowtowing and "please, sirs," and "sorry, sirs," we bow our way beyond the Uzis and into the prison complex, through the shantytown-like living quarters of the prison officers, past the military barracks and the central gate where the guards wave us inside, into the throngs of men milling about in sunshine-yellow uniforms, and through the concrete door of—a little library.

"Good afternoon, Professor Baz!"

It's the best greeting I've gotten all day—no, all week. Uganda has proven to be many things but welcoming isn't one of them; most days I am pleased to get a polite nod from even the hotel concierge, a professional at the art of service with a scowl. This greeting comes from a prisoner, Bafaki Wilson, aka Headmaster Wilson, aka Pastor Boma, all of which means that Wilson is a kind of peer-elected prison official. He's pastor of the "Boma" block of Luzira and lord of this library, erected by the London- and Kampala-based NGO African Prisons Project.

"How *are* you today?" Wilson asks, grinning as he always does, and looking long and hard at me with those eyes, surely the kindest eyes in all of Uganda. At thirty years old, Wilson is an uncanny combination of frail old man and lively little boy. His small, slim stature, unfettered smile, and spirited stare, not to mention floppy sun cap, fashioned from the yellow prison-uniform cloth and much too wide for his narrow face, all of these scream "boy." But the wizened old man shines through in Wilson's slow, wounded gait and, most of all, in his style of speech. Every sentence emerges slow and studied, finely crafted with pronouncements, as if lifted from the transcript of a Martin Luther King sermon.

"Wilson, I am well," I answer. Conjuring up my second smile of the day, this one genuine, I shake his hand. Then I make the rounds, greeting a dozen students with handshakes and broad hellos. They're assembled around a wooden table in the center of the blocklike library, scribbling on loose-leaf paper or flipping through random books they aren't really reading: *Speaking Norwegian*, *Hamlet*, *A Traveller's Guide to the English Countryside*.

Creative writing class is under way. Wilson sits to my left and reads, with studied enunciation, from the Maya Angelou poems I'd handed out yesterday:

> *You may write me down in history*
> *With your bitter, twisted lies,*
> *You may trod me in the very dirt*
> *But still, like dust, I'll rise.*

During my first class in Luzira I'd assigned the men personal essays, and Wilson told his tale. From rural Uganda, he was born into a polygamous marriage that produced over sixty children. His mother died when he was a baby and he was abused by his stepmothers, so he ran away. He committed crimes; he was too poor to pay either the fine or the bribe that could get him off the hook for these crimes. So he became one of the 35,000 Ugandans behind bars, living in prisons at six times their capacity—prisons created almost a century ago by former colonizers who used them as a form of social control and intimidation. More than a year later, Wilson has yet to be tried; this is not surprising, considering more than half of Uganda's prison population consists of pretrial detainees. Wilson took it in stride. He eventually found faith behind bars, transforming himself into Pastor Boma.

Did you want to see me broken?
Bowed head and lowered eyes?
Shoulders falling down like teardrops.
Weakened by my soulful cries.

Applause. "Baz, I must tell you," Pastor Boma begins. "This is indeed a beautiful poem. And indeed it speaks to our experience directly here, in this prison." The other students nod solemnly.

We spend two more hours indulging in pretty words. The class gaily crafts and shares their own poems; Wilson's, entitled "The Liberator," is a lament about the dictators who have lorded over East Africa, followed by a declaration of faith in Uganda's triumphant future. Another student writes a poem that begins, "AIDS, oh AIDS, why have you taken my family?"

When it's time to go, I gather up my papers and give Wilson another firm handshake, wishing him a good night's sleep.

"It is never a good night here, Baz. And there is no room to sleep." He says this with a radiant smile.

I step out of the library and arm myself, emotionally, for the world outside. Crime is a reality in Kampala, but it's the city's omnipresent security that really rattles me. East African terrorist organizations, like the one behind a bombing in 2010 that killed seventy-six people, are a persistent threat, so the country can feel like a ticking time bomb, laden with armed guards and military checks. Daily life here often feels like a grand obstacle course. Prison guards, then the dreaded *mzungu*-walk through the slum. Hoping today's taximan will show up and not leave me stranded; assuming he does show up, renegotiating a price we've already negotiated twice this morning. Kampala traffic, Kampala sweat, Kampala scowls, car-bomb checks, metal detectors. More guards growling and more Uzis and security checks, back at the hotel. Exhale.

No one said this global journey would be smooth.

––––

I'd recently embarked on a two-year pilgrimage to prisons around the world.

When I told folks I was going to take this voyage, most found it curious. I'm accustomed to people finding me curious, given my peculiar blend of identities. I'm a white English professor specializing in African-American cultural studies, a Caribbean carnival lover who is also a prison educator and criminal justice activist, a freelance producer for National Public Radio, a reggae fanatic, an agnostic New York Jew. I've worked as a journalist, a music critic, and an academic, and have produced two documentaries about hip-hop and the justice system.

I am curious because I am insatiably curious—which is how I ended up immersed in such diverse worlds. When I become fascinated by something, I delve in, headfirst and with zeal. When I fell in love with Jamaican reggae, for instance, I couldn't just be a fan; I had to become a sort of scholar of the music and frequenter of the country. And that fervent curiosity is what landed me in a Ugandan prison, armed with Angelou.

Growing up, prison was neither a fantasyland nor an everyday reality to me. I was raised in the Bronx, New York, bred, like so many others in my city during the 1980s and '90s, on hip-hop and reggae. I attended the City University of New York (CUNY), a massive public institution that's also massively diverse—one branch boasts of a student body representing 160 countries and speaking 127 languages. Like New York itself, CUNY cultivated my identity as a global citizen, molded by the multiplicity of cultures around me.

When I pursued my PhD in English I focused on African-American studies, specifically the boundaries of race in American culture: how these boundaries get drawn, who draws them, who boldly crosses them. Why did I focus on this? Because the very fact of race didn't make sense to me. I didn't understand how our world could be governed in so many social and political respects by an entity that's a construct and not a biological reality. There are more genetic similarities among so-called races than differences, so why does everyone seem to think these artificial categories are natural? Needing to explore this question led to my first book, a social history of real and fictional white people who passed as black.

Many of the book's ideas about racial crossover, hip-hop culture, the question of cultural ownership, and what it means to "claim" an identity reached outside academia, dovetailing with pop culture and the racial-musical zeitgeist of the early 2000s, the Eminem era. Then, during a year as a postdoctoral fellow at UCLA, for a *New York Times Magazine* cover story I interviewed nearly every rapper I'd ever wanted to meet and toured with Snoop Dogg; I convinced a *Los Angeles Times* editor who'd insisted that reggae had died with Bob Marley to let me write about contemporary Jamaican artists.

One of these artists was Jah Cure, a Rastafarian reggae star who'd become famous while serving an eight-year prison sentence for rape. I flew to Kingston, Jamaica, to negotiate with officials for interview access in prison, but was never granted it. My story eventually ran anyway because I couldn't let it go; I became riveted by Cure's case. He claimed innocence and said he was discriminated against because he is Rastafarian, which still carries a stigma in certain Caribbean class circles—but I also couldn't reconcile how this man, who sings some of the most beautiful, spiritual love songs I'd ever heard, could possibly have committed such a vile act. If he did, should he have the right to release music from behind bars? Playing his songs over and over again, I grappled with big questions about the complexities of human nature and the purpose of prison. Was it about correction or punishment? If liberty is the only right lost when one lands in prison, shouldn't Cure's music be permitted to roam free? And if he is guilty, I reflected, might his breathtaking love songs be a kind of public apology—a form of reparation, even?

These musings gripped me. And they came up again in two more pieces I published, one profiling a New York Police Department detective who founded a unit to monitor rappers and became known as the hip-hop cop, and another a *Los Angeles Times* cover story about the rising trend of rappers releasing albums while incarcerated. While in Los Angeles I partnered with a filmmaker to turn these two articles into documentaries, which eventually aired on various cable networks. Both were pop films designed for mainstream audiences. But questions about fundamental justice stayed lodged in my consciousness, so my research—especially for *Rhyme & Punishment*, which is essentially Prison Studies 101 meets

Hip-Hop Studies 101—started me on a serious and in-depth course of study.

As soon as I began looking, devastating statistics were easy to uncover. America is the world's largest jailer, with 2.3 million people behind bars, or one in one hundred adults. With 5 percent of the world's population, we're home to nearly 25 percent of its prison population. One in thirty-one adults, or seven million, are under some form of correctional control; up to 25 percent of the adult prison population suffers from mental illness. Swathes of our prisoners are serving long, hard time for drug offenses. In federal prison, that's 51 percent—only 4 percent are in for robbery and a mere 1 percent for homicide—and in the state system, 20 percent, larger than any other category of offense. Some 3,700 Americans who have never committed a violent crime are serving twenty-five years to life in California alone. Our country considers juveniles too immature to vote or buy alcohol but mature enough to live in adult prisons, where one in ten is sexually assaulted. Fourteen states have no rule against trying those under fourteen as adults.

I found myself confronting the mind-boggling racial inequities. More African Americans are under criminal supervision today than were enslaved in 1850. Blacks are six times more likely to be imprisoned than whites; as of 2001, one in six black men had been incarcerated. By the time he or she turns eighteen, one in four black children will have experienced the imprisonment of a parent. Ninety-four percent of children in America's family court system are black or Latino. Multiple studies have shown that blacks are treated less fairly than whites at all stages of the justice process, from pretrial detention decisions to prosecutorial judgments and decisions about community sanctions as opposed to prison sentences. A 2015 *New York Times* story reported on the "1.5 million missing black men" in America—"missing" because more than one in six black men aged twenty-four to fifty-four have disappeared from civic life, having died young or been sent to prison.

The length of our sentences also sets America apart. Just 20 percent of countries have life without parole sentences at all; the United States does even for single, nonviolent offenses. There are about 160,000 people serving life in the United States, as compared to fifty-nine in Australia, forty-one in England, and thirty-seven in the Netherlands. In 2005, Human Rights Watch counted more than two thousand Americans serving life without parole for crimes committed as juveniles; the entire rest of the world has only ever locked up twelve children without possibility of release. We are one of just nine countries who punish via both life sentences and the death penalty.

I couldn't get these statistics out of my mind. And when I moved back to New York to take a job as an English professor at John Jay College of Criminal Justice, a branch of CUNY where the bulk of the students are preparing for careers in law, social services, and other justice fields—and where I'd be teaching interdisciplinary courses about race, crime, and culture—the philosophical questions that consumed me now made their way into my classroom.

At the same time, letters from prison were making their way into my office. Penned by people who read my articles or saw my films, the letters were lengthy and handwritten: lives on paper, unasked-for confessions, intricate handmade cards. One of them came from the president of Latino en Progresso, a prisoner-run organization at Shawangunk Correctional Facility, and contained an invitation to be the speaker at their annual luncheon. I accepted.

I'd been in a prison visiting room before, but it was my first time visiting a prison as a volunteer, engaging in serious intellectual work with human beings living behind bars. I gave a talk about the social construction of race, reading excerpts from James Baldwin, Ralph Ellison, and others. Then I put my notes down and opened the floor to dialogue. Questions came at me with full force, a barrage of thoughtful critiques informed by learned references. The hours flew by, and too quickly it was time for the men to return to their cells and for me to exit the prison gates to freedom.

When I made that exit into the frosty air of upstate New York, a heavy burden weighed down my heart. I wasn't surprised that some of America's best and brightest were behind its bars. But for the first time, I felt irrevocably pained by this reality. I am not naive; I know that many of these men in green uniforms committed awful acts. But still I saw among them vast possibility, a collection of potentially great contributors to society. Why would we allow our greatest resource, our own brilliant citizens, to languish away in prison cells?

Around the same time, I was regularly trekking up to another facility to visit a friend spending his entire twenties in prison. He was practicing Judaism there, and I devoted many an hour to convincing prison officials that yes, prayer shawls are on the "permitted items" list. Visiting rooms became added to the list of things about prison around which I could not wrap my brain. That ugly barbed-wire-and-cinderblock structure, cruelly plunked in the midst of a Norman Rockwell-esque country landscape. The families mechanically lining up to show their IDs in exchange for time playing Scrabble with their fathers or husbands. The smell of the visiting room (ham sandwiches and nachos from the vending machines, heated up in a dated microwave); the sound of the visiting room (muffled echoes of change being deposited, sodas being cracked open); the surreal scene that is the prison visiting room: lockboxes of human emotion, thoroughly abnormal blends of the painfully public and the passionately private. I could not get over the bizarreness of the whole experience.

My initial curiosity, my instinct that something was very, very wrong with all of this, turned to gut certainty. I started to think, ferociously, about the institution of prison itself.

My students usually took it for granted. "Do the crime, do the time," they'd say. Prison is just a normal consequence of wrongdoing, like losing your voice if you yell too often. But actually prisons are relatively new inventions. Technically they've been around for centuries, but until the nineteenth century they were short-term holding pens for those awaiting trial or people facing minor charges; incarceration was a path to justice as opposed to justice itself. Mass incarceration, meanwhile, is only as old as the 1970s.

During months in the John Jay library I continued the research I'd begun while working on the documentary years earlier. Every revelation left me shaking my head more vigorously. How had I known so little about the evolution of a vital social institution, about pre-prison-era approaches to justice?

Israelites, I discovered, had a *beth ha-asourim* (house of chains) for holding debtors and those awaiting trial. Ancient Greeks and Romans called it a *carcer privitus*; during the Middle Ages a *carcer* was the monastery's room for delinquent clergy. The iconic jails erected in Europe—houses of correction in Amsterdam and Rome, Paris's Bastille, London's Bridewells—were primarily holding pens without distinctive prison architecture. Justice came in other packages, sometimes versions of the biblical eye-for-an-eye approach. In Athens, this meant confiscation of property, stoning, binding to a stake, consigning offenders to the gods via ritual cursing, or barred social interaction. Sub-Saharan Africa dealt with morality breakers by way of beatings, banishment, poison, or reparations of property, but the focus was on victims getting compensated, not offenders being punished. Among the Kikuyu in East Africa, for instance, nine sheep or goats was the price for committing adultery or rape, while one hundred sheep or ten cows was the cost of homicide. Banishment was a centuries-old justice vehicle. Many Africans exiled those who threatened the well-being of the whole community, like accused witches or habitual offenders. Europe made use of penal colonies across the globe. In colonial America, the stocks and the pillory were popular, as were the ducking stool and public whippings; all reflected a focus on public shaming as a form of justice, like the famous scarlet letter worn by Nathaniel Hawthorne's fictional Hester Prynne. China, until the third century, employed beatings and executions, while France, as late as the 1970s, subjected many of its criminals to the guillotine, which turned death into a well-oiled machine and executions into flamboyant spectacles.

During the late eighteenth century, things changed radically. Capitalism was born. Industrialization meant urbanization, which meant poverty and thus more crime. Thanks to the American Revolution, England lost a penal colony. Lawyers, writers, and freethinkers, filled with faith in humanity's capacity for engineering change, envisioned a radically different form of punishment, one that was neater, more contained, more rational—more in line with the so-called Age of Reason. They used the language of hospital reform, also popular at the time, speaking of crime as a contagion that could be methodically, scientifically cured. In the 1750s British magistrate and novelist Henry Fielding proposed "correction of the mind" instead of the body, arguing that solitude and fasting would bring "the most abandoned profligates to reason and order." In 1790 philosopher Jeremy Bentham submitted a vision of an efficient prison called the panopticon to the British parliament. He described a circular, tiered honeycomb of open cells placed around a tower through which residents are perpetually watched; such architecture would allow those running the prison to constantly monitor labor forces. As French philosopher Michel Foucault concludes in his landmark book *Discipline and Punish: The Birth of the Prison*, the world changed spectacularly when it was suddenly "civilized" for those who committed crimes to pay in time and isolation, not physical pain.

This thing we now call prison was very much a product of its era. Like capitalism's temple, the industrial factory, it demanded a distinct architectural look; Bentham's panopticon was in fact modeled after a factory his brother designed for Russia's Catherine the Great. Like capitalism, the prison system hinged on regulation of the body and the strict ordering of time, which came in monetary-like increments, meted out to fit the crime.

Freshly independent, avidly capitalist, and eager to prove itself more progressive than its former colonizer, America keenly lapped up such radical European ideas. And a grand irony was born. The birth of democracy was intricately bound up with the birth of the prison—freedom and the lack thereof in paradoxical union, in the new United States. Thomas Jefferson himself made some of the earliest prison drawings.

On our shores, theory was fast put into practice. During the 1820s the modern prison was truly born, as two competing American models opened their doors. Eastern State Penitentiary in Philadelphia brought Bentham's panopticon to life and employed a "separate system," which meant prisoners were in perpetual solitary confinement. In New York's Auburn Prison, the "silent system" was used. Laboring in factorylike settings, prisoners were whipped if they spoke, just like slaves. Here was another vile irony. Prison slavery was thriving just as the North was fighting to end slavery in the South. After all, the Thirteenth Amendment does not outlaw slavery, but rather makes it illegal *except as a punishment for crime.*

Having perfected its prison model, America exported it. Nineteenth-century European scholars made prison tours a vital stop on their visits across the pond. Fredrick William IV of Prussia was one of these prison tourists, followed by rulers of Saxony, Russia, and the Netherlands, and commissioners from France, Austria, Holland, Denmark, and Sweden. Alexis de Tocqueville and Charles Dickens were the most vocal visitors to US prisons, broadcasting the horror of what they saw there. Dickens called the American prisoner "a man buried alive; to be dug out in the slow round of years; and in the mean time dead to everything but torturing anxieties and horrible despair."

And so prisons weaved their way into the fabric of global culture, throughout Europe and, via its colonies, around the world, from Spain to Colombia, China to Japan and India—all imitating the American model. Which brings us to the modern era, easily encapsulated by two words: mass incarceration. Between 1990 and 2005, a new prison opened in the United States every ten days. How this dramatic shift happened is no great mystery; sociologists trace it back to the 1970s and the war on drugs. In 1980, nineteen of every thousand people arrested for drugs were sent to prison; by 1992, 104 of them were. Criminologist Todd Clear sums up the three trends that produced and sustained prison growth during the 1980s: reduction in the use of nonprison sentencing alternatives, increase in sentence length, and increase in the rate of return to prison for those under community supervision. Growth came in three phases. Phase one involved sending more people to prison; phase two, increasing the length of time they stayed there; phase three, ensuring that they served their full time via what's known as truth-in-sentencing legislation. Age, gender, race, and place, Clear explains, were critical factors. The "war on drugs" criminalized drugs associated with poor minority communities, specifically young black men in devastated neighborhoods, far more than it did "white" drugs, such as cocaine. Thus this "war" was less an attack on substances than a violent assault on racial progress made during the civil rights era, and an effective way to divert the public's attention from growing income inequality. Between 1979 and 1996, after all, 95 percent of wealth went to the richest 5 percent.

Trekking through prison history was a sobering expedition, leaving me feeling as if I'd encountered some insidious, and very expensive, worldwide plot. The United States spends more than $50 billion on corrections. In the past two decades, money spent on prisons has risen at six times the rate of spending on higher education; it costs $88,000 per year to incarcerate a young person—more than eight times the $10,653 to educate her. States spend upward of a million dollars each year incarcerating the residents of certain city blocks, dubbed "million-dollar blocks." Ultimately, money spent on the correctional system exceeds the gross domestic product of 140 foreign countries and is steadily bankrupting several states, which now face government mandates to reduce their prison populations.

Knowing all of this, it became impossible not to do something about it, even if it was a very small something. How could I know and not act? So as the invitations to return to the prison in which I'd given that first talk kept coming, I kept saying yes. And this turned into my starting an unofficial education program there. I taught one-off classes whenever I could, inviting interested colleagues to do the same. I came to know Ramón, the head of that prison Latino organization, quite well. He was an elegant, poised intellect from the Dominican Republic, and he told me at one luncheon that when he entered prison at the age of sixteen, he spoke no English whatsoever. This stunned me, considering I'd just seen him stand at a podium adorned by a Che Guevara poster and deliver a dazzlingly fluent twenty-minute oration about change, growth, and revolution. Ramón also told me that he spent three years in solitary, something I could not begin to comprehend.

While I chatted with Ramón, internally mourning the fact that yet again, here was a man whose tremendous gifts society has denied itself, a superintendent from Otisville Correctional Facility approached me.

"Why doesn't John Jay have a college program in any prison?" he asked.

I took the question home with me and posed it to Jeremy Travis, the president of John Jay College.

"I'd like to start one," I told him. He granted me permission. In 2011, John Jay's Prison-to-College Pipeline (P2CP) was born. It provides college courses and reentry planning services to incarcerated men within five years of release. These men begin their college journey behind bars and then, upon returning home, are guaranteed a slot in the City University of New York, where they complete degrees and embrace a new community. The idea is to make college the centerpiece of their new lives on the outside, so they can benefit from everything that a campus has to offer, from education to network building and free health, counseling, and tutoring services.

I teach English classes in the P2CP program and serve as its academic director. When I first started that job, I had little idea of what I was getting myself into. Running classes inside was in many respects the easy part. My students were so intellectually hungry that being their professor was nothing short of pedagogical heaven. What I was unprepared for was the psychological roller coaster that comes with this work; sometimes the ups and downs hit me with a force that left me emotionally leveled. When my students were denied parole, when they came home and had nowhere to live, when they were rearrested or even shot: these were traumatic events. But seeing a student on campus scurrying to class, when not too long ago he'd been my student in an altogether different setting—there is no greater joy.

Prisons lodged themselves at the heart of my emotional and intellectual universe. Yet still plenty of people in the world around me didn't seem to realize that, quite simply, there is no evidence that they work. It's this simple: prison populations in America have grown steadily since 1973 and do not correlate whatsoever with crime rates. And why *should* prisons work? Studies in probability theory and psychology reveal that deterrence is an illusion. Few people stop committing crimes because prison exists; the reality of its existence hardly factors into their thought process while criminal acts are occurring. As for incapacitation, prisons are schools of crime, and though they may lock people away from the general public, they also eventually return them to the community further criminalized and/or deeply marginalized, socially and economically. This is a recipe for an *increase* in crime, a fact that explains a 2014 NPR headline so counterintuitive it's delicious: "Crime Falls as U.S. Locks Up Fewer People, Attorney General Holder Says." Indeed, between 2007 and 2012, the states with the largest decreases in imprisonment rates had a 12 percent average reduction in crime. This is because of what Todd Clear and others call the "collateral consequences" of incarceration on urban communities. Prison, Clear writes, "has broken families, weakened the social-control capacity of parents, eroded economic strength, soured attitudes toward society, and distorted politics." Children of people in prison have been shown to be more likely to go to prison themselves. And prison time profoundly damages one's social capital and social networks. Can we really expect the manufacturing of such citizens to produce safer communities?

And what of the third justification, the word everyone exalts, rehabilitation? In 1954 the American Prison Association changed its name to the American Correctional Association, and prisons became Correctional Institutions. But programs that "correct" have grown few and far between. Only 6 percent of corrections spending is used to pay for prison programming. Between 60 and 80 percent of our prison population has a history of substance abuse, yet drug-treatment slots inside have declined by more than half since 1993; in 2012, the waiting list for drug abuse treatment in prison was 51,000 applicants long. Between 2004 and 2005 only about one-quarter of people in state prisons were involved in educational programming, fewer than a third were involved in vocational training, and about two-thirds had work assignments. Higher-education programs like mine, dramatically correlated with lower recidivism rates, were decimated in 1994, when incarcerated students were made ineligible for federal and state financial aid. Prison college programs, once numbering around 350, dropped down to seven in the span of a single year.

I knew all of this. I bemoaned it. Yet the thing about curiosity is that if you dwell on it for too long, it can lose its force. I felt this happening. Some of prison's bizarreness had begun to wear off. I was so routinely there and so often immersed in analyzing prison issues, I worried that my thinking had grown stale and that I was beginning to lose perspective. During one conversation with a funder, I caught myself using the words "at home" to describe how I felt in the classroom at Otisville. This appalled me. Did I really feel "at home" in a place once so alien to me?

I decided I needed a shock to the system, to unseat basic truths, to ask myself what I used to get asked all the time, before my world became overwhelmingly filled with people who shared my passions and premises.

Why care so passionately about the so-called wrongdoers of the world?

The plan unfolded in my mind's eye. I would find fresh answers to this question globally, seeing prison anew by seeing it around the world. And seeing the world by seeing its prisons. Invoking Dostoyevsky, Nelson Mandela famously said that "No one truly knows a nation until one has been inside its jails. A nation should not be judged by how it treats its highest citizens, but its lowest ones."

The journey would be a chance to rethink one of America's most impactful national experiments and global exports. Between 2008 and 2011, the prison population grew in 78 percent of all countries. Some 10.3 million people worldwide are behind bars, many convicted of nothing, waiting years to be tried and lacking access to adequate legal assistance. Yet the public conversation rarely seemed to turn from America's incarceration crisis to the global prison problem—something the United States built and then foisted on the world.

Justice should be loud and proud, a transparent system endorsed by all citizens. Yet prisons, the crown jewel of today's international justice system, are anything but transparent. They're invisible spaces, places most never see yet dimly accept as real and right. And how could anyone endorse what cannot be seen? On a very basic level, I felt an urge to expose the hidden places and forgotten people that exist in every country, across the globe. I hoped to be a witness in the world, and make my readers witnesses, too. Such a journey seemed, for myself and for my readers, a moral imperative.

From the get-go I envisioned a trek through human stories. *Human* stories. The language of corrections turns prisons into clinical, sterile spaces: "carceral" places, "correctional facilities" or "behavioral management units" filled with "inmates" and "offenders" serving "sentences" under "wardens." Such language makes it easy to forget that there is nothing facile about a facility. That inside these prisons—day in and day out, for years, for decades, for life—are living, breathing human beings. I wanted myself and others to lay eyes on them, to not look away, just as we could not look away during the crises at Abu Ghraib or Guantánamo, those rare moments when our nation's oubliettes, to borrow a fourteenth-century French term for prison dungeons—it means "forgotten ones"—violently pried their way into public view, demanding that we confront the human detritus of our justice system.

To minimize the inevitable anthropological rubbernecking, I would, when possible, volunteer in the prisons, working and doing instead of watching and writing. I'd take most of the trips during my allotted twelve-month university sabbatical, and fund them through both academic grants and journalism assignments. The assignments covering culture and travel would help, moneywise, but they'd also serve as prompts to explore a country's culture outside the prison walls. And this would deepen my understanding of the big picture, because justice systems and the societies in which they operate are richly intertwined. Prisons are dark mirrors, grand social doppelgängers, profound microcosms: life—distilled, caricatured, intensified.

I selected nine countries that might revolve around themes that defamiliarize foundational concepts about justice and prison, concepts we too often take for granted. After all, at panels and rallies, in newspaper editorials and exposés, I heard plenty of calls for reform, many of them driven by arguments about economics and public safety. These are vital reasons. But what about fundamental *moral* arguments about prison as an ethical concept—where were these in the public discourse? It was time to go back to the theoretical drawing board. I would re-ask the big questions about punishment, redemption, forgiveness, and second chances that had made me a prison activist to begin with and see if I might convert others not just into caring about such questions but—as voting, thinking citizens of a democracy—into becoming potential agents of change, too.

Perhaps I could make my zealous curiosity contagious, for the greater good.

First stop: Rwanda.

1.
Revenge and Reconciliation | *Rwanda*

*You can't have it both ways. You can't befriend that murderer
and expect to be our friend, too.*
—Crime victim to Sister Helen Prejean, *Dead Man Walking*

*See what a scourge is laid upon your hate
That heaven finds means to kill your joy with love.*
—Shakespeare, *Romeo and Juliet*

Brussels Airlines flight 1027 alights gently into the night at Kigali
International Airport. Immigration is a breeze and the lines are
short; Americans don't need visas to enter Rwanda. My suitcase
sits placidly, just outside customs. The man bearing the sign "Golf
Hills Residence" spies me at once and soon we're cramming my bag
into the trunk of his 1991 Nissan Sunny and cruising down remark-
ably traffic-free roads into the city.

Golf Hills sits elevated, above the so-called land of seven hills
in Nyarutirama, a tony Kigali neighborhood. It has the feel of a

suburban-style apartment complex, all russets and browns. As if to compensate for the genericness of everything else, "African" decor abounds: giraffes and tribal prints line the hallways, a leather Africa-shaped key chain holds the key to my room for the next six weeks.

One might suppose that I've launched my prison journey in Rwanda because Africa's prisons are in a dire state. In twenty-seven countries they average 141 percent over capacity. More than one-third of the continent-wide prison population, which comes to at least one million human beings, are held in pretrial detention; this means that in some countries, up to 90 percent of potentially innocent people are living behind bars—where, because most African governments spend little on justice, bribery, drugs, prostitution, and rape are rampant. In 1996, worldwide delegates met in Uganda to draft a report on African prisons, which were deemed to be having scant effect on crime. The result was the Kampala Declaration on Prison Conditions in Africa, which stated that prison conditions were "inhuman" for prisoners and "intolerable" for staff. Prison's overuse, the report concluded, "does not serve the interests of justice, nor does it protect the public, nor is it a good use of scarce public resources."

But I'm not here to dwell on the sensational. Instead, I'm interested in learning how cracks let in light. Across Africa, broken justice systems have produced avenues for radical reform. Crisis can be a synonym for possibility.

And I chose Rwanda, in particular, because one word comes to mind when the world hears "Rwanda." *Genocide.*

The hundred days in 1994 during which Hutus slaughtered nearly a million Tutsis, mostly by hacking or clubbing them to death, still defines this small East African country. It defines it over and above its newly acquired reputation for peace and political, social, and economic prosperity. Indeed, two decades after the killings Rwanda is a model of the so-called new Africa. Under the leadership of President Paul Kagame, Rwanda, Africa's third most-competitive place to do business, was ranked the second-best global reformer in the World Bank Doing Business Report for six years. Its gross domestic product has grown at an annual rate of 7 percent since 2001; literacy rates soar; national health care offers coverage for less than one hundred dollars a year per person.

Rwanda achieved this, goes the narrative, in part because it promoted reconciliation on a grand scale. I'd read about the country's postgenocide *gacaca* courts, community gatherings in which neighbors sorted through the slaughters committed by neighbors and, instead of punishment, determined a system of compensations. I'd heard about the national approach to justice supposedly being returned to its roots, preaching not of punishment but forgiveness and reparations. Genocide compelled the country to rethink its fundamental pillars, its prison system—and justice itself.

Here is a country where hundreds of thousands of victims and their offenders, the people who killed their fathers and mothers and sisters, live side by side, in some sort of reconciliatory state. It made sense to start my journey in this country because all conversations about crime should start not with those who committed the deed—even though that's how we always talk about criminal justice, asking Who did it? and How can we punish them?—but instead with devotion to those innocently impacted by it: the victims. Attention to the wrongdoer should never eclipse attention to the wronged. So before plunging into the global wrongdoer territory of prison, I needed to immerse myself in the pinnacle of wronged territory. Hence, Rwanda.

Determining this, I'd researched Rwandan NGOs, looking for one whose programs impressed me and might afford me access to prison. Such NGOs abound; peace, reconciliation, and rebuilding are the country's mantras and nonprofit selling points. Sifting through many mission statements, I'd gotten stuck on one, an NGO that works with college-age genocide survivors, all under twenty-five, many of them orphans. Some of these survivors, I soon learned from Skype calls and e-mail exchanges with the NGO's founders, want to visit prisons—where about 80 percent of the prisoners have committed the crime of genocide. The youth had talked about starting some sort of prison-visit program, I was told, but it hasn't catalyzed into reality yet. This is where I might fit in.

And so I have landed in Kigali to work with these students, genocide survivors looking to visit prisons filled with genocide committers. What these visits will consist of, what qualifies me to help coordinate them, how I'll overcome the language barrier—all of this is unclear. But I've arrived, inspired by the name of the NGO that struck me the moment I saw it. *Never Again Rwanda* (NAR). If my childhood had two words looming over it, if post-Holocaust American Jewry had two words looming over it, mantralike, they were those two, Never Again. Almost the entirety of my ancestral line was decimated in the Jewish Holocaust. In this connection might lie an entry point.

———

"Kacyiru. At the roundabout in front of the US Embassy, take your first right." I present these directions to James, a stout Rwandan whose English is as good as his Kinyarwanda, thereby making him one of the most coveted taxi drivers in Kigali.

The hotel manager puts an umbrella into my hand before I head out, odd since the skies are luminous. "Trust me," she says.

James pops in his CD. It's Konshens, a rough-tongued Jamaican dancehall artist.

"Too much love," James laughs. "Rwandans like too much love songs. I can't listen to the radio at all."

We find our destination with ease, across from the electric red One Luv Saloon, which might be called the One Seat Saloon, as it's essentially a concrete box with a lace doily for a door and All Star Zone spray-painted across the front wall. I make my way past the Never Again Rwanda sign and through the zinc gate. The offices are spare, with faded beige walls, a wooden desk or two, and several outdated computers. No one seems to be around; all I hear is the faint echo of Konshens, this time trickling out from the One Luv Saloon. I drift to the back room and find executive director Eric Mahoro hunched at his desk in a crisp white shirt and tie. He stands up to offer me a shy handshake and a halting "You are welcome."

"Would you like to meet your project leader?" Eric asks, leading me back to the front office. There stands Dukuzumuremyi Albert, known as Santos. Over six feet tall, twenty-five years old, and gangly, Santos has a languid gait that contradicts his hyperalert eyes.

We sit at an empty desk and get right to business. It's labor to converse. Santos's semifunctional English and my semifunctional French add up to moderately functional dialogue. Rwandan schools began incorporating English training after 1994, so members of the postgenocide generation speak it to varying degrees. Ironically, Rwanda is one of the few linguistically united countries in Africa. Hutus and Tutsis—unlike, say, the dozens of clashing ethnic groups in nearby Kenya—share a common tongue, Kinyarwanda.

Santos and I discuss the legacy of Rwandan prisons. German colonizers introduced confinement to the justice system here. When the Belgians took over in 1916, houses of detention proliferated in the form of *cachots*, informal detention huts consisting of guesthouses, back rooms, even kitchens in private homes. After independence in 1962, the Hutu regime used *cachots* to imprison masses of Tutsis, who were subject to constant arrest for the crime of being "vagabond" or "delinquent."

This meant that after genocide, there was no formal infrastructure to handle the mass numbers of killers. They were crammed into any available carceral space, and by 1995 prisons were at five times their capacity. Severe overcrowding produced ghastly conditions. Thousands were dying of TB and dysentery; layers of prisoners were literally piled on top of one another, rotting away from thirst and hunger. In the last six weeks of 1994 at Kigali Central Prison, 166 people died. In 1995 there were seven deaths per day there, and at Gitarama Prison, 900 deaths in eight months. Prisoners slept in toilets and in shifts; a *komeza* (literally, "continue") was someone who had nowhere to sleep and was relegated to walking through the night, wandering the prison like a golem.

President Kagame's response to this crisis was unusual. Let them go, he decreed. First the elderly prisoners, in 1998. Then, in 2003, a mass release of 24,000 prisoners, including the terminally ill, those who had participated in the government confession program, those under fourteen during the genocide. The second mass release in 2005 freed 22,000 more—all of whom, of course, still had to face their charges, clarified by a 1996 law outlining tiered gradations of genocide.

How can one even begin to enact justice in the face of such horror? The International Criminal Tribunal for Rwanda, established by the UN Security Council, prosecuted those bearing the greatest responsibility. It completed its work in 2014, finding sixty-five of seventy-five defendants guilty. Rwanda's National Court System prosecuted some ten thousand more suspects, twenty-two of whom were executed in the years before 2007, when the death penalty was abolished.

The rest, most, stood before the grand Rwandan experiment, which was really a return to precolonial forms of Rwandan justice. *Gacaca* means "grass," indicating that trials and truth-telling transpired on grand lawns, out in the open, overseen by community-elected judges. It's a scene I find almost impossible to envision, even as Santos describes it to me. Some 12,000 *gacacas* tried over 1.2 million cases between 2006 and 2012, handing down judgments and reducing sentences for the repentant and those seeking reconciliation with their communities.

In precolonial Rwanda, *gacaca* justice resulted in a plan for restitution, which could be material payment, beatings, or death. Postgenocide, sentences primarily called for time in one of about forty roving Travaux d'Intérêts Généraux (TIG) camps, established in 2005. *Tigistes*, as the 53,000 or so sentenced to these camps were known, make reparations through labor, building roads, schools, and houses for the homeless, including genocide survivors. *Tigistes* work three days a week, some commuting from home, and they are schooled, too, in construction skills, civic education, literacy, Rwandan history, and government policy. TIG camps saved Rwanda millions of dollars and reduced the prison population by some 53 percent, whittling it down to about 58,000. It's a relatively low number, yet still high enough to give contemporary Rwanda the world's seventh-highest per capita prison population. The Rwanda Correctional Service, though, continues its attempt to change this, and boldly aims to reduce fourteen prisons to nine.

I learn all this during hours of intense dialogue with Santos. He tells me that a team of NAR youth paid a single visit to the TIG camps about a year ago, which never became a full-fledged program. But the prison visits, which he and I will plan together, should be built into a sustainable program. I study the determined expression on his face.

"Santos, why do you want to do this?" I blurt.

"*Parce que…*," he starts softly, in French, then shifts to halting English. "I want to be the—how do you say it?—the root of peace. In Rwanda."

If he hadn't uttered it with such forceful sincerity, I'd have believed such a poignant response to be scripted.

Before heading back to Golf Hills that day, I ask James to take me to the Kigali Genocide Memorial. "Be strong," he says, smiling, as he drops me off. "Don't cry"—he is almost laughing as he says this.

Oh, do I cry. "Rwanda is a country of hills, mountains, forests, lakes, laughing children, markets of busy people, drummers, dancers, artisan craftsmen," reads the opening placard in the exhibition, before plunging into excruciating detail about the incomprehensible nightmare that was 1994. There is no Spielberg-esque heart-tugging here, but there is meticulous accuracy. Actually, many genocides preceded the massive one; in 1959 a series of massacres of Tutsis drove thousands into exile in neighboring Burundi, the Congo, and Uganda. Thirty-five years later women and babies were targets, and mothers were often raped and forced to kill their own children. Their sexual organs were mutilated with machetes, boiled water, and acid; they were deliberately given HIV. A twelve-year-old boy was made to rape his own mother in front of her husband. I stare at a chain that held a pair together as they were buried alive. Walking through a Children's Room in memory of "those who should have been our future," I find the listed causes of death revolting: "hacked by machete in his mother's arms."

I step outside. The hotel manager was right; sunshine has turned to torrential rain. There is a sign reading Please Do Not Step On The Graves. I start to sob. A grinning teenage boy is sweeping the water off blue tarmac blanketed over one of the mass grave sites.

"Hello! Are you married?" he calls to me.

Nonplussed, I shake my head.

"Where are you from," comes his reply, jolly as he absent-mindedly sweeps the graves.

New York, I mutter.

"America! You are rich!" he exclaims. He unpeels a corner of the tarmac. "Look—see graves!" It requires all of my willpower to keep from vomiting; the colossal pit is filled to the brim with skulls. Tens of thousands of skulls, like baseballs. Former human heads. Human lives.

I wander away in a daze. My mind follows suit. Is this teenager Hutu or Tutsi? Is it fair to wonder this, about everyone I meet? Whom does Santos live with?

How in hell am I supposed to face the men responsible for all of this?

Maybe they should rot in a Rwandan prison.

At the gift shop, I buy an English–Kinyarwanda–Kiswahili phrase book and one titled *We Survived Genocide in Rwanda: 28 Personal Testimonies*. "You wear black!" says the smiling man ringing up my purchases. "That is strange! Women like pink."

Outside, James glances at my book. "Excellent!" he proclaims. Then he proffers his story. Both of his parents were murdered in

1994 but he escaped to South Africa. He went to medical school in Kenya and worked in a bank, but corporate life bored him, so he moved back to Rwanda and started driving a taxi. It's hard for me to wrap my brain around the idea that this jovial man is a genocide survivor. Clearly I needn't have bought the book; personal testimonies are everywhere.

———

Over the weekend, I begin making friends. Through a New York connection, I'm put in touch with Eddy, an actor and activist. He shows up at Golf Hills in fitted black jeans, a leather jacket, and shades.

"You are welcome!" comes the outstretched hand. "You recognized me, did you?"

"Recognize you?"

"From the movie!" Eddy strikes a pose, arms crossed and face stern. Then he bursts into laughter.

Ah, yes. He played a prison guard in my friend's film *Kinyarwanda*, the first feature about the genocide shot in Rwanda.

We zip into town, through tricolored landscapes of electric-orange earth, emerald hills, and cream-colored homes. The air is crisp with drizzle. Pristine, traffic-free streets are littered only with omnipresent motos—motorcycle taxis, perilously zipping to and fro.

I tag along on Eddy's daily rounds. We visit a peace-building organization, a youth group whose logo reads Peace, Good Works and Patriotism, and a school, where he drops off donated books.

"Do you have a salary, Baz?" he asks on the drive back. Eddy has a disorienting habit of shifting emotional gears with zeal. One minute he's all smiles and the next, grave, eyes aggressive. I do, yes, I tell him.

"Not me. I make my living by donation. By giving. I am also a writer, but I love acting. That is my love, apart from my wife, who is my first love." The name of Eddy's book, which he also performs as poetry, is *Their Sin Is My Shame*. Eddy is Hutu.

"There are many books by and about the survivors," he explains. "But there is no voice for we who were the perpetrators, who did not kill but are stained by what our people did, the ones who did kill. The shame of it, that is our lives."

It's a profound point, and it makes me think of John Jay College, where I often show my students a documentary called *Beyond Conviction*, about three crime victims who choose to meet and dialogue with the men who wronged them. One is a woman who was raped by her brother, when he was high on psychedelics. Their meeting is wrenching to watch. She exhibits debilitating emotional scars and he convulses with sobs, so overwhelmed with shame and self-loathing that he cannot even glance at his sister. Finally he does, at her request. She hugs him. And through tears, in one of the most powerful, believable reconciliation scenes I've ever seen, she says that she forgives him and it will help her heal and move on, but he will also have to learn to forgive himself.

I ask my students an awful and ultimately unanswerable question: Whom would you rather be in that scene, the victim or the offender? The offender, of course, they all say. Who would choose to be a victim? I press them. Are you sure? You'd rather walk around for the rest of your life carrying that cross, knowing you committed a wholly revolting deed?

To recognize one's sin and thus forever bear the burden of that horrific deed—this is natural justice, a prison truer than any man-made one. Being a victim is a nightmare, but there is at least honor in that nightmare. Being a sentient offender—in this there is only lifelong indignity.

I'd brought a copy of *Beyond Conviction* with me, along with a mini-library of books about victim–offender reconciliation dialogue. I'd thought they might come in handy during meetings about the prison visits. I give them all to Eddy, as he drops me off.

———

Do you want to talk about genocide?

It's the first question on the list of talking points for today's meeting with the prison-visiting group. Others include, Why are you here, and How do you feel about punishment? I'm nervous. How could I not be? I'm a *mzungu*. Yes, I have experience working in prisons and bringing young people inside them. But that's America. This is Rwanda, and this is genocide.

When I show up at the Never Again Rwanda office, the students haven't arrived yet but there's a secretary at the front desk. Grace, twenty years old, works at NAR three days a week. I try to engage her in a chat but YouTube proves more engaging. Until I drop the right word.

"You are a writer. That is my dream!"

Soon we agree that she'll write some essays for me, to practice her English, and her first assignment is to define her generation.

"My generation?" she asks. Then, "Oh, you mean the genocide?" She says this casually, offhandedly. "Me, I lost both my parents."

Such words crash instantly and ferociously to the floor, even when coolly uttered. I hear them again and again from the fifteen youth members in our group. They trickle in and shyly shake my hand.

I introduce myself, with a staff member translating. There seem to be five Kinyarwanda words for a single English one, making me feel as if I'm missing half the conversation. I tell them about John Jay and the Prison-to-College Pipeline. As part of it, I escort undergraduates into prison once a month to take class alongside the incarcerated students. These learning exchanges, as we call them, have a profound impact on both sets of students; the incarcerated ones are inspired to experience a "normal" college classroom while the outsiders are usually stunned to discover that their "inside" counterparts are a lot more like them than they'd imagined. The Rwandan students' ears perk up. *We want to meet them,* they tell me. *Let's set up a joint Facebook account.*

I ask the students what they want to do during their prison visits. They look at me in silence. Santos jumps in and explains that behind bars, he doesn't want to talk about genocide. We are tired of talking about it. We do not want to address the crime but to come as a gesture of peace and reconciliation. This is the explanation that slowly emerges. So what *do* they want to do? More silence. Write it down, I say. In any language.

This works. They scribble away, producing a list of suggestions: Play football. Sing. Dance. Have debates. Watch movies. Comedy. At our next meeting we'll vote on which activities make sense for the monthly visits. We choose a name for the program: Never Again Rwanda's Prison Visiting Project, aka NAR's PVP. This is the land of youth groups and peace-making organizations, all wearing acronyms.

———

Santos, fresh from church, is in his Sunday best. I'm wearing jeans and sneakers. Before our Sunday meeting with the PVP group, we sit down to discuss the selection process for prisoners who'll participate in the visits. I write down "reentry," a prison buzzword used to sum up the process by which people in prison return home after serving their time. Santos nods animatedly.

"Yes, Baz. We can select the ones who are soon coming home." He eyes me, coyly. "Baz, I can ask you something?"

"Sure," I say.

"Baz, what is the name — 'Baz'?" I explain that it's a nickname, given to me by my sisters when I was a baby. My real name, which no one ever uses, is Bathsheba, from the Bible.

"That is a queen!" declares Santos.

King David, I joke, always steals the spotlight — everyone knows his name but not that of his wife, mother of Solomon. "In Hebrew it actually means 'daughter of seven' or 'daughter of good fortune,'" I tell him.

Santos likes this. He takes my notebook and, in block letters, slowly prints a word, UMUNYAMAHIRWE.

"This is your Kinyarwanda name," he says. "Daughter of good fortune."

The group trickles in, all of them, too, in church wear. Eugene, who speaks the best English in the group and is the least timid, tells me that his mother works in Shalom Village, a sizable orphanage two hours from Kigali. In the corner sit Jean and Nathalie, coupled up and giggling; like many of the others, Nathalie is a business management and economics student at Kigali University.

The students are again reticent, and the translation, by Santos and Eugene, comes haltingly. We're still debating the activity game plan for the prison visits, and soon I'm left out entirely; the democratic process takes over and everyone is vigorously deliberating. Every now and then Santos lets me know what's being agreed on. One part of the visit will involve discussion groups around current events. They like my suggestion about breaking off into smaller groups that mix the incarcerated with the nonincarcerated, an approach I use in my American program.

Suddenly things become animated. The students are listing topics for the discussion groups, and Santos has proposed "How to keep the country peaceful." Matthew, who led last year's visit to the TIG camp, is glaring at Santos, squinty-eyed. He hasn't come to any of our meetings until today, and he's said little until now. Finally, he spills forth a question in English, directed at me: "How can I ask these criminals, these *genocidaires*, about how to keep the country peaceful?"

The elephant lands, with a thud, in the center of the room.

Criminals. Genocidaires. Words that have thus far been drowned out by prettier ones. *Peace. Forgiveness.*

Thankfully, Santos jumps in, in Kinyarwanda, and the discussion flows on. We draft an agenda. Later, Santos tells me what he said to Matthew to quiet the storm.

"Baz, I told him, I said, 'We are visiting—because we want to move past what has happened, to give them second chance.' Because they will come out of prison one day. Do we want them to be angry and full of *haine*? They will live *avec nous*, together in our villages with us. Like you say, *reentry*."

Again I must convince myself: Is Santos a figment of my liberal imagination?

————

Days pass and I settle into Kigalife. "The world comes to Kigali," reads the Heineken billboard up the road from Golf Hills. It's true. And they come, mostly, as volunteers. I meet them at Golf Hills and at local hangouts: the doctor from New York, here to train Rwandans in sonogram use; my new friend from Holland, working on a microfinancing project involving local women; the Canadian-Somalian doctor pursuing real estate opportunities.

I spend my afternoons at NAR, most evenings with friends, and my mornings on the balcony at Golf Hills, where I grow accustomed to hanging out with my laptop, sipping pungent Rwandan coffee and reading the local paper. There's at least one genocide-related story per day, whether about proposed amendments to the law against genocide ideology or the trial of Jean Uwinkindi, a former pastor responsible for the death of thousands. It's as if 1994 was yesterday.

Between NAR visits I try to get a handle on the cultural life here by seeking out musicians and talking music with everyone I meet, for an NPR story. It proves yet another way of talking peace and reconciliation. Again and again, musicians in their twenties describe their songs as perpetually positive, sans talk of politics, genocide, or anything too solemn.

"Love. We sing about love," says Kamichi, a gently handsome, soft-spoken Afrobeat star. "I was there, I survived—I saw everything. Why would I want to sing about that? I would go crazy if I did. And who wants to be always reminded?"

Even the rappers I speak to, performing in a genre known for voicing what no one else wants to say, argue that they'd rather not wax lyrical about politics. No country knows the value of silence like Rwanda, where speaking the wrong way about ethnic groups is a crime, because not too long ago, speaking the wrong way about ethnic groups produced the unspeakable.

"Freedom of speech can be overrated," Kamichi declares. "Before the genocide, people said what they wanted—and almost a million were slaughtered because of it. So, you know, not everything needs to be said." Indeed, renowned musicians were prosecuted for their hateful anti-Tutsi lyrics, and even today, people are careful not to be in contempt of laws against genocide ideology. After the genocide, the National Unity and Reconciliation Commission created *ingando*, national solidarity camps. Released prisoners spent months there before *gacaca*, getting indoctrinated in Rwandan ideals of peace, unity, reconciliation, and antivengeance. These days the government encourages and sometimes requires Rwandan citizens from diverse walks of life— students, politicians, church leaders, prostitutes, ex-soldiers, ex-combatants, *genocidaires*, *gacaca* judges—to attend *ingando* for periods ranging from days to months.

Some have called this brainwashing, or political propaganda. I try my best to put my skeptic's cap on and see things from this angle, to muster up my American freedom-of-speech self. I scour every conversation for what isn't being said, for moments of mental programming, but in the context of genocide, "brainwashing" loses some of its negative connotation. The line between education and indoctrination can be thin. If Rwanda created a peace-loving national narrative by dabbling in censorship and tampering with freedom of speech just a tad—given the circumstances and the miraculously harmonious end, is all of that such a dreadful compromise?

Finally, the big news comes from Eric at Never Again Rwanda. He and Santos have a meeting at the Correctional Service tomorrow and will have in hand the proposal and letter I've drafted.

"But it is better if you don't come with us," he says. "If they see you, they may grow—" He pauses. "Maybe concerned. Who is this American professor and what does she want?" I nod. Keep me posted, I say. I'll be anxiously awaiting word.

In the meantime, at Bourbon Coffee, the Starbucks of Rwanda, I chat with Eddy's perfect foil of a best friend, Ishmael. Like Eddy, he's an artist, a filmmaker working on a film called *The Divorce*, about the rift between his and his parents' generation. Unlike Eddy, though, he's Muslim, and a survivor.

"You are really going inside the prison?" he asks me, as I explain why I'm here.

"I like this," he says with a nod, his tender eyes fringed by long lashes. "I do not want to go in, if I went to the prison, and see angry, miserable people. They will come home, and then they will be angry and miserable in our communities."

Ishmael was inspired to make his film, he explains, because he felt that genocide was something his generation should not dwell on, as the older generation does.

As Ishmael reflects on his childhood, I have my own flashbacks. I am eleven years old. It's the night before Yom HaShoah, Holocaust Remembrance Day. This means a big day ahead, at Hebrew school tomorrow. Dress code is all black. No regular classes, just Holocaust-themed workshops and films. Every hour on the hour activities will come to a halt and over the loudspeaker, the principal will read a litany of names, student family members who were murdered and the concentration camps in which they perished. Compiling our list, my parents are arguing about who was slaughtered where.

"No, no. Rachel Surah was in Auschwitz, not Buchenwald," insists my mother.

"I'm staying home," I announce.

My father spins around to glare at me.

"I don't have anything black to wear," comes my protest.

"You don't have *anything to wear*?" shouts my father. "Do you know how much of your blood was spilled, how many slaughtered, and you have *nothing to wear*?"

I knew how many, all too well. Six million ghosts occupied our home. Auschwitz nightmares were a regular part of my sleeping life. I'd grown up in a household where my mother regularly played the *Schindler's List* soundtrack in the living room. Where *Zayde*, my omnipresent grandfather, who lost his entire family in the Holocaust, instructed us to never, ever set foot in Hungary because the Hungarians were worse than the Nazis — *The land is soaked with your blood*, he said. I can count the times I saw *Zayde* smile, and the times he hugged me; I cannot count the times he argued viciously in Yiddish with my father, howling across the Sabbath table, or told us the story of the Hungarian Nazi sympathizers who dragged his father out of the yeshiva and literally beat him to death on the street. *Zayde*'s cousin was the only one in the family to survive the camps, and she grew up in my father's house; I knew the story of how her twin brother didn't make it, but she, with the right combination of guile and luck, did. When I went to Europe, I lied to my parents about going to Germany. I still taste the guilt that seeped down my spine during that train ride across the border.

I was tired of the Holocaust.

Not tired — exhausted. Haunted. Enslaved. It hung like a sinister cloud of mental illness over my family.

I share my flashback with Ishmael. The look in his eyes tells me he knows much, much better than I how this feels.

"Many times I say I would rather be a victim than a survivor," he admits. "I'm a survivor, I know this, but I don't want to be a survivor for life. I'm a survivor for my history, but not for life. So let me enjoy my life, let me hold my life in my hand." He goes on, voice slow and trembling. "Members of the family cannot be replaced. I will never find someone to replace my mom. I will never find someone to replace my dad. Never. But I don't have them now. Who is my mom, who is my dad? My country. So let me enjoy my country—let me enjoy what is there. I don't want to forget that person but I don't want to always sit in a room and cry. I need to *live*."

The next morning, as I strap on my iPod, set out on my daily run, and marvel at the picture-perfection of my route—implausibly rich orange soil, women peddling clay pottery and guerrilla sculptures on the roadside, flamboyant Skol beer ads—I cannot banish Ishmael from my thoughts.

Ishmael and my *Zayde*. Survivors, victims. I run. Tears stream down my face. It's the first time I've felt visceral empathy for *Zayde*, mourning his—our—loss. Ishmael and my grandfather: both survivors, yet such radically different spirits.

"Man to man is so unjust," sings Bob Marley in my ear.

I have another childhood flashback, to the holiday of Purim, which celebrates the time Jews eluded the potential genocidal plot of evil Haman, adviser to King Ahasuerus. Our house is congested with *shalach manot*, celebratory gift baskets from the community, brimming with food, wine, and grape juice. My father is doing a public reading in our living room of the Book of Esther. Each time Haman's name is read, we shake our noisemakers as if to cuss him out, per Jewish tradition. And when my father reaches the part where Haman is eventually caught and hanged, along with his ten sons, he reads loudly and in one breath, another tradition meant to underscore the triumph of revenge.

But today I balk. Is revenge a triumph? To harm someone who has harmed you, is that not hypocrisy, perpetuating a wretched chain of wrongdoing? We justify legal violence with the word "deterrence," but one would have a hard time arguing that it is effective, considering the fact that putting 2.3 million behind bars has hardly eradicated crime. This utilitarian approach to justice, using the lives of offenders as a means to our end—safety—is, as criminologist Deirdre Golash argues, vastly immoral. "We may require wrongdoers to compensate their victims for the harms that they have done," she writes, "but we may not harm them in order to prevent future harms by others."

I've been absorbed by Golash's work lately, in my quest to unravel the dilemma of punishment. Turning off my iPod, sitting down on the side of the road, I start scanning my mental library, overloaded with the words of those grappling with the so-called problem of punishment. It's a problem because, as sociologist Daniel Boonin aptly puts it, "How can the fact that a person has broken a just and reasonable law render it morally permissible for the state to treat him in ways that would otherwise be impermissible?" Prisons, see, are revenge on a grand scale. And while *correction* makes sense, is retribution ever a justifiable aim? Enter Seneca, another thinker populating my "punishment" library. "'Retribution'—an inhuman word and, what is more, accepted as right—is not very different from wrongdoing, except in the order of events," he says. "He who pays back pain with pain is doing wrong; it is only that he is more readily excused for it." Finally, enter psychologist James Gilligan, who speaks of punishment as "that collective violence which any society defines as legal, just as crime is the individual violence that we define as illegal." Punishment, he goes on, "does not prevent or inhibit further violence, it only stimulates it."

Ultimately, revenge cannot undo; it merely does again. It arises from a feeling of helplessness, from the need to re-create a painful situation with roles reversed. It welcomes wrongdoers into our orbits and hands them tremendous power over our souls and spirits. Punishment is backward-looking. Forgiveness, on the other hand, is forward-looking, liberating us from a violent cycle and from the one who's wronged us. He who forgives, goes the proverb, ends the quarrel.

I rise up, turn around, and jog back up the hill.

Ishmael and my *Zayde*. One exudes the freedom and serenity that come from letting go; the other, the injurious, contagious consequences of bitterly holding on. I'd read a multitude of studies about the value to human health of forgiveness and the damage done by vengeful unforgiving. But here were live case studies.

———

Later that week, still awaiting word from Never Again Rwanda about prison permissions, I anxiously await another result, the US presidential elections. At the Car Wash restaurant my friend Noreen and I join an all-night election party. I'd met her on my second night here, hanging out with a crew of expats working to get the national airline on its feet and living at Golf Hills. She'd seemed a mirage, this twenty-four-year-old Kigali local in towering heels and chic sundress, appearing in the crisp night.

Tonight Noreen throws back one too many drinks and begins to share her personal story. Her family is Pentecostal. They let her read nothing but the Bible and banned all secular music in the home. Her family is also Tutsi, one of many who fled to Uganda during the genocides prior to 1994, changed their name in order to pass as Hutu, and then returned years later, along with nearly a half million other exiles, to find whole family lines demolished.

Noreen speaks of her childhood as if recounting time served: hours locked in the bedroom crying, wishing for a normal teenage life. She eventually won a scholarship at a college in rural Canada and was overjoyed to leave the country, but then discovered, on arrival, that she was the only black person for miles. Alienated and alone, she fell into a deep depression and medicated herself with drugs and alcohol. She eventually gave up and came home but refused to move back into her parents' home and is now finishing her degree at a local university.

As Noreen opens up to me, I contemplate the word "victim" — so misleading, so minimizing. It implies that crimes have a singular impact, when in fact their damage radiates outward, poisoning individuals, families, communities, a whole network of those wounded in myriad ways by the trickle-down effects of trauma.

"For so long I wanted to kill all Hutus," Noreen admits. She still often feels angry. Sometimes she doesn't even know why. There was the night she had to be escorted out of the club, after she got drunk and called someone who stepped on her toes "a fucking Hutu." Clearly the healing process is still very much a work in progress.

I wake up to good news and bad. CNN informs me that Obama is still my president. Eric's news is far less promising. "Rwanda Correctional Service has said—they said no, it is not possible, our project," he tells me. Procedure did us in. Corrections officials felt slighted by our approach. It is not our place to tell them what should be done. They are the arbiters of this. We should have come to them asking, not telling. I'm crushed. Eric had assured me, before I arrived in Rwanda, that permission would be sorted out, but we knew there was no guarantee.

"Maybe I can meet with Mary?" I implore. Mary is a top-level corrections official. Eric says he will try to organize a meeting for this afternoon.

Closing my laptop, I grab my purse for an excursion with Jean de Dieu, "Jean of God." His organization? Shalom: Educating for

Peace—yet another Hebraic connection. I'd been researching groups that do prison work here, because I was worried about precisely the disappointing news I got today. Jean and I had lunched at one of Rwanda's ubiquitous buffets, and between gap-toothed smiles, he told me his story. Like countless others, he was making a living off peacemaking, or at least trying to. He'd completed his doctorate in South Africa, where he studied the relationship between justice, peace, and anticorruption efforts, and Shalom educates young people about such issues. I did not ask him directly, but later learned that Jean is "mixed"—his mother is Tutsi and his father Hutu. His wife, who lost her mother in 1994, whose brothers survived by hiding in a basement for weeks, is mixed, too.

"Would you like to see a peace village?" Jean had asked. I'd said yes, with no idea of what such a thing was.

This morning Jean picks me up in a 1981 Toyota that looks and sounds as if it can barely make it up the hill, let alone to Rulindo, two hours from Kigali. Sure enough, after we pick up Tarsis, a politician in charge of good governance for the Rulindo district, the car comes to a sputtering halt. It's fine, Tarsis and Jean say. We will leave the car here and take the bus. A bead of sweat trails down my spine. You will definitely be back in time for your meeting with Mary at RCS, they assure me.

We cram ourselves into a minibus decked out with a Che Guevara logo, where I find myself all but sitting on my neighbor's lap. The ride is jaw-droppingly beautiful, carrying us past Mount Kigali, up, up, and up into the lush greenery, ascending to what's surely the most resplendent hill in the land of a thousand hills. The bus pulls into a clearing in the forest, encircled by lanky pine trees, and the rhythm of drums greets us.

Some three hundred people are assembled, seated on the ground, wearing voluminous T-shirts and colorful cloths. On chairs in front of them sit three men in baggy suits and cowboy hats. The village has been awaiting our arrival; singing and clapping commences. I clap, too, and make out the word *amahoro*, which means peace. Jean leans in with a translation. "Have peace, unity, reconciliation. The genocide ideology, root it up and burn it."

"This is a village meeting," Jean whispers. "They are planning activities for official reconciliation week, later this month. Tarsis is here to oversee." I nod.

"He"—Jean points to the elderly villager speaking—"is describing what the village has planned. Planting trees. Food and drink. Celebration." Tarsis, taking the floor, emphasizes the value of good governance. He goes on. And on. Jean rolls his eyes. "Politicians," he murmurs.

Suddenly, a dozen villagers stand up. The others applaud. They sit down.

"These people have now been forgiven, officially," Jean explains. "They have paid off their debt. They have been forgiven and fully welcomed back into the community."

I'm stunned. Nineteen years ago, this village was a slaughterhouse; these people, Hutu and Tutsi both, were murdering their neighbors. Now, thanks to confession, restitution, and vigilant efforts to promote peace as a community staple, they live together in harmony.

"You will speak next," Jean whispers to me. I will? "It is a tradition. A foreigner comes to the village, they must speak."

What does one say to a living miracle? First, drop a *murakoze*, an expression of thanks.

"She is Joan?" one of the villagers calls out. No, Jean explains. Joan was another *mzungu*, last month.

I conjure up *Zayde*, welcoming his spirit to this sacred space. I claim a status I have never claimed before, telling the villagers that I am, in some very small and distant way, also a victim, a survivor. And through Rwanda I have come to unprecedented empathy for my ancestors. But the survival I grew up with did not feel as this place does. Forgiving. Peaceful. Benevolent. There was love, yes, but much bitterness and pain in my living room. Inherited scars remained raw. No one stood up and sat down, as they do today. I wish they had.

I wish, too, for my country to be as forgiving as this village. In America we prefer punishment. Our grudges take the form of millions of prison cells, a culture of incarceration that Alexis de Tocqueville and Gustave Beaumont, who visited the United States in 1831 and marveled at our prison population, dubbed a national ritual that Americans see as "a remedy for all the evils of society." It's true that, as the philosopher Emmanuel Levinas put it, "a world where forgiveness is almighty becomes inhuman," but a world where punishment is almighty becomes barbaric. In America we don't brainwash in peace; we mostly make justice a synonym for revenge.

Alas, the pillars of this place are not the pillars of the place I call home. These pillars are literal. I discover this after the meeting is over, as Jean and I pose for photos by the village's peace pole, planted in the heart of the circle where village meetings take place. *Amahoro N'aganze Kw'isi Hose*, reads the pillar. *May Peace Prevail on Earth*.

The journey back is sticky and dusty. I join Tarsis and Jean for a buffet lunch near the bus station, and before I run off to my meeting with RCS, Tarsis jots something down in my notebook: *Umugabo mbwa aseka umbohe*.

"It is a Rwandese expression," he explains. "It means, 'A foolish man laughs at prisons.' You have a serious job to do."

The clock is ticking as I meet Santos at NAR. Another crowded minivan ride later, we are late, trekking up the stairs of a concrete slab of a building. "Justice, Corrections, Knowledge, and Production," goes the RCS motto, which strikes me as impressively progressive, efficiency-minded—in other words, classically Rwandan. Rwanda's "poo-powered prisons," as BBC News dubbed them, are a prime example of such enlightened thinking: some are 75 percent powered by human waste.

"No ID, no entrance," proclaims the stern, stolid woman at the door.

"But please, we have an appointment," I implore. Santos gently lets forth a fountain of Kinyarwanda. I smile sweetly and mentally bow before this woman.

She relents. We climb the next set of stairs and await Mary, whose office is adorned by a giant portrait of President Kagame.

"This is not how things are done here," comes Mary's pronouncement, after I explain what was already said in the letter about our intentions.

"Your permission is denied." She delivers this with stern finality.

Santos leans forward to respond; I cut him off.

"Yes, you are right," I concur. Santos looks at me, confused. "We have done this wrong. You have procedure; we violated it. We are very sorry for this." I take out my John Jay College business card and place it on the glass coffee table between us.

"But I do hope that when you come to New York, you will come visit my university, and give a talk to our faculty about the progressive work you do here. You are a leader in the field."

Mary picks up my card and inspects it. "John Jay," she says to herself quietly. To me she says, "That is a prestigious school, yes?"

"One of the top criminal justice programs in the country. I do hope you will be in New York soon."

"John Jay," Mary repeats.

I'd told her which university I was from before, and it was also stated in our request letter, but it's visibly sinking in right at this moment, card in hand. Pause. Then, miracle.

"Let the professor in," she declares to her assistant. "It is not about victim and offender, not one person but a whole community harmed, and a whole community that must be put back together," she says. Santos's eyes grow wide.

"Your program is needed because it is about restoring communities. Yes, we will let the professor and the students inside. Friday."

"Actually, might tomorrow be possible?" I entreat. "I unfortunately leave Friday."

Yes, it is possible. Mary and her assistant exit the room and go next door. Santos gives me a look that walks the line between confusion and awe.

"I am so happy right now, Baz. My heart is—it is—very full. I don't know how it is—how you did that."

I don't know how, either. But as thrilled as I am that permission has been granted, I'm saddened by how it happened. Prison decisions—life-and-death decisions—can be as arbitrary as this. I've seen it back home, again and again, parole rulings holding my students' futures in their hands, made with no apparent rationale or explicit justification. Beyond the force of my status, there's no rhyme or reason here in Rwanda today, just as there is no rhyme or reason why Theo from New York, who's served twenty-two years with perfect behavior, who has a job and a college game plan lined up for release, who has three children waiting for their father to come home, is denied parole, while Steven, who bears the very same rap sheet, is granted it. "Nature of the crime," the parole board stamps, with cold finality.

Mary returns with an official letter on the stationery of the commissioner general.

> Reference is made to the letter dated 5 November 2012 from the office of Never Again Rwanda, requesting Rwanda Correctional Service to facilitate your team of eleven people to visit Gasabo Prison with the purpose of rehabilitative impact on the prison population throughout the country. I wish to inform you that you have been granted permission to visit Gasabo Prison during the normal visit hours.

There is an agenda. Santos has printed it, I discover on arrival at NAR the next day. The students, giggling and joking, load boxes of water into the van.

"This is *le jour*—the day," he greets me. He wears a white polo shirt with an NAR logo that reads, across its back, Empowering Youth with Opportunities to Become Active Citizens.

Forty minutes later we have arrived. Gasabo Prison is a stately orange-brick structure, laced in barbed wire and crowned by a turretlike guard tower, rising from the back alley of a suburban Kigali neighborhood. It looks medieval, much like the prisons of upstate New York. This is no accident. African prisons are Western impositions with roots in various colonial sources: "gaols" set up in coastal forts and garrisons by trading Europeans in the sixteenth century, devices of bodily restraint and confinement used in the slave trade, military lockups used in imperial conquests since the 1880s. Early twentieth-century prison building across the continent represented colonial efforts to exert control and reinforce hierarchies in the most literal of ways, creating dramatic, segregated spaces in which black bodies were contained, subjugated, and humiliated. The very look of prisons spoke a thousand words. Orderly, Western-looking edifices sought to impose order on those unruly natives, amassed in collective cells. This building I'm looking at, then, is a classic instance of prison as brutal Western imposition, left to fester even after the colonial masters took their leave, declining to clean up the carceral mess they made.

Our stroll through the gates is smooth and casual. We're permitted cameras and cell phones and ushered into the superintendent's office to await instructions. The students chat animatedly, unruffled. On the wall is a framed portrait of President Kagame, a map of Rwanda with the location of its prisons marked, a chart detailing the chain of command here, and a chalkboard listing a series of numbers. As Eric and Santos converse with the officials, I pick out the English words "never again," "genocide," and "peace building."

The superintendent, a vigorous woman, enters and beams as she says, "Professor Baz, you are welcome." Hands are extended. She points to a number on the chalkboard, 4,528, and explains that it represents today's Gasabo population.

The superintendent leads us out of her office, through the prison, and into a warehouselike space annexed off to the side, like a garage. As we walk, throngs of prisoners, strolling about, throw barely a glance in our direction. They wear candy-colored uniforms, tangerine orange for those who have been sentenced and cotton-candy pink for those awaiting trial. The place feels calm and controlled. I sense none of the tension that lurks in furtively eyed hallways behind the walls of American prisons.

Inside the annex, nearly one hundred prisoners sit serenely on long wooden benches, some looking as young as twenty and others well past middle age. We sit on benches directly facing them. Eric takes the microphone and offers a greeting filled with *murakozes*. Next comes singing and clapping. One curly-haired, sweet-faced corrections officer, handsome in his khaki uniform, introduces himself to me as Rolfe and appoints himself my translator. He murmurs in my ear.

"We come because of love," Santos announces. Applause. "Today we will talk with you about current events. We will discuss the topic of gender. What is the meaning of equal rights?"

From there, lively dialogue erupts. Students take turns at the mike but Santos is clearly the leader, and very much in his element. I marvel at the way he's abruptly transformed from shy and gawky to buoyant and garrulous—a teacher and a leader.

"Should the nation be run by a woman?" Santos asks.

"Never!" calls one prisoner. "Our prison used to be run by a woman. Now it is run by a man and it is far better."

"Women are too subject to moods to run a country," calls another prisoner.

Howls of disagreement erupt from all sides.

"This is entirely a lie. Women and men are both subject to moods," a prisoner to my left says, finger in the air. Everyone is animated, ardent, and at home. I am happy to sit where I belong, on the sidelines. The students and prisoners break off into groups to debate the issue further.

"Where is your gun?" I ask Rolfe, the corrections officer.

"We do not carry guns," comes the reply. There is almost no violence here. Order is maintained via a prisoner-run government, led by a *capita general* and an array of *capitas* under him, who govern individual blocks. Rolfe laughs as he tells me that one prison has a "Block Texas," so named because it's occupied by wealthier prisoners. The *capita* in charge of security is called the *commissaire*, and there's little need for the corrections officers to even enter the prison. Elections are held regularly. Most *capitas* are *genocidaires* and highly educated. Most *genocidaires*, after all, were highly educated.

I cannot lie. I do look at the men in prison uniforms and think, *skulls*. Almost a million of them. Corpses. Rape. Machetes. Murder. *These men did all of that.* And yet here they are, looking like— *human beings.* Being warm and gregarious with the survivors of their atrocities, who are in turn kind and gracious beyond measure. Is such a thing really possible? My mind reels, and so does my heart.

"American prisons are harsh, isn't it?" Rolfe asks. I nod. "And I hear that they have no Internet connection, yes? How can that be?"

I don't know how it can be, Rolfe, but indeed it is. Rolfe gapes at this. He explains that there's a prison economy in which services like laundry and goods are for sale. Most prisoners have jobs on the outside and keep 10 percent of their pay.

"They're permitted to go on work leave?" I ask, surprised.

"Of course." Rolfe gives me a "silly *mzungu*" stare.

"Here, we play football with them. There is no difference between these prisoners and us. The only difference is—how do you say?" He fingers his uniform. "The cloth."

"But," I cannot resist asking, "aren't some corrections officers, aren't they survivors? Isn't it hard for them to be here, you know, to play football with the *genocidaires*?"

A second stare. "No," says Rolfe firmly. "There is a word called—how do you say?—*forgiveness*."

Silly *mzungu* me.

Do not take me for naive. The cynical New Yorker in me looked hard for the flaws in this Rwandan facade, searched for greedy, self-interested motives lurking beneath the peace agenda. I struggled to find them. *There is a word called forgiveness.* Indeed. Even if there were cracks in the facade, even if there did exist persistent social divisions, ways in which the *gacaca* system had failed, excessive government censorship, the ease with which this mantra, *forgiveness*, rolls off every Rwandan's tongue, the way it has firmly ensconced itself as the crown jewel of this country's national narrative—this was striking. Lip service has value. Say "forgiveness" often enough and eventually behavioral psychology kicks in and divine actions follow; preach punishment and watch bloody hell break loose.

The prisoners and students reconvene to present their group's findings. There is more speechifying, handshaking, and laughter. We are out of time before I know it.

"We have much to learn from you," Rolfe declares as we say goodbye, muttering something about high-tech security measures and official prison procedures. "But I hope you also have something to learn from us." It's a grand understatement.

As we file out of the prison, through throngs of men in uniform who pass us unperturbed, one student hugs me and slings her arm through mine. She is giddy; the visit has gone better than expected and she cannot wait for the next one. She wishes there was more time with the imprisoned men, who were so bright and interesting, with many good ideas.

"The visit was, like, amazing," another student, beaming, says during the ride back. "When we meet those guys they were very, very happy. As we were discussing in groups their ideas were really amazing. They are bright. I am very excited to meet those guys. They show us that they have new things to teach us." Adds Santos, when we reach the office, "We have to make a better world. This is a part of peace-building—making sure that those guys who are in prison, they are human beings like others. They will come home and we all live in peace."

Santos is real. All of these students are real. They are survivors of genocide. They have just returned from a dynamic visit to a prison housing the kinds of people who slaughtered their parents— maybe even the very people who slaughtered their parents. And they return dizzy with joy, awed by the discovery that "they" is actually "we," that the men inside have committed monstrosities yet are not monsters, that, as Rolfe put it, it's the cloth that divides.

How can I say such a thing? How can I equate the skulls in those pits with the people whose unfathomable cruelty created them? Alas, the twentieth century alone, in which more than 50 million people were murdered by "civilized" government decrees—during Nazi Germany, the Armenian genocide, the Soviet regime, and so on—has proved how easy it is for good people to turn mass murderers. This is the era of Abu Ghraib, where naked prisoners were stacked high in a pyramid so that American soldiers could photograph each other grinning over their human pile. And more naked prisoners were put on dog leashes and made to perform oral sex acts while these same soldiers gave each other high fives.

This reality—the human capacity, our capacity, for evil—should not distance us from those who commit atrocities. Quite the contrary, it should remind us of a fine line: if not for some grace, there go we.

I say goodbye to the students, knowing that the Prison Visiting Project is in good hands. The visits will continue now that the structure is in place, official permission has been granted, and a sponsor has been found. Santos tells me that future visits, to prisons across the country, will be longer and will include movies, sports, and culture. The program will flourish and grow, he's sure.

———

Inside Bourbon Coffee at Kigali International Airport, awaiting a delayed flight, I take out my book, Desmond Tutu's *No Future Without Forgiveness*. "Forgiveness does not mean condoning what has been done," Tutu writes. "It means taking what happened seriously and not minimizing it; drawing out the sting in the memory that threatens to poison our entire existence. It involves trying to understand the perpetrators and so have empathy, to try to stand in their shoes and appreciate the sort of pressures and influences that might have conditioned them."

I have, in Rwanda, seen Tutu's words take life, along with those of all the academics and thinkers I'd consulted on the road to this trip. I've seen empathy, restitution, and reconciliation in unfathomable doses. Now I have the right to bear witness, to say, *Don't take my word for it—take their word for it.*

In the end I spent just one day in prison in Rwanda. But really I was in prison the whole time I was here. Most of the country is a liquidated prison; those who did not pass through the opened gates into freedom were victims of the ones who did. Rwanda is a grand courtroom putting justice to the test and shattering the very foundation of the concept we call prison. Most imagine that after harm must come punishment. But here lives a radically different paradigm that involves healing, restitution, and that pinnacle of humanity called forgiveness. Rwanda has been a trial. I bore witness to some of the worst atrocities imaginable, and left maintaining my belief that in a world without prisons, the pain of victims and survivors can be treated in radically reimagined ways.

Rwanda has also allowed me to launch my journey the way any reassessment of justice should begin, spending most of my time with survivors and victims—those who ought to be our focus when we think about crime. Now it's time to make an entrance into the world of so-called offenders: Pollsmoor Prison, South Africa.

2.
Sorry | *South Africa*

When a man sins against another, the injured party should not hate the offender and keep silent. It is his duty to inform the offender and say to him, "Why did you do this to me? Why did you sin against me in this matter?" And thus it is said, "You shall surely rebuke your neighbor." If the offender repents and pleads for forgiveness, he should be forgiven. The forgiver should not be obdurate. —Maimonides

I land in the pages of a Jane Austen novel. At least it feels that way, especially coming from Rwanda. I see an eighteenth-century manor and a backdrop of cloud-cloaked mountains, with guinea fowl poised picturesquely on the lawn. My room at the Steenberg Hotel feels like a royal carriage house, with creaking mahogany and a four-poster bed. The air is al dente; the setting sun casts crimson light over the exquisite mesas that ring Cape Town, South Africa, like beatific fortresses.

Helping to fund my stay here is the travel piece I'll write about Constantia, a posh Cape Town suburb and winemaking region that happens to be just a stone's throw from Pollsmoor Maximum Security Prison, among the largest prisons in Africa, home to some 7,500 men, women, and children—including, from 1982 to 1988, Nelson Mandela.

In other words, when I'm not in prison, I'll be immersed in luxury. It's an ironically uncomfortable, yet also apt, way to experience one of the world's most unequal societies, not simply in the glaring contrasts of black and white wealth, but also in the skewed balance between the masses and a rising entrepreneurial super-class. My South African experience will take me from one end of the racial, social, and economic spectrum to the other, and will, I anticipate, be pertinently discomfiting.

These extremes are colonialism's and apartheid's legacy; centuries of grand inequity left a sea of poverty and crime in its wake. The statistics are staggering. South Africa's rate of violent death for men—in 2012, some 16,000 cases of homicide were reported— is eight times the global average, while the female homicide rate is six times it. Over 40 percent of men report having been physically violent to a partner and more than one in four report having perpetrated rape, three-quarters of them before age twenty. In 2012, 64,000 rape cases were reported to the police; even the country's president, Jacob Zuma, a man with four wives and at least twenty children by a host of women, once faced that charge. More people are reputedly knifed to death in Cape Town's townships than in any other metropolitan area.

But as in Rwanda, I've come to engage in forward-thinking work, this time to further explore restorative justice. It's an alternative paradigm for thinking about crime, not as an offense against the state that demands punishment but as an injury done to another that calls for healing and restoration. If Rwanda was about forgiveness and reconciliation on a grand scale, South Africa, where I'll spend a week observing a long-standing restorative justice program inside Pollsmoor, offers a glimpse of these things on a person-to-person basis—individual "sorry"s, not collective ones. Here I hope to examine, with a close and critical lens, the entity at the heart of almost all of my interactions in Rwanda, that strange and powerful force known as forgiveness.

———

My plan had been to walk to Pollsmoor in the morning. It's only yards from my hotel's driveway, sitting on land once owned by wealthy Afrikaner farmers, then sold to the Cape Command for use as a World War II military base, before finally becoming a prison. But the concierge insists I be chauffeured in a Mercedes limousine bearing the hotel logo.

"I bet I'm the first guest you've carried to Pollsmoor," I say to Wilbert, the hotel driver, who has yet to emerge for even a split second from the yoke of high-end formality.

"Yes, ma'am, you are the first," he replies, unflustered.

Welcome To Pollsmoor Correctional Facility: A Place Of New Beginnings, reads the sign. We pull up to the gate, where the officers toss an indifferent glance my way and wave us inside. I'm early, so none of the others I'm meant to meet have arrived.

"Are you certain you'll be fine, ma'am?" Wilbert asks with a worried look. Pollsmoor has an outsized reputation for vicious violence, mostly due to its highly ritualized gangs, known as the Numbers. It's said that the 26s are responsible for gambling, smuggling, and accruing wealth; the 28s are organized around the keeping of sexual partners, or "wyfies," and fighting on behalf of all three groups; and the 27s are the peacekeepers and guardians of gang law. I've been told that stabbings at Pollsmoor are practically a daily occurrence; in 2011 there were forty-seven suicides and murders behind South African bars, and the corrections department owed billions in damages to prisoners and former prisoners, mostly for assault and rape. The government has no policy on the prevention of sexual violence in prisons, and infecting a prisoner with HIV is said to be a form of gang punishment. The tuberculosis transmission risk is 90 percent a, and 32 percent of prisons lack a doctor or nurse.

Assuring Wilbert that I will be fine, I take a seat on a plastic bench beside the main security booth. I survey the area. Built for 4,500 people but home to nearly double that, Pollsmoor still resembles a massive military compound, a compendium of bastions and barbed wire. There's even a renowned on-site restaurant, staffed by prisoners, where curious civilians can order chicken cordon bleu and beef schnitzel. The backdrop of exquisite mountain ranges is staggering: the whole prison is reminiscent of refuse discarded in the middle of Eden.

Another American volunteer arrives. He's from California and he wields a Bible. "God called me here," he explains, as if saying "I caught the red-eye." The two of us take a ten-minute walk along the rims of the barbed wire toward Medium B, our home base for the week. The door is at the end of a narrow, fenced alleyway. There is no metal detector or dress code for us volunteers, and no one confiscates my cell phone. We enter a mess hall–like room, where my nose reacts to the fusty air, thick and mildly rotten. A banner reads, "Restorative Justice: Working Toward Reconciliation And Reintegration."

I lay eyes on something depressingly familiar from American prisons: a sea of black and brown faces above uniforms—less than 10 percent of South Africa's prison population is white. The uniforms are tangerine orange, stamped with CORRECTIONS in a circular design. Many uniforms have been styled out, tailored into funky vests and blazers, with zippers and buttons; one man has sewn on a Nike swoosh. Most men are blanketed in tattoos and many are missing their front teeth, a style favored by Numbers gang members. They rush forward to shake our hands vigorously. This, too, is familiar. It's prisoner–volunteer fraternizing, friendliness fused with boundless optimism over something to be gained from the encounter. There is camaraderie with the wardens, smiles, jokes, teasing. I suspect that it all belies the angst at the core of this place.

Seven tables are swathed in floral tablecloths and labeled with names spelled out in three tongues—English, Afrikaans, and Xhosa, the language of a Southern African Bantu ethnic group. On one side I spy Accountability, Confession, Responsibility, and Repentance; on the other side, Restructuring, Forgiveness, and Integrity.

A rail-thin, sixty-something prisoner with a shaggy salt-and-pepper mustache greets me warmly. Decades ago he served time on Robben Island, he tells me, because he was a freedom fighter. Postapartheid, he returned to his township and found that little had changed; there were no jobs but plenty of drugs. So he resorted to crime and eventually earned a fifteen-year sentence.

Pastor Jonathan Clayton takes center stage, and the rest of us, our seats. Mine is in the back of the room, at a table for nonparticipant observers.

"We apologize for the delay!" comes Jonathan's welcome, in thunderous tones.

"There was an escape yesterday, so security for the prisoners is heavy today. But"—he runs a hand through slicked-back hair, jet-black and faintly dotted with gray—"we are here now, and we are glad to be here!"

In crisp blue Hugo Boss shirt, ivory tie, and handsome slacks, Jonathan cuts a sharp figure. Americans might dub him "Indian," but in Cape Town he is known simply as "colored," a term that rankles my American mind. As the catchall category for anyone who belies the easy black or white, it includes mixed-race individuals as well as those with roots in India, Malaysia, Madagascar, and elsewhere.

Welcome is repeated in sonorous Afrikaans.

"We speak three languages in this room," Jonathan explains. "I will speak English and Afrikaans. Peter"—he points to a white man with a Santa-style beard seated at the Accountability table, surrounded by black men—"will translate to Xhosa for those of you who need Xhosa. You will understand this process. You will understand it in your own language, yes? And we have other ground rules. Is everyone here voluntarily?" Pause.

"We cannot allow you to participate in this restorative justice week if you have been forced to be here." No one protests, so Jonathan continues.

"This program is based on Christian principles but we accept any religion. If you are Muslim, very good. If you are not any religion—that is just fine, eh?

"You have full and total confidentiality in this room. You may be free to speak your mind and your truths at all times, yes? Total confidentiality. But if you confess a murder, and in this confession you tell us things, details, such as the location of the body, we will have to pursue what you have told us. We must do this to help you and the victims be healed, due to the evil things that happened to them and their loved ones. Yes?" Jonathan delivers an Afrikaans translation of this, then goes on.

"This process is very confrontational. Are you prepared for this confrontation? Is anyone *not* prepared for this confrontation? You may speak now and we will escort you out, no questions asked. Remember, this process must be voluntary and free—no forcing here." He surveys the room, which does not stir.

"Last rule of this restorative justice week." His voice is booming now. "You are not an offender. A prisoner. A criminal. You are a *person*, loved by God. You are not an *inmate*—you are a *client* of the *Department of Correctional Services*."

And with that, the program officially begins.

"I declare this restorative justice week open!" Jonathan sounds off, as if the horses are at the gate. Singing commences.

Through you the blind will see,
Through you the mute will sing.
Through you the dead will rise,
Through you all hearts will praise.
Through you the darkness flees,
Through you my heart screams,
I am free, yes, I am free.

Jonathan is at the helm again, distributing the worksheet for today. *Discover You*, reads the heading. *Examine the effects of your hurt, pain, and anger: Who am I? Why am I here? Who hurt me? Who is responsible for my hurt/pain?*

"Who wants to talk about family right now?" Jonathan asks the room.

"I don't talk to my family," one man calls out. Others concur, nodding.

"Why don't you talk to your family?"

"They don't want to listen," comes one voice.

"I have no family," comes another voice.

"I am ashamed," comes another.

"Tomorrow we will phone your families," says Jonathan. "Who gives us permission to do this? Tomorrow you will hear how your family is hurt. Who gives permission? Stand on the bench if you do and identify your name. Please."

Jerome practically leaps on the bench, all hip-hop swagger in his brown Timberland boots. He looks to be in his early twenties and wears his uniform jumpsuit unbuttoned down to his waist, white undershirt visible beneath it. At the Confession table, Gerswin rises; "Al Capone" is tattooed in gothic letters across the back of his skull. Finally, twenty-something Yahiya from Responsibility climbs on his chair and adjusts his white *takiya*, onto which he's slapped a pair of Ray-Bans.

"You are brave. We will hear from your families tomorrow. Thank you, gentlemen. You may take your seats once more." Jonathan proffers a slight bow.

"Tell me," he asks. "What do you want to get out of the process this week?"

Answers spill forth. *Healing. Change. Be a better person. Take responsibility. Peace with my victim. Be part of my community again.*

I want to be a father to my children: this from a solemn, small, elderly man, tattoos covering every inch of his wizened face. A teardrop is imprinted on his cheek.

"Tell me your fears!" Jonathan thunders.

They flow forth. *My children won't recognize me. My children will end up in prison like me.*

Pastor Jonathan Clayton morphs into Professor Clayton, breaking down the principles of restorative justice, complete with a PowerPoint presentation and citations from Howard Zehr, the Minnesota-based father of the movement. Crime is disrespect and irresponsibility, goes the lesson. We don't need more punishment; we need to address broken relationships. He hands out a short poem about the illogic of a prison-based system of justice.

We want them to be responsible,
So we take away all responsibilities.
We want them to be positive and constructive.
So we degrade them and make them useless.
We want them to be nonviolent,
So we put them where there is violence all around them.
We want them to quit being the tough guy,
So we put them where the tough guy's respected.

Instead of asking, as traditional criminal justice does, what laws have been broken, who broke these laws, and how we can punish those who broke them, restorative justice—the philosophy behind such US organizations as Bridges to Life in Texas and Common Justice in New York—asks altogether different questions. Who's been hurt? What are their needs? How can we meet those needs? Some restorative justice programs operate as community courts, which a 2007 University of Pennsylvania study found were more effective than prison at reducing recidivism. Most involve "circles," in which victims and offenders meet and engage in dialogue about the crime;

many are Christian. For all, the goal is victim empowerment of the sort that traditional criminal justice systems leave by the wayside. Study after study has shown that trials, public rituals though they are, are rarely therapeutic for victims. Quite the contrary, they prolong the life of traumatic wounds.

Jonathan approaches to ask if I will go sit at the Confession table and help Gerswin fill out his self-assessment form. Like many in this room, he is illiterate.

I take a seat beside Gerswin and offer a handshake. He gives me the once-over. I notice a star tattooed between his eyes.

"Have you experienced the following," I read aloud from the form. "Anger?"

"Yes," comes Gerswin's answer.

Gangsterism? Yes. Childhood abuse? Yes. Drug addiction? Yes. Depression? Yes. How old are you? Twenty-six. Did you know your father?

"No. Only once when I was a teenager. He was a drunk and my mother, she threw him out. He would beat her up, all bloodied. I would wipe up her blood." I write this down.

"What happened when you met your father?"

"I—" Gerswin pauses. "I wanted to kill him. I almost did." I keep scribbling.

"When did you last speak with your family?"

"Three years ago." Gerswin delivers all of his answers in deadpan fashion. He's just another kid from the township, three bullet wounds to prove it. Now he's just another Pollsmoor Numbers gang member. His narrative isn't exceptional, and clearly, he knows it.

We finish completing the form. Waiting for others to do the same, we study each other awkwardly. Lunch, salty sausage in a stale bun, is passed around. I resort to my usual icebreaker.

"You listen to hip-hop?" This elicits a smile.

"Yes, hip-hop. American hip-hop." Gerswin raises his shirt to reveal an unsurprising tattoo: "Thug Life" across his stomach, à la Tupac Shakur. I tell him I never met Tupac, but I did tour with Snoop Dogg for an article once. His whole face lights up. He's suddenly a childlike fan.

"Have you ever"—he leans in, eyes gleaming, mouth full of sausage—"met Lil Wayne?"

We're interrupted by Pastor Ron, the heavyset, sleepy-eyed facilitator at our table. "I must leave for the afternoon," he announces abruptly, folding up his glasses and his lunch bag. "You may take over," he says to me.

And so I am given a new role for the week: part-time facilitator at the table of Confession. Home to Gerswin, Ebrahim, and Anthony. And, when they feel like showing up, Pastor Ron and sidekick Dennis, who stays silent as a stone, his function unknown. All three incarcerated men at my table are admitted gangsters belonging to different Cape Town generations. Gerswin is a member of the 28 gang. Ebrahim, in his thirties, with piercing green eyes, narrow cheekbones, and pencil-thin mustache, belongs to the 27s. Anthony is in his fifties; he was once a member of the Americans, a notorious Cape Town gang, but is now a born-again Christian.

All of the facilitators are, with two exceptions, white. This reality reminds me of the unfortunate, too-familiar white-savior-of-black-souls dynamic, but for the week I have little choice but to stomach it.

"I have four children," Anthony reads from his sheet. "I buried one of them several years ago. One of my daughters is here, in Pollsmoor. She was caught with her boyfriend's drugs. I caught sight of her once, is how I knew she was here." Then the bomb dropped: "I raped my stepdaughter. I was so high on drugs, I didn't know what I was doing or who she was."

And for the remaining hours of the day, the room erupts with narratives of pain. It becomes an aural fun-house mirror, in which stories echo and reverberate. *My mother was high on drugs and alcohol when I was a baby. I was shot seven times. I saw gangsters kill my father. My father died of AIDS.* The tales of poverty and crime, gunshots, drug addiction, and abuse might well be set in Brooklyn, New York, or South Side Chicago. Only here they are monstrously exaggerated, everything that lives in American prison narratives but *more*—more violence, more drugs, more abuse, more wounds. *I killed my stepfather. He abused me and my mother one too many times so I stabbed him.* This from Peter-John, aka PJ, a formerly incarcerated facilitator.

Jonathan is getting the men to see themselves as victims in vicious cycles of violence, which is critical. People often forget that all over the world, most offenders are also victims. The 2015 Boston Reentry Study, for instance, found a strikingly high incidence of childhood trauma among people returning from prison, with more than 40 percent having witnessed a homicide and half having been physically abused by their parents. But still I do have my moments of skepticism, during which I wonder about, say, the man who tearfully declares that he dealt illegal diamonds not because he wanted money but because he was desperate for his father's love. Really?

"We spend today," Jonathan concludes, "so you realize that you are victims of hurt. You are not only offenders. You are victims. You have been deeply hurt."

And with that, day one is a wrap. I say goodbye to Gerswin, Anthony, and Ebrahim and file out of Medium B. Outside the barbed wire, a Steenberg limo awaits. Climbing in, I feel tremendous shame.

This is work, I tell myself. This limo is not mine—it belongs to my assignment. An assignment I'm privileged to have. Privilege cannot be discarded when convenient, however many barbed-wire fences one crosses. In fact, denial of privilege is the ultimate mark of it.

I repeat this mantra as evening descends and I take in the oak-lined streets and colonial mansions of Constantia. At a lavish dinner, I look around me. Whiteness. Everywhere, except for my waiter. If this is Cape Town postapartheid, I can only imagine the look of things at the height of it. Ghosts of my day begin to invade an elegant evening. Gerswin scowls at my foie gras; PJ sips my Smirnoff. These men are products of the posh world I'm indulging in, conditioned for crime and prison by a society founded on inequality. It began with the Dutch regime, which used local jails to incarcerate those violating the country's "pass" laws, requiring them to carry passports stating their race. During the late nineteenth-century period of British colonial expansion, prison labor fueled the country's workforce, so between 1916 and the end of apartheid in 1986, 17 million blacks and coloreds were imprisoned, subjected to corporal punishment, and made to work in the country's diamond and gold mines for companies, like De Beers, who made fortunes off their backs. Pollsmoor was born primarily for capitalist purposes, not criminal justice ones. After World War II, when the area's farms demanded prison labor, it made sense to set a prison in the area.

This is true of prison history as a whole. For centuries the institution has expediently produced what its birthmate, capitalism, demands: a perpetual labor force. The process was to criminalize "others" by tilting the law against them, then incarcerate them and put them to work. In the United States, where prisoners produced goods for the Union army and then became the South's postemancipation labor force, so-called black codes criminalized such things as loitering and joblessness, which meant that by 1870 in the South, black incarceration rates tripled those of whites. For centuries in Europe, confinement had its greatest vogue during times of unemployment, when it made sense to withdraw labor from the overstocked market and put it to work for the state. It's striking that so many early prison drawings, detailed charts and diagrams about where to situate all those bodies, are eerily reminiscent of slave ship renderings. Slavery, prison, capitalism, and race have long been a deadly global cocktail. Prison was a way to subjugate natives or former slaves while serving the white economy's best interests.

Our workshop at Pollsmoor hinges on owning choices and working to change them. But considering this history, and the extremity of what I've been seeing here in Cape Town, my cynicism about this thing we call choice intensifies. What is choice in the context of slavery, prison labor, apartheid, segregation, townships? Is all this talk about taking personal responsibility and saying one is sorry clouding the reality of systems designed for some to dramatically fail and others to succeed?

Capitalism rests on the notion of the individual standing alone, over and above social factors. That's the essence of the American dream: "I" over "we." *Pull yourself up by the bootstraps*, goes the mantra. But what of the classes and colors who weren't provided with bootstraps to begin with? We like to talk about giving prisoners second chances, but what about *first* chances? It's easy to lap up glorious stories about the exceptions, the ones who overcame the race-and-class odds, because it's more fun to celebrate the exception than lament the rule.

The word "scapegoat" flashes across my mental screen, from my favorite essay about prisons, by economist Glenn Loury. "Our society—the society we together have made," he writes, "first tolerates crime-promoting conditions in our sprawling urban ghettos, and then goes on to act out rituals of punishment against them as some awful form of human sacrifice." I cannot vanquish that scapegoat image, in its literal, biblical sense: a creature onto which all of society's sins were thrust and who was then tossed over a cliff to absolve the rest. Sixteenth-century philosopher Thomas More wrote as much in *Utopia*. "If you suffer people to be ill-educated, and their manners to be corrupted from their infancy, and then punish them for those crimes to which their first education disposed them, what else is to be concluded from this, but that you first make thieves and then punish them?"

"Check, please," I tell my waiter. He bows.

———

"Reconciliation Is the Journey from Truth to Justice." So reads a headline in the *Cape News* the next morning. In between the how-far-we've-fallen-since-Mandela stories making up much of the South African news, here's a story about Olga Macingwane, recipient of the Institute for Justice and Reconciliation Award, victim of a racially motivated bomb attack in 1996—a woman who publicly forgave the white men who maimed her.

Minutes later, I'm inside Medium B, noting how sunny and bright it is. Under apartheid this was Pollsmoor's white prison, boasting more windows than the black or colored units. That fact also explains its double hallways; racial comingling of any sort was not permitted. The very architecture of colonial African prisons thus transmitted a weighty message about racial superiority.

Inside the gym, Anthony gives me a warm handshake and a toothless grin. Ebrahim and Gerswin offer circumspect nods. Facilitators sit serenely, reading their Bibles.

Objective: Understanding the crisis/damage/hurt/pain caused by crime, reads the handout Jonathan presents me with. *The inmates will understand in detail the effects of their wrong decisions. Other people are experiencing a crisis because of their wrong actions.*

"I am free," I sing, in unison with the prisoners. Then Jonathan begins today's session, and true to form, he knows how to immediately grab our attention.

"Twenty-five years, forty days, and thirty-five minutes ago, I was a Pollsmoor resident like you," he declares.

"That is my confession today. I was once a prisoner, for three years. I stole, I lied, I did wrong, eh? But I stand before you today, a different man. I knew no English whatsoever when I first came to prison, you see? Only Afrikaans. I learned everything inside and I turned myself around. This process is the beginning of your doing as I did. It starts with confession. This day you will confess, eh? You will confess so that you become free."

Papers are distributed.

"We will get unreported crimes. We always do," Jonathan whispers to me as the men log their confessions. "Once even a guard confessed, to running a smuggling ring." He scans the room with an eagle eye.

"For seven years, I did this alone. Just me alone, with no facilitators, and fifty, sixty prisoners," he goes on. "The handbook was fourteen pages then—now it's eighty-five. I would call the prisoners 'sir'—the authorities couldn't understand this, for years, the way it's about treating them as human beings, as people. Even these white tablecloths, the authorities couldn't understand those. Sit around a proper table and have a meal like humans, I said." He pounds his fist on the table. Then he breaks down the full dimensions of the program, for my benefit. After these six days there's a once-a-week follow-up with the men; during these months he'll locate the men's victims and arrange dialogues with them.

As the prisoners scribble away, a fired-up Jonathan goes on with a nutshell history of this workshop and his Hope Prison Ministries, now operating in nine prisons. By 1994, Mandela's election to the presidency represented the final nail in apartheid's coffin. In 1999 Jonathan was a prison chaplain, but as the Truth and Reconciliation Commission left its potent mark on South Africa—"this unbelievable process of dialogue and confession and reconciliation about apartheid crimes, our country found a healing through it"—he became obsessed with restorative justice and traveled to a peacemaking institute in Vermont to earn a certificate in it. Then he returned with a request for the prison authorities. Let me introduce restorative justice to Pollsmoor, he suggested. Give me your toughest prisoners and let me work with them, bringing volunteers inside to do the same.

His request came at the right time: as apartheid was being dismantled, the South African prison system was radically reformed. Pollsmoor became desegregated in 1991. Shortly thereafter, the Prisons Act was amended. Prison Service became DCS—the Department of Correctional Services. Solitary confinement and corporal punishment were abolished and DCS pledged to respect the fundamental rights of all people in prison. In 1997 a renowned warden, Johnny Jansen, took over Pollsmoor and for the first time opened its doors to a host of NGOs, eager to make the place more humane. The Victim–Offender Dialogue program was introduced and is still touted on a DCS Web site saturated in the vocabulary of restorative justice.

Along these lines, Jonathan continues, South Africa opens the doors of many parole hearings to victims and encourages prisoners to reach out to their victims. In fact, Jonathan explains, those who've *not* attempted to engage in dialogue with their victims severely diminish their chances of getting parole. This adds up to a great deal of pressure on the man who is, due to budget cuts, Pollsmoor's lone restorative justice show in town. The administration wants prisoners to get parole—not from love of mercy but because there's simply no more room in the overburdened system for everyone.

At Pollsmoor there's one social worker for every three hundred or so prisoners. They avidly refer prisoners to Jonathan, who doesn't accept everyone and promises nothing, including the coveted letter of support that increases chances of parole. But he does sometimes find himself scouring the nooks and crannies of the townships like a crazed bounty hunter. *Have you seen this man they call Nordling? Do you know the mother of the man who was murdered here two years ago? The girl who was raped outside that shebeen seven months ago?* He's searching for victims in the hopes of getting them to attend parole hearings or dialogue with their offenders, anything that will make him feel he can in good conscience endorse his prisoners as genuinely remorseful and thus worthy of release.

But how do you know who's genuinely remorseful? Saying sorry—and this is the bête noire of restorative justice—leaves potential for what philosopher John Drabinski calls "obstinate narcissism," which has us hurrying past another's pain "in order to 'promote,' for lack of a better word, this new self that has (allegedly) emerged after the harm we've caused." Jonathan's task, an impossible one, is to play God with a prisoner's heart and figure out who's professing cheap grace.

"The men, they tell me, 'I want to say I'm sorry. I was wrong. I am so sorry.' And I tell them, 'It's not about you! It's about your victim. Not *your* needs. Your victim's needs.'

"Parole once asked me to set up a mediation involving a guy who killed the son of a high-profile gangster. They said, 'We need this done quick quick!' and I said, 'Hold your horses! This is delicate stuff. Dangerous stuff, eh? I need six months.' I talked to that gangster's men. I did homework in the community. Then I went to the gangster himself and paid respects—I followed protocol. By the end of it, they sat together and they shook hands. He did get parole. There have been no killings since." Jonathan shakes his head vigorously. "That was a rough case."

He returns to the helm and collects the confession logs.

"How did this feel? To write these confessions, to talk about them at your tables?"

"We are opening up and revealing things we cannot talk about," Jerome calls out, sounding much like a student hungry for the teacher's approval.

"For all my life I've never had someone I could talk about feelings with," interjects Yahiya, Ray-Bans still coolly perched on his white *takiya*. "Now I can think that my life is not only a—" He slips into Afrikaans.

Jonathan: "He is using prison language—it means a flop, a disaster. Your life is not only a flop, yes?"

Gerswin rises. "I confess that I made promises to my family, to stay out of prison. But then they disappoint me and I react and I am violent. And then I end up in prison again."

Jerome, again: "I confess that I stole. To feed my girlfriend."

"To feed your girlfriend?" Jonathan presses him.

"Well, some to her. And to party," Jerome admits.

"And what else?" Jonathan sees right through him.

"Well, drugs." Methamphetamine is an omnipresent staple of township life, inextricably tied to crime there.

"Are you still together with this girlfriend, who you stole for?" Jerome shakes his head.

"See, this"—Jonathan air-jabs lean fingers at Jerome, who's now hanging his head—"is a perfect example of what we call a *thinking error*. Yes? He is blaming someone else, when really who is to blame? Himself. You stole so you could do drugs. Not for someone else—for *you*."

Then it's time for phone calls, as promised yesterday.

"Gerswin, do you still want me to make this call?" Jonathan asks. "You didn't make an emotional decision—you are ready for this?" Gerswin nods, but looks manifestly uneasy. Jonathan whips out his BlackBerry.

"Hello! Is this—who? Maria?"

"That is my mom," Gerswin calls. He's rocking back and forth, his right leg quaking.

Jonathan switches into Afrikaans on the phone. "*Ja, Ja*," he nods. More Afrikaans. He hangs up.

"She says she is cooking and working now so she can't talk. But she says we can call her back later and she will talk. She asked me right away, when I said her son's name, 'What did he do?'" Gerswin looks wholly deflated.

The next call is to Jerome's mom. She does much of the talking; Jonathan paces with phone to ear, repeating "*Ja, Ja,*" and running a hand through his hair.

Jonathan hangs up and announces, "'I'm sleeping well now,' she says. 'But when he's here, I don't. I worry about my safety when he is here, and I cannot sleep. He brings trouble and violence. I do not think I will come to the visit on Saturday—he knows why.' She says to you, Jerome, 'I love you but I don't want you home.' She hopes you stay in prison because she cannot be safe if you are out and she says you and the family will end up dead."

Her words slice ferociously through the room. Jerome grips his head in his hands.

"How do you feel?" Jonathan asks him.

He says nothing, hands still cradling his head. Then, softly, without looking up: "It makes me want to give up. To go back to that lifestyle, to do crimes."

Jonathan puts a hand on Jerome's shoulder.

"You're not alone," he tells him. "We support you, sir. We believe you can change."

Such change demands confrontation with victims, and often restorative justice programs use a stand-in, a violent crime victim whose pain represents that of all those wronged by prisoners' actions. At Pollsmoor today it is Robin Crawford. Small, gray-haired, and grandfatherly, he speaks softly and almost detachedly of the day he was viciously attacked by a gang in Johannesburg.

"'We're going to give you AIDS, you fucking white bastard,' they shouted at me," Robin says feebly. "They pulled my pants down to my ankles and sodomized me. I was screaming. Blood was gushing out of every orifice. I spent four weeks in the hospital recovering, in a trauma unit. There was a hole in my ankle, made by a concrete slab that was aimed at my head. I couldn't sleep because I was rigid with fear. I couldn't pass urine, could not have a bowel movement. I refused to look in the mirror. Friends came to visit me and told me that my face looked like a piece of raw liver."

The room stops breathing for a moment.

"Responses to this?" Jonathan asks. Robin looks forlorn. The men in orange are silenced.

"I feel sick at these crimes in my own country," one facilitator calls out.

"If this was your victim, what would you say?" Jonathan asks. No one stirs. "Anyone have the courage to say something?"

"Sorry," Jerome calls out, faintly.

"Not enough!" Jonathan thunders. The responses trickle in.

"You are very brave."

"God bless you."

"I'm sorry and please forgive me. But I need to change my life."

The men are instructed to write letters to Robin, expressing what they might say to him and their own victims. I move back to Confession to put Gerswin's words on paper.

"'Dear Robin,'" Gerswin begins. He is ready, words hungry to be released. "I hope you will continue to use your pain to give us strength. Thank you for sharing your pain with us. I am sorry for your pain." We fold the letter and wait.

Gerswin gives me yet another once-over. Then he begins to talk to me. First, about his life at Pollsmoor. Like most residents here, he shares his crammed quarters with more than three dozen others; he's locked in there daily from 4:00 p.m.—when guards take leave and the place becomes a notorious free-for-all—until 6:00 a.m. Then he begins to talk about his life on the outside, the street stabbings, the number of men he thinks he's murdered, he can't be sure how many. About the Numbers gangs, to which he belongs — "we came to be as a good gang, to fight apartheid, originally." Legend has it that the Numbers were born when two Zulu men, Po and Nongoloza, set out to rob colonial outposts in an effort to redistribute the country's wealth. During apartheid, they fought for prisoners' rights on the inside, demanding beds, decent food, the right to wear watches and thus have some control over the passing of time.

Gerswin says he cannot count the times he's been behind these bars. And he knows he's wanted on the streets of his township, so much so that he refused parole last time because he knew he'd slip right back into his old lifestyle.

Lunch is passed around. Gerswin asks Ebrahim for a halal meal.

"Six months ago I became Muslim," he explains. "Some say it's a skill—how do you say?—like a hustle. Like I am pretending. But I know the truth." He pounds his chest.

Chomping into his baloney sandwich, he explains that he goes up for parole next month. Then he describes his drug habit, how it consumed him, destroyed him, ran his life. He puts his baloney sandwich down and looks me in the eye. I notice a deep scar between his brows, below the star tattoo, like a permanent crease.

"When I needed drugs, Baz, I would do anything. I would have shot Pastor Clayton right in his face. *In his face.*" I believe him. But is this a confession or a boast?

"How do you feel about the phone call, to your mother?"

"Her response will be worse than Jerome's. I told him so. She will say worse things about me."

"How do you feel about that, though?" He shrugs.

"I am over it."

"Really?" He nods, chewing, his face like stone.

"Sometimes," I say, "we think we're over things, but it's impacting us in all kinds of ways—we don't even realize." He shrugs again, leg shaking.

Robin, meanwhile, begins reading the letters. After the fourth one, he looks up.

"I am touched beyond words," he announces, tenderly. He continues reading. Later that day, he proclaims that he'd like to volunteer as a facilitator in this program. It's a breathtaking moment, a flashback to Rwanda, an act of forgiveness and reconciliation that many deem impossible.

But I know the data that say it is possible, psychological studies proving the power of "sorry" and rethinking what victims really want. Restorative justice literature outlines the four needs of victims: truthful answers; empowerment; restoration of respect, usually achieved by the repeated telling of their stories of harm; and restitution, which can be a statement of responsibility or a literal payback. Such needs are best met through dialogue, not punishment and trials, which usually marginalize victims, turning them into passive observers. A study of Chile's National Commission for Truth and Reconciliation, for instance, conducted in 1991 to address the human rights abuses that occurred during the Pinochet regime, showed that hardly anyone wanted vengeance; they wanted justice and truth, and to honor lost loved ones, and assurance that the atrocities wouldn't happen again. Victims who participate in victim–offender dialogue are again and again shown to feel less fear and to experience high levels of satisfaction with the criminal justice system.

Philosopher Hannah Arendt called forgiveness "the only reaction which does not merely re-act but acts anew and unexpectedly, unconditioned by the act which provoked it." Forgiveness is a miracle—a life-enhancing one. Social, developmental, and clinical psychologists began mapping this miracle in the 1990s, defining it as a state in which the offended is no longer negatively driven by avoiding the offender or taking revenge on him, and instead is fueled by constructive, prosocial motivations. Tools such as the Forgiveness of Others scale and the Forgiveness Inventory were devised to gauge merciful and vengeful impulses. One study showed that feelings of victimization incur passivity, making people less efficient with everyday tasks and quicker to give up. In 1998 two psychologists surveyed survivors of childhood sexual abuse and, finding better marital relationships among those who scored higher on the forgiveness scale, concluded that forgiveness in one realm translates to another. And a 2008 study reported in the *Journal of Personality and Social Psychology* found that far from producing closure, vengeance increases one's unsettled aggression by making one fixate on the wrongdoer.

Participants in another study were asked to recall a specific offending event and engage in four types of imagery: focusing on the hurt, nursing a grudge, empathizing with the offender's human qualities, or forgiving. During the latter, subjects' forgiving feelings manifested physiologically—they showed less elevation in systolic and diastolic blood pressure and lower heart rate when recalling the event. In another trio of studies conducted by psychologists in 2002, participants were asked to envision themselves as robbery victims and then imagine receiving, the day after their victimization, an apology, restitution, both, or neither. When victims received strong apologies they reported feeling less vengeance, anger, and fear, and more forgiveness; when they received both apology and restitution, effect magnitudes about doubled.

Ultimately, retribution has a backlash effect that harms us all. In one 1999 experiment, male undergraduate students were led to believe that they'd unintentionally broken a piece of lab equipment. Then, from the experimenter, they received forgiveness, retribution, both responses, or neither. The experimenter next asked participants to deliver materials to various offices on campus. Participants who received forgiveness showed greatest compliance with this request, whereas those who received retribution showed the least compliance. The giftlike quality of the forgiveness received by the wrongdoers made inequity so tangible, it compelled them to restore equity by performing a positive act of restitution. In other words, punishing people perpetuates destructive actions—and thus increases crime—by amplifying resentments. Forgiveness promotes social order and peace.

———

It's time to ring Gerswin's mom. She can talk now, and she does, in rapid, emotion-laden Afrikaans, which Jonathan shares with all of us after hanging up.

"People are looking for you in the community," he begins, gravely. "Your two sisters live in fear because of your gang affiliation. The word they use for you is *buta*—big brother—your sisters call you that. There is that kind of a respect for you, eh? Your sisters miss having their big brother."

Gerswin's face has gone white. His leg trembles in double time. Jonathan continues.

"Your cousin was shot ten times, his friend eleven times. Your mother, she wants you out of prison but has no guarantee she can keep you out. Your sisters need you. This is what she says. She does not think she can keep you out of prison; the family is not safe if you are home."

"But I tried," comes Gerswin's protest, blurted out with angst. "I tried to reach out. She always, yes? She makes excuses for why she won't see me and talk to me."

"How long?" asks Jonathan. "How long have you tried to reach out to her for?"

"Three years since I have seen them."

"I will bring your mother and sister here tomorrow. I will send a car for them and they will come here for you to talk to." Jonathan walks over to our table and puts a hand on Gerswin's shoulder.

"You are crying inside. Crying for a mother. I will bring her to you tomorrow."

Gerswin looks overwhelmed: emotionally at sea, as if he's been handed a set of tools for a job but doesn't know what the job is or quite how to use the tools.

"Baz, I never gave myself the chance to talk to people like this," Gerswin proclaims, exhaling with relief.

"How do you feel?" I ask.

"Great," he says, his face lit up. "Now my mother—she cannot run away, she will answer. She will have to answer. Finally. Tomorrow."

Leaving Pollsmoor that day, I get lost in memories of New Year's, 2005. I was in my twenties, unprecedentedly in love with a quite wonderful, quite flawed man who'd moved to the United States from the Caribbean only about a year earlier. Jon made me very happy until the day I got a call from his wife about their son, both of whose existence was news to me. I was floored. In time, I healed; we all do, eventually, once we get over our selfish sense of being singularly wronged by the universe. He and I were back together, on-again, off-again, for a number of years, during which he blamed his mistakes on totally legitimate yet wholly exasperating excuses: racism, lack of education, a hideous economy, and the travails of getting a green card. And for years, I lusted after a single thing from him, an apology. Our love took too long to get over because it required me to forgive a man whose owning of mistakes came in fits and starts and, ultimately, too late.

Why does my petty heartbreak remind me of Pollsmoor? I have no right to connect something so minor with something so major. Yet Gerswin somehow reminds me of Jon. Both are products of a system stacked against them. Yet both are still tasked to slowly don the mantle of responsibility, own mistakes in fleeting bursts that inspire but, because they tend not to last, potentially disappoint. Both have inherited an inherent flawedness, for lack of a better word, of a whole lifestyle. I'm blessed to have never been a victim of a major crime, and I have no right to compare any experience to that one. But I have been the victim of emotional harm by another.

So have all of us. Surely you know at least one living, breathing scarlet letter—someone who erred, maybe even gravely, maybe even against you, and is laboring to come correct. And sometimes not just correct but uber-correct, revising and remaking themselves in ways even those of us with the best of therapists can merely aspire to. Call them modern-day St. Augustines, Malcolm Xs, Mary Magdalenes—there's a reason religion and lore are filled with sinners-turned-saints; formerly flawed souls come clean in the noblest of ways. So however far you live, literally and metaphorically, from a prison, you've had to grapple with making mistakes, with forgiving and being forgiven. This is why prisons aren't

really foreign to anyone; they're something we can all, on a theoretical level, viscerally comprehend.

———

"O Faithful One": a new hymn has slipped into the morning song list.
I've been trying to keep my religious biases in check, my feeling that
in prison religion becomes the road to complacency and passivity,
because I do recognize that it can also serve positive ends. America
recognizes this, too; in 2003, Florida became the first state to dedi-
cate an entire correctional facility to a faith-based model, opening the first of four Faith-Based Character Institutions. In these,
about 3,300 men devote their day to religious activities including worship, scriptural study, mentoring, and character development programs related to parenting and anger management. Staff
and volunteers reported improvements in prisoners' attitudes and
behavior, while the prisoners themselves described the FBCIs as
less stressful and more conducive to self-improvement than traditional prisons.

Pocketing my skepticism, I scan the daily objective, which is
"to instill the core values of honesty, respect, trust, and integrity." Pastor Ron, sporting shades, is with us today, as is Dennis.
Gerswin, wearing a white *takiya* that matches Yahiya's, gives me
a hearty handshake as I sit down at our table for initial discussion. Anthony offers his signature toothless grin and Ebrahim nods
coldly in my direction.

When asked to address feelings about his victim, Gerswin says
flatly, "Well, Pastor Ron, I felt very bad." Do I detect a smirk?

"I don't want to talk about my victim," says Ebrahim.

Lifting a hand off his rotund belly, Pastor Ron touches Ebrahim's cheek. "You will be ready to heal soon, my son," he sighs.

Then, hand lightly placed on Gerswin's chest, by his heart: "You too, my son."

"You are both Muslim, yes?" he continues. The two prisoners nod.

"You are truly Christian, in your hearts." Hand on cheeks again. "I see it, yes. Christians. You love Jesus, deep in your souls. In your hearts." Hand on cheeks, hand on hearts.

"Let us pray for Gerswin," says Dennis, head low and eyes half-closed. I swallow my mounting exasperation and bow my head. A moment of silence for Gerswin's lost, non-Christian soul.

Heads up. "Are you ready to give up your number, Gerswin? No more gangsterism?"

"No, Pastor Ron."

"Will you still carry a firearm?"

"It's not so easy, Pastor Ron. But Pastor Ron, I will not use it. I will be a good man when I come home."

The pastor has already moved on to Ebrahim. "Will *you* give up your number?" Ebrahim hangs his head, a mischievous look in his green eyes. He says nothing. Pastor Ron mumbles something about Jesus saving and continues. "Ebrahim, when you leave this place, will you give in to peer pressure?"

"No, Pastor Ron."

"And Gerswin, where will you live, when you come home?"

"With my old community. With my old friends but also my enemies. This way I can show them the path that is right, that I have changed."

"Excellent idea, Gerswin!"

Terrible idea! I can't contain myself anymore.

It's break time, but Gerswin and I stay put as everyone else makes restroom runs. I ask him, point-blank, if he's just going through the motions, telling the pastor what he wants to hear. He shakes his head vigorously. But Gerswin, let's talk about your game plan. The debate turns heated. I tell him that when my students in America come home, they avoid their former neighborhoods like the plague, lest they fall back into old lifestyles. Many of them want to work with at-risk youth and share their hard-earned wisdom, but they realize that they have to be sure they've saved themselves before they set out to save everyone else. He's adamant that he can resist and insists that he has a calling to guide the youth in the right direction.

Finally, at a standstill, he asks me if I will come with him to meet his mother this afternoon. She's on her way. Jonathan had someone pick her up and escort her from the township.

That afternoon, Jonathan and I head to the building entrance area to greet Gerswin's sister and his mother, just a few years older than I am. She gives us dense, grudging hellos and sits down with a huff on the bench in the waiting room. His nineteen-year-old sister, wearing jeans and a tight red top and headband, promptly bursts into sobs. I sit down beside her.

"I didn't want to come," she tells me, a river of tears streaming down flushed cheeks. Her mother stares blankly at the wall. I hand her a tissue. You're in school, I ask? No. Work? She shakes her head.

"I just, you know. Hang out," she sniffles.

Jonathan guides us to the social worker's office. She greets us warmly, in booming Afrikaans. Her military-style prison uniform resembles the one worn by guards, combat boots and all. She just learned about this reconciliation meeting this morning, but she'll do her best.

Gerswin enters. No one moves a muscle as he plunks himself down between his mother and sister, whom he hasn't seen in three years, and looks straight ahead, stolid.

"*Drukkie!*" commands the social worker. Gerswin obeys and gives his mother a stiff hug. As he embraces his sister, her sobs return. Gerswin is visibly moved and does not let go of her. His mother continues to stare at the wall and his sister's tears leave broad wet spots on the shoulder of his orange uniform. He grips her hand and she grips a tissue as the social worker orchestrates a dialogue, Jonathan intervening every now and then to translate for me.

It's an emotional Ping-Pong match. Mom came in drunk one night from the shebeen, husband in tow, and tried to stab her own son. Son has been committing crimes since age ten, when he sold the new clothes Mom bought him for school and used the money to buy drugs. Yes, she's struggled with drugs and alcohol, too. But she had him when she was fifteen years old, after she was raped by the man who would show up drunk on her wedding day.

"He is twenty-six now!" says Mom, finger pointed and voice raised. "He has a daughter who is eight. She is in danger! So are we!" Anger fills the room like hazardous smoke and Gerswin wears a face I haven't yet seen on him: sullen, pained, confused, lost.

"You never protected me from any of those men you took home!" Gerswin grips his sister's hand even more tightly. "You never protected *her!*"

Suddenly, deeply feeling my not belonging here, I signal to Jonathan that I'm ready to head out. Let the professionals and the family members work privately. I conjure up a supportive smile for Gerswin and exit the gates.

———

Days and hours at Pollsmoor march by, thick with narratives and pain. There's the moment Anthony owns his mistakes toward his wife — "when we were married I'd watch rugby instead of going with her to weddings, to gatherings" — then shakes his head and goes on, owning up to far grander wrongs. "I spent my life chasing after women and money. *I raped my own stepdaughter.*"

There's the moment Gerswin, calmer and more somber after the meeting with his mother, admits to being emotionally upended.

"I feel — what do you say? — two things at once. I see that my mother is a victim, too. I had to see my baby sister, she loves me and I hurt her. I see the ripple effect of my actions and my crime." I'm struck by his use of restorative justice vocabulary; apparently the lessons are sinking in.

"But I feel angry, Baz. And so I think, why should I stop my actions? And it is this, see — I want — a father. I am jealous of these happy families. What did I have? Zero. Drugs."

And there is, too, the afternoon at a coffee shop, post-Pollsmoor, when I ask Jonathan to tell me the long story of how he came to devote his life to restorative justice.

He grew up in Paarl, near the Winelands outside Cape Town. His grandfather lost his farm under apartheid land seizures, and the only white people he ever saw were those who came to preach in his ultra-strict church, all the while refusing to acknowledge apartheid as a moral wrong. He was taught to revere them. "Back in those days, if a white person smiled at you, you'd think it was God himself," he laughs.

When his mother was pregnant with him, her neighbor was pregnant, too — from the same man. His father then had an affair with the housekeeper before eventually abandoning his wife and seven children altogether. Dropping out of school in the tenth grade to work in a factory and support his mother, Jonathan discovered he'd become just like his father.

"I loved women. Entertaining women, being in the company of women. And to do that I needed money." He took it wherever and however he could, via credit-card schemes, petty thefts, small hustles.

"When I finally got arrested, my mother came to the police station and said, 'I'll pray for you, my son.' Another cousin came with a Bible and I almost spit in his face. I wanted nothing to do with religion." Handed a six-year sentence, he eventually landed in a maximum security unit of Pollsmoor, the only colored section with available beds. He learned English behind bars.

Good behavior earned him early freedom, in 1990. At the gates waiting for him was the one woman who'd stayed in contact with him throughout his incarceration, a childhood friend named Jenny.

"She said two things were on the agenda for that day, the day of my release." Jonathan grins broadly, as if greeting the memory. "'One: my mother prayed for you every morning—you will join her for prayer. Second: I'm going to take you to your dad.' I said, 'Jenny, you're mad.' I hated that man with a passion—he never even came to visit me. *Hated* him, eh? But I did what Jenny said. We went to my father's house and I walked in, and a five-year-old boy ran to me and put his arms around my neck and called me *buta*, 'great brother.' I was thirty-one years old and I embraced him. I took my father's hand. That was my first experience with restorative justice, without knowing it."

"Meet my wife!" Jonathan announces at Pollsmoor one day. Jenny, all smiles in her pink lipstick, wears a chic black-and-white suit and her raven-colored hair is pulled back into a neat ponytail. She's Pastor Clayton, too, a minister who runs restorative justice workshops in Pollsmoor's women's prison, next door. Jonathan had painted their courtship to me in sparkling detail. He'd known her during his rebellious, womanizing days—"I threw eyes at her when I was at my girlfriend's house. She wouldn't have any of it, eh? But we became friends." They stayed in touch, even after his arrest. And on January 1, 1989, after he'd been incarcerated for just under a year, she surprised him by showing up. They corresponded in long, detailed letters, and Jonathan kept painstaking notes of her every visit. After his mother's death, he began addressing his letters to "my loving Jenny." But all along he'd assumed he was pushing the envelope. She'd never marry, he thought. Her life would be devoted to the church. So he merely dropped hints, even postrelease, while he worked grueling hours driving a truck for a bakery and they spent every day together. Even, too, after he set his hand on her leg and she didn't remove it. And even after he took her to dinner, hid a diamond ring in her dessert, yet couldn't bring himself to propose. Finally, in 1991, Jenny turned to Jonathan and said, "The answer is yes. Do you remember the question?"

The prisoners gaze at Jenny, awed, as she narrates a slide show: *The Claytons*. Amy Joy is eighteen, Kara Chloe fifteen. "I never told them to serve God. They choose to live righteously as they do," she says. Here they are going to prom, in dresses resembling red-velvet cakes. Here they are in their church best, all smiles and grace. Jerome and Gerswin's eyes grow wide as they behold the picture-perfect family that neither they nor a single man in this room have been privileged to have.

"And these girls," Jenny continues, glowing with smiles, "they are not shy to say their daddy was in prison. You know why?"

Why? The men, entranced, practically shriek.

"Because what you are today is more important than the past. This is what I say to you, my friends. Every day is a new chance to make a correction for yesterday."

———

That ultimate day of correction finally arrives. It's a moment of reckoning. The men in orange will put their week of soul searching to the test by confronting those most acutely impacted and victimized by their deeds, their families. Anthony greets me with the news that he's been denied parole yet again. I tell him I've recently gotten the same news from America, where a parole board consisting of political appointees has decided that twenty-three years is not enough punishment for one of my most promising students, who's been in prison since age eighteen. "The victim wants more time from you," they'd told my student. Do they also want a pound of flesh? I'd angrily wanted to shout at the board. What kind of justice system cultivates such profound levels of vengeance?

"There isn't much out there"—Anthony gestures toward the window, the barbed wire, the Constantia mountain range, with a shrug—"for someone like me. I'm probably—I probably belong here. I'm old." He shrugs again. "Maybe I will die here."

Anthony's family members did not make it today. But many others did. Wives, fathers, mothers, grandmothers, grown sons and daughters trickle in and take seats on benches in the middle of the room. It's a reunion scene of awkward handshakes and suspicious once-overs in lieu of warm embraces. Jerome, whose phone call with his mother had taken a toll on him days earlier, looks nervously around the room and strokes his chin, where faint traces of a beard have begun to sprout. Will his mother show up?

"Welcome!" Jonathan booms. "Welcome to your opportunity to restore broken relationships! It is *your* time. Come forward and make statements. Tell them, tell us, how you feel, eh? You can say, if you want, 'I am sad.' Or 'I am angry.' Or maybe you want to ask questions: 'Why?' 'How long is your sentence?' This is your chance to have them answered, everything you wanted to know. Not to degrade, but to restore. Come forward!"

They come. Eagerly. First, big sister of Yahiya. She faces the gangster who is her brother, who stands with hands on hips, shifting his weight from one leg to another. Yahiya has spoken all week of being hated, rejected by his broken family. During public sessions he has animatedly detailed the feelings of rage that this caused him.

"I don't know you. We weren't raised together. I never wanted to know you because I thought, he is a criminal." She sizes up her brother. He adjusts his shades.

"But now I say to you: You are loved."

Suddenly the gangster collapses into sobs. He hides his head in his hands and cries uncontrollably as his sister goes on. "We will try now to restore that bond. My brother, we will try." They are both sobbing now. Then, at Jonathan's command, they are embracing.

The white prisoner hasn't seen his mother in five years. Mother, widowed just weeks ago, grips his face with both hands. "Look me in the eye, my son," she says. "I unconditionally love you." Son falls, tearfully, into mother's arms.

Watching these narratives broaden before my eyes takes my breath away. It happened when I sat with Gerswin and his mother, too: "apology" in the root sense of the word, from the Greek *apologos*, meaning "story." I've been listening to stories all week, confessions about childhoods, criminal acts, family wrongs, but when offender and victim are reunited, these stories are suddenly infused with fresh dimensions, supplied by family members who were critical protagonists in them, too. In Xhosa, in Afrikaans, in English, the prisoners are solicited, one by one, by the people they love. *Tell me the truth.*

You have made me a failure because I cannot raise my own son.

How could you have stolen from your own wife?

"Resentment is a story-telling passion," writes philosopher Charles Griswold. Restorative justice involves widening and deepening that narrative to include the narrative of the wrong-doer, which does not excuse but does explain. Two architects of restorative justice, Barb Toews and Howard Zehr, propose that the meaning of a given crime must be actively determined through dialogue, and meaningful justice can only emerge when "co-authored by the victim and the offender."

Today's tears thus have a reddish tint; they're a bloodletting. Again and again comes a resounding chorus of those tremendous words. *I am sorry.*

Hardened gangsters collapse, bawling, in their mothers' arms. Fathers confess love for sons they never really knew. Tattooed faces grow puffy and damp. Shame is rife and hours pass; the line grows longer as family members decide that there's more to say, more to ask. Some extrasensitive confrontations, like the wife facing the husband who raped her, are relocated, to be handled privately. But the rest are public acts, a cleansing ritual like nothing I've ever witnessed.

Will you buy me that bicycle, Papa, so we can ride together, like we used to?

Jonathan halts the proceedings. "We can spend all day here," he says. "I can spend the next lifetime here, restoring. But I want everyone to have one hour with family, just to spend time. Don't talk about the weather! This is your quality time. Continue to connect."

Jerome's mother never made it. Jonathan later lets me know that when the car arrived to carry her here, she was too much under the influence to take the ride. He's slumped at his table, disappointment and emotional exhaustion having annihilated the gangster swagger he once exuded. I sit with Gerswin, who makes a declaration.

"Baz, I have decided I will not take parole," he says, nibbling on a meat patty. "I am not ready. I know now that I will react badly. I need more time to work on my anger. I need to work with my family. I will cause trouble if I go home now."

I ask him if he's heard of Malcolm X.

"Is that a rapper?"

I give him the rundown on the gangster-turned-leader who educated himself behind American bars.

"Baz, I will make you a promise," he says. "I will learn to read. I will enroll in the literacy classes. I promise...I feel sorry, Baz. For my family. For my life."

All apologies are promises, so-called performative utterances— words that are also actions. Their ultimate meaning thus hinges on the future, which is why the Jewish sage Maimonides defined true repentance as a scenario in which the sinner faces the same temptation to wrongdoing, yet this time resists it. I believe Gerswin's apology and take his promise as sincere. I also believe many of the apologies I've heard all week long. But forgiveness rarely comes in one fell swoop, rather in fits and starts. So only the future will lend all of these words their true dimension.

The day concludes with a climactic return. On day one of the program, Jonathan had sent one of the guards to purchase three chocolate bars from the shop and presented them to Gerswin, Yahiya, and Jerome. Would the three men in orange return the much-coveted chocolate on the last day? Could they be trusted not to eat or sell this precious commodity?

Gerswin stands proudly on his chair, displays his chocolate, and speaks in steady Afrikaans. "I never allowed people to trust me. I came to realize how many people I hurt in the past. This—it looks like a simple chocolate, but the thought behind it has a lot of significance." In English: "I feel, see, convinced about myself." The room erupts into a standing ovation: three gangsters, standing on chairs and wielding chocolate bars as if they're MVP trophies.

PJ, the facilitator and former Pollsmoor prisoner, closes out the day with a hip-hop performance in Afrikaans. He then shares, in stolid tones, his story of abuse and murder, prison and religion and redemption. Jonathan embraces him and turns to the families.

"I want you to look at him," he says, "and see your son. *This is a good man—and this is your son.*"

That afternoon Wilbert the hotel driver takes me home from Pollsmoor in the limo.

"You will not go to Pollsmoor tomorrow, ma'am?" he asks.

"No, today was the last day."

"Ma'am, I hope you don't mind if I say that I have enjoyed taking you there every morning."

"Thank you, Wilbert."

"Ma'am, yes, it was inspiring to see you come in and out safely every day. See, ma'am"—he pauses and lets out a slight cough—"it is only this close that I did not end up there myself." He holds two fingers up from the wheel.

"The judge said he would give me a second chance. And ma'am, I have done well. It is two months I am on this job. No more crime. I am a new man."

And just like that, two universes collided.

———

I hang around Cape Town for a week after the workshop ends. After all, I'd seen the prison and its uber-white antithesis,

Constantia, but not the world beyond either fortress. I visit the one prison more infamous than Pollsmoor, Robben Island, where Mandela spent eighteen years. Even mass tourism could not dim the profundity of this place. Riding the tour bus I chant songs from Pollsmoor, which refuse to take leave of my consciousness. *I am free, Lord, I am free.*

On my last day, I return to Constantia and knock on a glass office door marked by a small sign, African Prison Ministries: Serving the Forgotten Prisoners of Africa.

"Come, let us go!" Jonathan rushes out. He wants me to see the whole of Pollsmoor, not just the area where the workshop takes place, so we take the five-minute drive to the prison for a full tour. I find it profoundly deflating. Restorative justice offers magnificent promise, but Pollsmoor itself offers nothing in the way of redemption. Nearly one-third of the prison population is on remand and the country's recidivism rate is at 80 percent. We pass through the area known as "Afghanistan"—fighting here is sheer warfare, Jonathan explains— and through the next double hallway. "I spent nine months in that section, right there, downstairs," Jonathan says.

En route to Medium B, Jonathan sends the guard to produce Anthony and Ebrahim. They bring smiles and thanks; I wish them safety and blessings. But where is Gerswin?

"Come this way," says the guard. We amble down sterile halls resounding with echoes, congested cells and aging eyes peering out at us. And here's Gerswin, sleeping on the top bunk at one in the afternoon. One of his forty-four cellmates prods him awake.

He opens his eyes, leaps down from the top bunk, and buttons his shirt. Through the bars, he takes my hand. *I remember my promise to you, Baz. I won't forget it. I won't forget you.*

En route back to America, Jonathan's e-mail lands in my inbox:

> We had a very exciting and meaningful follow-up session on
> Thursday. We spent two hours just to debrief especially with a focus
> on Saturday. Yahiya stood up and said, "I am very involved with
> the Numbers gang inside prison. There is a lot of pressure on me
> after Saturday because I became quiet. I want to get out BUT"—we
> all thought he would make an excuse but he said, "I will need your
> help if I get out and move on." Wow, the room was in silence.

From my airplane window, I try to conjure up Anthony, Ebrahim, Yahiya, Jerome, and Gerswin, somewhere in the backwaters
of the South African prison system, shuttled from Pollsmoor to a
longer-stay facility and then, in all likelihood, from that facility
to yet another one. With every transfer and every day that passes,
their weeks of restorative justice work and emotional progress
recede farther and farther into the distance. I ask myself a question
that's also a silent prayer, inspired by Rwanda and South Africa
both. What would the world look like if restorative justice were not
some ancillary to the justice system—but the very thing itself?

3.
The Arts behind Bars |
Uganda & Jamaica

Returning to New York City after my time in Africa, I check in with my Prison-to-College Pipeline students. Ray had been released while I was overseas and though I'd called him as soon as I'd heard his "I'm home!" voice mail, giving him a welcome-back hug is a joy. Like all students in the program, he visits campus within days of leaving prison. Like all of them, too, he stands wide-eyed before John Jay College of Criminal Justice, awed by the school to which he already belongs—he's been taking classes in prison, after all—and which represents his new life, here on the outside. Ray's goal is to start classes in six months, and thus far it seems a reasonable possibility; he's calmly shouldering the bureaucracy of postprison life, from parole officer meetings to anger management and vocational training classes.

But Ray, just twenty-seven, has also returned to the same Brooklyn neighborhood that steered him toward gangs and drug dealing in the first place. Seven years later it's a more gentrified version of that neighborhood, yes—"I never seen 'organic' stuff in my bodega before, Baz," he says, laughing—but beneath the hipster veneer of whiskey bars and artisanal cheese shops, the Bed-Stuy that paved Ray's path to prison survives. I don't know how to help him transcend the past. All I can do is encourage him to focus on the big picture, and his future, which involves a college degree.

"I'm your English professor," I tell him as he leaves campus for the subway back to Brooklyn. "I know your talent. I've seen your highest self." I have glimpsed this higher self because I taught him writing, a creative art. I've seen the language arts work magic in my New York prison classroom. And since the 1970s it's been an accepted reality in America, certified by projects like the international PEN Prison Writing Program, that verbal and artistic expression has profound cognitive-therapeutic impact, especially in a prison context. Organizations like Michigan's Arts in Prison, for instance, have offered programs in writing, along with music, gardening, yoga, and visual and performing arts, for decades, and studies continue to endorse their value.

But I wanted to assess their worth in a more intense, concentrated fashion. What sort of rehabilitative power do the arts really posses? And what might they accomplish in prison, outside the framework of a college program like the one I run? Rwanda and South Africa had allowed me to rethink the very foundations of justice, to reflect on revenge and forgiveness while glimpsing possibilities of what could be. They'd shown me their own versions of what corrections could look like. I came home eager to see how another vehicle of correction, the arts, might also be used as a healing agent in exceptionally punishing conditions. For that I would return to Africa—to Uganda.

Some 35,000 people are incarcerated in Uganda, about half on remand, all housed in a system built for 15,000. In 2004 the Uganda Prison Service's self-assessment painted a gruesome portrait of these brimming infernos. Prisons designed for twenty-three people were home to 265; half of all prisoners had no access to safe water. This led to some reforms, but in 2011, Human Rights Watch declared conditions only slightly improved. According to the Human Rights Watch report, 41 percent of prisoners were being beaten, some by other prisoners at the warden's command; those refusing to perform hard labor—including the elderly, people with disabilities, and pregnant women—were caned, stoned, handcuffed to a tree, or burned; others were stripped naked and thrust into cells flooded by ankle-deep water. HIV and TB were said to be almost twice as prevalent behind bars as in the general population, but as of 2011 treatment was available at only one prison in the country and just 63 of 223 prisons had any on-site health care worker.

I'd been heartened to learn of the African Prisons Project, a London-and-Kampala-based NGO engaged in education, leadership training, and health initiatives behind bars. The organization, open to volunteers, was responsive to my ideas about coordinating something new for them and for Uganda: a creative writing class.

After arriving at Entebbe International Airport and spending three hours in traffic, I reach the apartment I'd put down a deposit on. It turns out to be a dark, dusty cell in a crumbling compound, encased in barbed wire and shielded by a man with a scowl and an Uzi. I spend the night sleeping, literally, atop my suitcases in the sooty apartment. The next day I negotiate a decent rate at the Sheraton, the hotel where Idi Amin's palace once sat, its sprawling green lawns host to many a bloody execution. Then I stop to change money.

"No, ma'am, we cannot take this twenty dollars, it is a bad year."

"Bad year?" I ask.

"Yes," comes the explanation.

I buy a SIM card for my cell and put fifty dollars of credit on it. I try to make a call; no credit.

"That is because yours is an old corporate account, ma'am."

"How can that be, if I just bought it? So I just threw away fifty dollars?"

"Yes," comes the explanation.

Finally, I head back to the hotel, where a bomb check awaits at the gates. Ever since the 2010 suicide bombings that left seventy-four dead in Kampala—a Somali militia with supposed Al Qaeda ties claimed responsibility—random checkpoints are de rigueur here. The stern stares from behind a gun, the popping of the trunk, the opening of the glove compartment, the waved hand for entrance: all of it leaves me skeptical about their ability to prevent a bombing, but they are effective at generating perpetual unease.

"I will pick you up at 8:45 tomorrow," the taxi man tells me.

"But I don't have to be at the APP office until eleven. Isn't it only half an hour away?"

"Jams," he replies.

———

Bright and early Monday morning, en route to the office in bumper-to-bumper traffic, I sweat through my dress. Even in February Kampala is blisteringly hot. Out of my open window I spy bustling crowds, cave-sized potholes, military uniforms, and Marabou storks, like drones in the sky. I take my phone out to snap a picture. My driver straightaway shuts the window.

"Thieves," he says. "They will pretend to be walking. And they will reach in and take your phone."

The APP office, a small cottage on a hill, is manned by a security guard who writes our names in a book. Handshakes go all around as I greet five team members. A map of Uganda hangs on the wall, thumbtacks marking each of the country's 223 prisons. I craft a callout for my writing class, to be circulated behind bars: *Are you a creative person? Do you enjoy stories and poetry? Do you want to express yourself through writing?*

My syllabus includes a range of genres, from personal essays to drama, fiction, and poetry. I make my assignments as general as possible and select readings from both classic African-American texts and Kenyan, Nigerian, and Ugandan works I'd discovered in the bookstore over the weekend. Then, as I await my taxi, my phone rings.

"Yes, madam, this is David." My taxi man. "I cannot make it. But I have sent another taxi. He is also called David. He is in a jam but he will be there soon."

"Soon" means an hour. Jams add another hour. I reach the Sheraton, pass through the metal detector rigmarole and, exasperated, make a beeline for the Paradise Grill. A *sheesha* pipe and a Nile Special beer later, I stroll down Nile Avenue, past a bar blasting Jamaican dancehall music. Beautiful prostitutes, dressed to the nines, have the run of the place; posted at every table, they survey customers like ornate owls.

The next morning, one of the prostitutes shares the elevator to the lobby with me. On the way out the door, I scan the odd batch of books for sale in the hotel shop: *Birds of Uganda, Eradication of Gun-Based Violence in Uganda, Sixteen Deadly Women: How to Recognize and Avoid Them.*

"People think just because you are in prison you are a sinner," says David, my taxi man, narrowly avoiding a collision with a swarm of boda-bodas (motorcycle taxis). "I know this is not true, sure? Mistakes can happen."

At the gas station, Jean from APP picks me up. I haven't been officially approved to work in Luzira Prison so she'll be my escort, and the plan is to enter through the side gate and hope no one asks questions. We take a turn off the main road, into a vista of crumbling brick and rusty zinc roofs. The ground is swathed in scraps: wood chips, newspaper, dirty cardboard. Tire tracks produce rivers through mud and chickens dart out of the dilapidated Betterlife Medical Center. The scent of frying breadfruit and samosas tickles my nose.

Jean stops to buy chapati from a vendor. She's several years younger than I but seems twice my age; perhaps the powder-blue polyester suit adds years. As we walk, she tells me that she grew up in Kampala, went to university here, and used to be a high school teacher.

"Now I live in prison," she says.

I nod. "It can feel that way sometimes, yes?"

"No, I live there. *Live*, sure?"

Jean's husband is a prison officer and they, along with their two children, have a one-room hut on the prison grounds.

After slipping through the gate, essentially a hole in the barbed-wire fence, Jean points out where officers live. Then, as we head down a rocky path toward the prison interior, we see the sunshine-yellow uniforms, like daisies in the dirt. Prisoners are tilling fields.

"The head of the prison, his garden is looked after by the pris-oners," Jean explains.

Luzira, which has units for convicted, remand, women, and death-row prisoners, was Uganda's principal colonial prison, built in 1927. Throughout the colonial world such prisons served the aims of whites, extorting money by way of bribes to stay out of prison and obtaining free labor from prisoners for cotton produc-tion. Here, too, colonial powers adroitly manufactured reasons to put bodies behind bars. In the 1930s, about 60 percent of those in Uganda's native authority prisons were convicted of tax default or adultery. African prisons thus became instruments of social con-trol, often combined with corporal punishment, which lasted in British African colonies like Uganda until the 1930s.

At the main gate, an elderly prisoner in yellow shorts and flip-flops sweeps the hedges with a makeshift broom. Jean and I are waved inside by an officer in a military-style uniform of red beret, khaki skirt, and bobby socks.

"You may put your bags in there," she directs, pointing to a small hut serving as an entrance tower. I hang my purse on a rusty nail, beside a stack of old, handwritten gate passes, crammed on a large skewer like shish kebab.

Outside, a manicured garden full of verdant bushes is being tended by prisoners in yellow uniforms darting to and fro. I can't help but be reminded of a scene in an American classic we'll be reading during class, Frederick Douglass's slave narrative, in which he describes his master's Eden-like, bountiful garden as a dreadful source of temptation to hungry slaves, resulting in many violations and ghastly whippings.

The officer in charge shakes my hand, takes out his badge, and sets it on the table before me. He looks me up and down, then mutters something about permission for the professor to work while her official permission is cleared. One more handshake and it's agreed.

We go through another set of gates and along a pebbly alleyway that leads to the ramshackle housing blocks at the gut of the prison. Pieces of yellow uniform are scattered about, drying in the sun—pants on the bushes, a top dangling off a branch, as if the barren trees have sprouted flowers. Eyes peer through windows of concrete huts; Jean explains that between 7:00 a.m. and 4:00 p.m. the incarcerated men can essentially roam free on the compound. We follow several men to the life-size concrete box that is our destination. They remove their flip-flops, as if entering a holy space.

"And you are welcome to the APP library," Jean pronounces.

A wooden table rests in the center of the room beside three antiquated computers, and a dozen men sit on benches, the backs of their uniforms displaying stenciled-on words like REMAND, WARD 23, DEBTOR, CLEANER. Other men mill about, quietly shelving books. I spy Arthur Miller's *The Crucible*, a Star Trek cartoon, *Mathematical Methods*, and *The Hotel Guide to Greece*. Printed on the blackboard is one line, "Marriage Disadvantages: it can bring poverty." Today is the last day of the Functional Adult Literacy program, and Wilson—Mr. Headmaster, as he's known—is wrapping up the class. He'll shortly be one of ten men certified to teach his fellow prisoners about finance, social skills, and family planning. Exhibiting the enduring patience and commanding presence of a veteran teacher, Wilson immediately impresses me as a leader here. He and the men in his "train the trainers" class will also be my creative writing students.

"Yes, Tom. That is correct," affirms Wilson, animated and enthused. "Marriage can bring one great financial distress. So this is to be considered when one chooses a wife and a time to be married."

Jean gathers the men around the table and introduces me as a professor from America who'll be their new writing instructor. One of them, with a hard stare that radiates gravitas, raises his hand.

"I am very pleased to hear of this. Your class will be welcome. I myself am a great fan of the novelist Thomas Hardy. But"—he raises his hand—"madam professor, why only one week? Why not a complete college program?"

"What he means," Wilson intervenes, "is that many people have come and gone here, with good intentions, like yourself. They bring programs, they depart. Why cannot you create a program that remains?"

"That's what I'm hoping," I tell them. You all can be trained as writing facilitators, and then run the class once I'm gone. Tom nods thoughtfully. A stocky prisoner with red and squinty eyes, a mustache, and a grand pot belly, enters the library and is presented to me.

"This is Chairman," says Wilson. Luzira is a self-governing entity, and the man in charge must endorse all programs.

"I approve of this class," he affirms, with a sturdy handshake. "Creative writing? I will come sit in."

My future students pepper me with more questions about earning certificates and receiving grades. Then it's time for them to be counted, yet again, and we file out, and I'm back through the prison gates and then the metal detectors at the Sheraton.

———

The morning of our first class, I am sipping bitter coffee at the hotel when my phone rings.

"Madam, I cannot come today," says David the taxi man. "I must visit the hospital. But I will send Hakeem."

Hakeem arrives, and, dropping me off, cheerfully demands more shillings.

Safely inside the prison library, I await my students. Never-ending head counts steal precious class time but they trickle in, one by one. Hassan ran a construction company and has a business degree. Nicholas, from the Baganda tribe, was a soldier. Grave-looking Tom, who likes golf, completed his A-levels in law and is known among the prisoners as Magistrate Tom. The senior welfare officer, slumped in her seat beside Jean, offers an indolent grin; I wonder how this lethargic-looking woman has the energy to look after her own welfare, let alone anyone else's. Mohammed, seven feet tall and surely no older than twenty-one, says he writes music and gives us a sample, breaking into a reggae song.

Oh how woman suffers so, goes the chorus.

"By words the mind is winged. Declared by one Aris-tophanes," Wilson reads aloud from the syllabus. He looks up. "The concept of this wise statement is that even if one is behind bars, one can be free with a pen. One's mind is free, all times."

"Has anyone heard of a slave narrative?" I ask.

Blank stares.

"America was founded on slavery," I explain. "And slaves began to write about their experiences, and publish them to great success. Why might they want to do this?"

"To expose the injustice!" Mohammed calls out, finger in the air.

Tom sonorously reads aloud the words of Frederick Douglass, author of America's most celebrated slave narrative, published in 1845:

*I have no accurate knowledge of my age, never having seen any
authentic record containing it. By far the larger part of the
slaves know as little of their ages as horses know of theirs, and
it is the wish of most masters within my knowledge to keep their
slaves thus ignorant.*

"He does not have knowledge of his own birthday," declares
Wilson.

"Is this not sad?" I ask. Casual nods all around.

"What is noteworthy here," Tom begins, "is that he begins his
life story not with what he indeed does know about his life but what
he does *not* know. Unusual."

We read another excerpt, in which Douglass witnesses a bloody
whipping.

"It is gruesome," Wilson declares, flatly. He notes Douglass's
well-crafted language of restraint, along with his rhythm, cadence,
and biblical references. The men are engaged yet blasé. I ask them
to start writing the first pages of their own autobiographies. As
distant drumming outside grows louder and they scribble against
the din, I read their preclass assessments: *I hope to get knowledge. I
hope to keep my mind refreshed all the time, and be creative. I expect
to learn team spirit in writing and my creative potential will be ener-
gized and reawakened.*

Half an hour later, the students share what they've written.
One writes of war in Mogadishu, and coming home to discover that
his mother, father, and son have all died of AIDS.

"Life was difficult," he concludes. It's an understatement of the
sort repeated again and again in the men's narratives today. Wilson
titles his "From Trash to Throne," and reads, "I am of the youth

that believes to be the less privileged, being born into a polygamous family of Mr. Bafaki and seven stepmothers. As a result of this my father gave birth to very many children, about sixty of them, and I was the thirty-seventh and alone in my mother's womb."

His mother died when he was five, Wilson goes on, and he was raised by abusive stepmothers "who all practiced witchcraft." In exchange for school tuition he did manual labor for a wealthy man from a neighboring village, but shortly after he started, his coworkers managed to make him the fall guy in a scheme that caused the company to lose money, which led him to spend a year and a half in remand before being sentenced to thirteen months or a US $600 fine. Whether or not Wilson is innocent of his crime, it seems clear that he has endured a life of poverty, abuse, and trauma.

So have his peers. These students were nonchalant about a slave narrative because it really wasn't very shocking to them. Shuttled from one abusive home to another, begging for food, battling excruciating poverty and homelessness and disease—this is life for my students. Even Jean from APP, participating in the exercise, has a sad tale.

"The only thing I had in life was abuse, beatings, and miserableness," she reads aloud. "So since then I am psychologically disturbed because whenever I remember the mistreatment I went through, tears roll."

Tom reads last. His earlier references to Charles Dickens and Thomas Hardy had indicated that he's no stranger to formal education, and his eloquent essay confirms it. He writes about growing up in relative comfort in Entebbe, landing in jail for a white-collar crime, and being deserted by those he considered friends.

"I am now looking ahead and focused on improving things and positive change. I will never keep those who abandoned me in my hour of need as hostages in my heart because my heart is too small to keep old issues. I will never fail in my quest to be a better man."

I leave our first class moved by my new students' words, impressed by their willingness to reveal their own stories, and heartened by how well they're taking to the assignments. But I also feel weighed down by the anguish of their lives, past and present. What can simple words do in the face of such devastation?

————

I spend the weekend with Al, a twenty-something friend of a friend. We share a love of reggae, which is astonishingly popular here. Like Uganda's population, three-quarters of it under age thirty, the country's music scene is extraordinarily young, essentially born since 1986, when Yoweri Museveni took power. After the brutal reign of Idi Amin, after a series of military coups and political instability, the peace of his regime provided space for culture to grow. So the music is still finding itself, and much of this involves diligent copycatting. After a night out with Al, from one over-the-top nighttime palace to another, I decide that Ugandans are more Jamaican than Jamaicans.

Perhaps because I'm something new and foreign to spice up his routine, Al generously appoints himself my tour guide. Saturday morning he picks me up in a silver Mercedes with a crack down the windshield and a missing side mirror.

"A boda-boda took it off last month," he explains. "We'll just have to avoid the police since I'm not meant to drive without it. Sure?

"Have you seen the slums?" he goes on. "*Mzungus* always want to see the slums. They always have many projects there."

We visit Old Kampala, up in the hills, where impalas once roamed, then haggle over entrance fees to the Lubiri Palace, the compound of the Buganda king, where a guided tour includes a peek at Amin's torture chamber and Rolls-Royce. Uganda's ubiquitous hustle has me watching my back at all times, but there's an endearing earnestness to Al that allows me to let my guard down, for the first time since arriving. He showers me with questions about life in America, mostly about how much it costs. He schools me on the social scene here, criticizes local homophobia, and explains that like many Ugandans, he has Rwandan roots—his family fled here after one of the early genocides. Then he tries to convince me that Ugandans are preferable to Rwandans.

"In Rwanda they may smile at you a lot but then they will kill you. Here, you know what you are getting. Sure?"

Suddenly Al turns frantic at the wheel.

"Quick, pass me some shillings!"

"Huh?" I reach for my pocketbook.

He pulls over by the side of the road and rolls down the window.

"Hello, Officer!" Broad smile.

"Hello, sir! And how are you on this lovely Women's Day?"

"I am wonderful, sir! I will soon cook for this woman right here!"

Al proffers his hand to the grinning policeman and the two shake firmly.

"Enjoy your day!" And to me: "Happy Women's Day!"

Then we're off, without having to pay a fine for the missing mirror. I've just witnessed the friendliest bribe of all time.

"I am just glad we are not in Rwanda. I could not do that in Kigali, sure? I would never want to live in a place so proper."

Monday morning, I dive into the local paper. There's a story on Museveni and corruption, one on a bombing two hours from Kampala and one about a twenty-year-old, HIV-positive woman who lives with her one-year-old son inside Luzira Prison, still on remand after three years now. Her charge? Stealing a mobile phone. I share the story with my students at Luzira that morning, but they seem unmoved.

"How many of you are behind bars because you could not afford the fine for your crime, or the bribe to elude it?" I ask, describing my police encounter over the weekend. Nine prisoners raise their hands.

Corruption is endemic here. In the East African Bribery Report of 2012, launched by Transparency International, Uganda registered the highest number of bribery cases in the region, with a rate of 40.7 percent. That same year, $12.7 million in donor funds to Uganda's Office of the Prime Minister—earmarked for rebuilding northern Uganda, ravaged by a twenty-year war, and Karamoja, Uganda's poorest region—were funneled into private accounts, prompting the European Union to suspend foreign aid to the country.

Uganda isn't alone. In various incarnations all over the world, money and justice are bonded together in unholy matrimony. Take the United States, where it's an accepted reality that your case is as strong as the lawyer you can afford, not to mention the bail money that gets you out of jail, in a better frame of mind and thus far less likely to take a plea bargain. Is that not a form of bribery? Justice is, ubiquitously and dispiritingly, not only for sale but also costly. Consider the Michigan teenager who caught a fish out of season and landed three days in jail, or the homeless Iraq War veteran who served twenty-two days for getting drunk and climbing into an abandoned building. In both these cases, jail time wasn't for punishment but for failing to pay the ever-increasing fines associated with the criminal justice system. Fees for arrest warrants, court-ordered drug and alcohol treatment,

DNA samples, jury trials—are these not a kind of legally sanctioned extortion, too?

We turn to Wilson's autobiographical essay from yesterday, for peer criticism.

"Pastor," Tom begins. He always begins. Tom is as insightful about literature as he is somber—I have yet to see him smile. "You seem to imply that polygamy has not served you or your family well. Or am I reading this wrong?"

"Indeed this is correct, Tom."

"So how can you *show* your reader this?" I nudge, rolling out a writing mantra: show, don't tell. Wilson takes a deep breath.

"The financial stress. The fighting among siblings. The pain of being hated by your stepmothers. Beaten by them, as well. Every day, with belts and paddles. This wears on one's spirit." He sighs.

"And what of the manual labor, when you worked for the rich man? How did that feel?" Tom is adopting the mantle of my co-instructor, and I welcome the assistance.

"I am a grown man so I will try not to cry when I remember. But it was painful. You are doing things you do not have to do at home; you are abused year upon year, and you turn your hands to God. It feels as if you have been forgotten by him."

Wilson pauses and shakes his head.

"This is painful, to write. It is to remember. To remember is pain."

"In the pain is a healing," Tom, the temperate intellect, tells him.

Wilson shrugs, fingering his yellow floppy sunhat. As the week moves on, I come to know more of Wilson's pain and slow healing. One morning he sits down on the bench beside me and, before class begins, details his life plan. When released he'll start a prison ministry and help people coming home from prison find work on a farm. Steadily, in his usual sermonlike tone—he's Pastor Boma, indeed—he sums up conditions behind bars.

"I sleep on my side for lack of space. Lice and scabies inhabit my blankets. The food is insufficient. There is no clean water, so among many it is a commodity traded for acts." Sex acts, he means.

"Even my mother would be shocked to know I am here," his classmate Mohammed, eavesdropping, interjects. "At first I cursed and cried, I am an innocent man in prison. But I learned to survive."

The call comes from outside; a student looks up from *Slavery in America*. "Come, let us go again for the count before they come with the canes."

The thought of canes makes me shudder. And perhaps because of the frustrations with the count, today's class is slow going. No one has done the reading—excerpts from Mandela's *Long Walk to Freedom*—or written their dramatic dialogues, because they haven't grasped the assignment. So when the students return from the third count, I try a writing exercise.

"I was happy," I print on the board, instructing the men to rewrite it by *showing* that they're happy instead of saying that they are.

Roderick raises his hand. "I was happy when I at last got a trial date," he reads.

"But *how* were you happy?"

"How about 'I was happy when I became free'?" asks Siraj, finger in the air.

"I was happy when I was no longer begging for food!" Chairman calls out.

Finally, Wilson stands and announces, "I was so happy I jumped up and down."

"Yes!" I exclaim. "This *shows* us an image and an emotion." The men nod silently.

"I was surprised."

Mohammed: *I was surprised when my father beat my mother and she ran away.*

Hassan: *I was surprised when I had to be a soldier and hold the heavy gun.*

Extracting visible emotion from such flat accounts of trauma proves a colossal challenge.

The call comes again and my students scramble to gather their things.

"Off to our wards," Wilson mumbles. "Do you know why they call it that, Baz? It is the language of hospitals. They imagine that we are sick and they are healing us."

———

As the days pass I find things to enjoy in Kampala. Go where the foreigners go and there's a burgeoning arts scene, late-night shee-sha bars, and white-sand beaches framing Lake Victoria. But still the haggling and hustling, the Uzis and bomb checks, the hostile glares from strangers and familiar folks alike, all of the things that make up daily life for me here—they take a toll on my spirit. So does my time in Luzira, land of inspired students and dreams deferred. The daily walk from the taxi to the prison, through the heartrend-ing slum, fuels my cynicism and alienation. It's as if the work I did in Rwanda and the optimism it inspired about possibilities for change, globally and back home, came from another life. Did those possibilities even exist at all? The rumors I'm hearing here about Rwanda's dark side, about politically motivated detentions and

disappearances attributed to the Rwandan army and police, target-
ing those critical of the government, deepen my depression. I begin
to wonder if progress is a mirage.

Yet still I enter the prison and behold that beautiful sight of
students hunched over the wooden table, too busy writing to greet
me. Luzira's conditions and deadening bureaucracy shred my
optimism, but our writing course diligently labors to sew it back
together. Class by class, the students' journals fill up with lively
letters. When they try their hands at short stories, Wilson mes-
merizes the class with a tale about a snake and a caterpillar who
crash a party, only to get beaten up and tossed out.

"At this point, the snake blamed the butterfly for deceiving it
with the idea that everyone admired them," he reads. "Little did
they both know that the snake never really changed, apart from
pulling itself from the old skin."

"That's what we call a fable," I say. "Is there a moral?"

Tom raises his hand and finally lets forth his first half-smile.
This morning I'd run into him while making my way through the
prison gates and he told me he'd be late to class because the officer
in charge wanted to speak with him.

"You're a gifted writer, Tom. You really must know this," I'd
told him.

"I'm humbled," he'd said, head bowed, still sans smile. "I truly
wish you would run a proper college program here, though."

I'd mumbled something about trying to help him get his work
published. Knowing the inadequacy of such a response—a talent
like Tom deserves far more than I can offer—I'd rushed off to class.

"If I am not mistaken," Tom says to Wilson, "the story's moral
is that some changes are merely superficial."

"And, too," Wilson interjects, "that people can be like the but-terfly. Find wings. Change. Grow. Reinvent ourselves, as some of us are doing here in this prison."

Chairman volunteers to go next. His story paints a picture of a Sunday outing to Lake Victoria with his family. The boda-boda ride is behind "clouds of dust that stretch from a fleet of luxury vehicles going to eat money at the beach." The fishing boats come alive; so do the sun's rays on the water, the dangling of dusty feet in the sea, and the "beautiful girls trained to trap money, very busy asking for orders of drinks and well-roasted tilapia fish."

Here he abruptly halts and slams his paper down on the desk.

"That is all I wrote," Chairman says. "The memory grew too painful."

"Painful?" asks Wilson. "You have just taken away our pain by transporting us to the beach today. This is beautiful!"

"I would love to eat that fish now," Mohammed sighs.

"And a Nile Special with it," Hassan adds. Chairman, looking pleased with himself, absorbs the compliments and says he will write the rest tonight.

"The writing has taken us out of this place, if for a moment," affirms Wilson. "With words, we are winged."

———

Later that week, Al arrives with a friend to take me for dinner along Acacia Avenue in Kololo, Kampala's tony expat district. We've fast become close; Al has proven himself a patient, inquisitive sounding board for my struggle with local customs, and a wingman ever in the know about where good reggae can be found. He's the one person I can count on to treat me like a friend, not a *mzungu* novelty item, though I do remain something of a curiosity to him, this woman who's come all this way to spend every day in prison.

"You are truly working in the prison?" Al's friend in the passenger seat asks, turning to face me. He speaks with an American accent, acquired at college in California, he explains. And then, "You must meet my father."

We promptly take a U-turn and land in an alternate Kampala universe, where the streets are lined with trees, the roads are devoid of potholes, and the mansions are American-style. Our car pulls up to an iron gate manned by two armed guards; inside, a velvet rope is lifted and we're ushered into a gleaming indoor-outdoor dining area where half a dozen people are seated on mahogany chairs.

Al greets his friend's father, a stately man wearing a crisp striped shirt, seated beside a woman in a sumptuous headwrap. He looks me up and down.

"Who is this American?"

"I am a professor in New York, and—"

"Sit," he commands, pulling out a plastic-covered chair. A plate of chicken and coleslaw is set down before me.

"Eat!" he decrees, brandishing a pinky ring and depositing a bone on his plate.

"We are celebrating his release," his wife explains.

I discover I am having dinner with Captain Mike Mukula, former state health minister, onetime fellow at Harvard's Kennedy School of Government—sentenced to four years at Luzira for embezzling some $84,000 of donor funds earmarked for immunization campaigns. He's home tonight from two and a half months in prison, having won an appeal. Plate clean, he looks up.

"So you are working in Luzira?"

I nod.

"That place is terrible. It must be fixed. We must fix it." He slams a fist on the table. "The men in there, they are smart. They can be made to learn a trade. Chicken farmers! Something! Learn a trade. They can serve community service instead of prison. It is a disgrace."

As he cracks open a Coke, I think of Bernard Kerik, former New York City police commissioner who spent three years behind bars for tax evasion and came out railing against the system, writing a book and telling every press outlet that mandatory minimum sentencing sets prisoners up for failure.

"I have never heard him so passionate about something like this before," Mukula's son marvels after dinner, after I've given the minister my card and told him I'd connect him with colleagues who might collaborate with him in large-scale prison-reform work. "He never thought about prisons before he went to one. Now it is all he talks about." I wonder if it still will be, after the shock has worn off.

———

It's a good thing it's my final day at Luzira, because I never did get official permission to enter, and today's confrontation with an aggressive guard means I can no longer fly under the radar at the side gate. Narrowly negotiating my way past the Uzis, I enter the library. Wilson raises his head from *Great Expectations*.

"Professor Baz, what is your religion?" he asks.

"I don't have one."

Jean, shocked, looks up. "What do they call it in New York, to have no religion?"

"My religion is to do good and seek justice," I say. It's a too-pat answer, I know, but it's the best I can do without broaching a thorny subject. Wilson smiles knowingly and grips me on the shoulder.

"Even without Jesus, you are on the righteous path, Baz." This show of tolerance, in a country steeped in conservatism and tradition, is just the sort of gracious move I've come to expect from Wilson.

We delve right into their argument essays. The topic is the Marriage Bill, and Roderick is insistent about its horror.

"It devalues marriage, sure? The Bible does not speak of cohabiting—it speaks of *marriage!*"

"But cohabiting and partnership for many years, this can be just like marriage," Tom insists. "After all, as they say, if it walks like a duck it is a duck!"

"No!" cries Wilson. "Marriage is a sacred act and we cannot tamper with it."

"I am aware of the cultural rigidities," Tom declares, his voice rising. "But as we are mutating as a nation, we cannot stick only with the old. We need to graduate from cultures holding us hostage."

Tom carries on evenly and imperiously, as if Parliament is in session.

"We cannot hold our women hostage to old customs," he states. "What Uganda needs are peaceful households. The use of bride-price is turning our girls into assets. We cannot resort back to the 1920s."

"But to do away with bride-price," Wilson objects, "this adds up to a man enjoying free goods. You will care for your wife more knowing you paid good money for her!"

I'm forced to pause the discussion because the clock is ticking and the game plan is to end our day, and my time in Luzira, with African-American poetry.

"Poetry," declares Wilson, as if burnishing the word. "It means, ideas married to meter and rhythm."

Nicholas reads from Maya Angelou:

The caged bird sings
with a fearful trill
of things unknown
but longed for still
and his tune is heard
on the distant hill
for the caged bird
sings of freedom.

Wilson hangs his head so close to the page of the poem, it's as if he wants to collapse into its pauses.

"And we at Luzira, we are also caged birds," he sighs.

Our remaining hour becomes a quiet meditation, a serene space between words.

Wilson reads Maya Angelou with heady enunciation and a broad smile across his wizened, youthful face.

It's the fire in my eyes,
And the flash of my teeth,
The swing in my waist,
And the joy in my feet.
I'm a woman
Phenomenally.

"This is the power, beauty, of strong womanhood. Of person-hood," Wilson beams.

The whole class is enraptured. So am I. In all my years of teaching, I have never felt language carry me up and out of a place as dramatically as it has during today's poetry reading. I suspect it's because our longing runs so deep; if I am hungry to be out of this place, my students are ravenous to be out of here. Such intense longing leaves one's heart open to the transformative power of literature and art in profound, even desperate, ways.

I instruct the class to turn poets themselves. Without an ounce of hesitation, they rise to the occasion, proudly reading their creations. Mohammed's poem is titled "Poverty" and it's full of force:

Do it! Push it! Bring it!
Put it down! Lift it up!
Shuck it! Take it there!
Poverty, Poverty, Poverty!
Why don't you go back where you came from?

Jimmy's poem concludes with a moving command:

People, When shall we wake
Up and try to avoid our
Selves from being culprits
Of prison? Get concerned.
Time lost
Is never regained.

Finally, Peter's verse:

Oh AIDS, AIDS, AIDS,
Oh what a strong killer disease.

You stole my parents and my brother and sister
AIDS how can you leave me alone
In this world?
I wish you knew how difficult it is
To stay alone on this earth.
AIDS I wish if you could hear me
You would come for me too.

Silence.

There is no adequate response to such words. And I'm bowled over by how quickly, how expertly, these students took to a genre that was essentially foreign to them before today.

"God bless you," Mohammed whispers. Our time is up and the sadness is palpable.

"You must greet your prisoners in New York for us," says Tom, with flat resignation.

"Why don't you stay another week?" Wilson asks. "You have shown us something wonderful, but now you are taking it away."

Guilt and grief wash over me. It's the same sadness I feel every time I leave class in a prison, as I get to escape to freedom and my students must trek back to their cells, but it's more intense now because I'm not only leaving students I've come to care about behind, I'm leaving them for good—and I'm leaving them *here*, in this living nightmare of a place. As for the guilt, it's because Wilson is right. I foster a spirit of humanity, creativity, and intellectual freedom, open up emotional scars, then parachute right out, back to business as usual. I hope but doubt that our creative writing program will indeed live on. What good is a week of transcendence if it can't be sustained?

"Let us just go," says Tom glumly. He takes Wilson's arm and they, along with the other students, exit the library and turn prisoners once more.

I look down at the seminar table, empty save for one syllabus with a Ray Bradbury quote on top: "You must stay drunk on writing so reality cannot destroy you."

Our class has indeed imbibed all week long. It's been more than just escapism, though—real emotional gains were made here. A 2013 study revealed that subjects assigned to read literature scored higher on an exam asking them to look at photographs of actors' eyes and read their emotions; researchers concluded that reading literary fiction enhances the skills and thought processes critical to intricate social relationships and functional societies. A 1990 study of so-called bibliotherapy argued that among the outcomes of behind-bars writing programs was an increased ability to tolerate frustration and disclose feelings of pain, guilt, and sadness. The writing process itself, with its stages of revision and peer review and self-criticism, was found to promote an ability to explore value systems, bolster self-esteem, and foster empathy.

All week I've watched these men critique, debate, and dialogue with one another in generous, thoughtful ways. I've watched them excavate their emotional pasts and presents, and refine their ability to listen to and feel empathy for another man's struggle—even when one man's horror story always seemed to outdo the one that came before.

"Reading taught me to deal with my anger problems," Carl, my incarcerated student back home, once told me. "Because I have to finish any book I start. And sometimes I get frustrated with a book, I don't understand it—I get mad. Frustrated. But because I know I

have to finish I stay patient. And patience is the antidote to anger."
In California, I heard an incarcerated student in a writing class sum
up the experience this way: "I not only learned that I could write,
but that I can be my own therapist."

Indeed, people in prison can also, while engaged in beauty and
the arts and intellectual discourse, be their noblest selves—"born
again," as my incarcerated student Korey once put it, deem-
ing our classroom a place in which he could finally manifest the
higher self that the rest of the world, forever labeling him a convict,
won't allow for. He felt that as his professor, I glimpse his princely
humanity in a way few others could.

"Human beings are not built in silence, but in word, in work,
in action—reflection," writes Brazilian philosopher Paolo Frere.
Dialogue, he continues, is "an act of creation" that requires
love and faith "in humankind, faith in their power to make and
remake…faith in their vocation to be more fully human." This is
the essence of what it is to read and speak and write from behind
the barbed wire, however extreme the conditions: to resurrect a
sense of humanity. To become winged through words. To return
oneself to language and thus to the very identity that prison powers
seek to annihilate, to reclaim the mind even as the body is contained,
to exist again not only as an "I" but, in a classroom brimming with
pooled words, a mighty "we."

The day before I fly home, Al and I take a day trip to Jinja, which
claims to be the source of the Nile. We're extracted from Kampala's
jams and land in rural villages, pine forests and fields of pineapple.
A rowboat carries us to a lodge, built tree house–style on a rocky
island in the river. Nestled amid aloe plants, marveling at how the
sound of rapids can be so soothing, I wrestle with the overall value
of my stay, weighing the gains against the guilt of having ignited

something likely to die with my departure. Is reform valuable if its impact is a mere drop in the bucket?

I return to the question that struck me after the first day of class at Luzira: What are words in the face of sheer devastation? Arts-in-prison programs are potent agents of individual change, yes. But are they also in some way a distraction from the whole social order itself, from the powerful forces at play in the criminal justice system as a whole?

———

In search of a resolution to this quagmire, I set off to Jamaica a few weeks after I return from Uganda. That Caribbean country might offer me a fresh angle on the arts behind bars, this time involving a different genre, music. Touted as rehabilitative in prisons from the United Kingdom to India, music behind bars also has a storied American legacy that includes slave songs, prison blues, and the iconic Angola Prison, where folk legend Lead Belly honed his art.

"It's become quite official now—there's European money behind it," Jamaican activist and educator Kevin Wallen says of the Rehabilitation Through Music program. We're having lunch on the sand at Hellshire Beach just outside Kingston, and he's filling me in on the history of the program I've come to witness.

In 1997, he and Harvard professor Charles Nesson began building programs inside a Jamaican prison. They established a library, computer lab, radio station, and music studio. This last one generated international headlines, as it produced Jah Cure, the reggae artist I'd never gotten permission to interview in prison, years ago. Now I'd finally been cleared to visit the prison where he'd recorded some of my favorite love songs, to learn about the program that made him a star. Organizing my access is Carla, an effervescent Italian, who took over the program from Kevin several years ago.

The next day a taxi carries me from New Kingston, where skyscrapers and strip mall–like boulevards evoke Anycity, USA, to the less tourist-friendly face of Jamaica's capital, ramshackle downtown. Kingston is divided into uptown and downtown, a demarcation that refers as much to class as to geography. In this car-friendly sprawl, the wealth gap is baldly visible, and gang-related violence, which has plagued Kingston's "garrison" communities, or politically aligned ghettos, since the 1970s, means that for the past decade Jamaica has had one of the world's highest murder rates. The island of 2.7 million people has seen a thousand-plus killings every year since 2004, and the conviction rate for homicides is 5 percent. Unsurprisingly, nearly half of all prisoners here are serving time for nonviolent offenses. According to a study conducted in 2012 by the Jamaica Constabulary Force, the "typical inmate" is under age thirty-four and faces his first arrest before age twenty-four for breaches of the firearms act, which generally adds up to not paying the registration fee for a gun.

"To GP," I tell the driver. General Penitentiary. "Ever been there?"

"Yuh mad or wha?" he replies in Patois.

From across the street, I ogle the fortresslike prison, Jamaica's largest: some 1,700 men live in a facility designed for 650. Bloodred brick and concrete, with a graceful sentry box and twenty-foot-high walls, it's touted by a government Web site as an example of "exquisite Jamaican Georgian architecture." The structure dates back to 1845, seven years after the full abolition of slavery in Jamaica, but it was not the only form of punishment used here. The 1865 Corporal Punishment Act, better known as the whipping bill, made larceny punishable by up to fifty lashes, while the Penal Servitude Act, a precursor to America's convict lease system, rented out predominantly black, formerly enslaved prisoners to employers at a price per head. John Daughtry, Jamaica's general inspector of prisons between 1841 and 1861, modeled GP after Philadelphia's Eastern Penitentiary. In 1985, when the Rehabilitation Offenders Bill and the Corrections Acts revised "prisoner" to "inmate" and "prison officer" to "corrections officer," the place was rechristened the Tower Street Adult Correctional Centre. GP, though, stuck.

"Me like your eyes," a young man with scattered yellow teeth tells me as I wait for Carla in the parking lot. He's here to collect his brother, who will be coming home after seventeen years. Because he hasn't been notified about his brother's time of release, he's been here since sunrise. He tells me prisoners are permitted two face-to-face visits a month, but relatives can drop off food and supplies every Wednesday. Today their first stop will be a doctor's office, where his brother will be thoroughly examined and fed cleansing tea.

"Me live inna Jamaica now but used to be inna Brooklyn," the young man says, adjusting his Yankee cap.

"Otisville?" I ask, referring to the New York prison where I teach. It's part guess, part read-between-the-lines.

He nods. "Six years, all over. You name it. Otisville? Elmira? Riker's was worst, yuh see me? So much fighting. But still, America is Club Med next to this place. Seen?" He cocks his head to the side.

Carla arrives, salt-and-pepper dreadlocks tied like a rope down her back. She's all business, giving me a curt wave and marching with determination to the gate.

"Come, come, we're late," she calls to me. "Let's move."

"Find out when my brother comes out, seen?" scattered-teeth cries as I follow Carla.

A copy of my passport is affixed to the concrete wall at the guard station, just below the dress code. My phone is deposited in an enormous safe, atop a mountain of Nokias. The officer checking me in produces a ruler and, in perfect cursive, imprints my name in a giant sign-in book.

Through metal detectors that beep wildly we make our way outside to a courtyard area where khaki uniforms hang on clotheslines, flapping in the breeze. A sign on the fence reads Thank You Lord for Another Day.

Em-press!

Shor-ty!

Whi-tie!

Pssssst!

Prisoners holler at me from every angle.

Me like you!

Me waan talk to you!

Em-press!

It's a first, these catcalls in prison. Universally, the prison interloper is stared at, occasionally waved to, but she always half-exists in this land of the buried alive. In GP I am decidedly present. It's unnerving, landing me in the heart of this hell in a far more immediate way than I've ever experienced before—there's simply no looking away. Chaos bubbles to the surface like oil from a curry pot. Prisoners here are resurrected from confinement for only four and a half hours a day, and during those hours they are, clearly, very much trying to live. Din is indomitable; everything and everyone is on display. The place is essentially a massive football field encircled by minuscule, medieval-looking cells.

Carla's assistant, George, whom I'd later meet in her office, would detail his three years inside those cells.

"It was quite a revelation to me, to say the least," he declared. "Three to five people in one tiny, tiny space. There is no toilet; you must urinate in a water bottle. If you have to defecate it can be a real problem. You notify cellmates that you have to do so and you use a newspaper. But only if you're a *badman* or recognized inmate are you given that privilege; otherwise, they will tell you to hold it inside until you are let out of the cell. This results in many prisoners defecating on themselves or becoming ill.

"On the cell floor is room enough for two, so the other persons build a hammock. 'It's gonna cost you,' the tailor told me when I arrived. Without a hammock, see, you stand to sleep. Mind you, you cannot lie down beside a man—Jamaica is a very homophobic society." This is an understatement. In 1997 comments made by the commissioner of corrections about condoms for prisoners led to a guard strike and prison rioting, during which sixteen people were killed. The commissioner resigned. Separate sections were created for prisoners labeled as gay. A culture of fear paralyzed HIV-prevention efforts behind bars.

"Sometimes men will stand up night after night, until they reach family who can help," George recalled. "And yes, I did witness many stabbings, sometimes for a simple thing like stepping on someone's toes."

Shor-ty!

Em-press!

Hsssssst!

The soccer ball whooshes through the air, and Carla greets the prisoners in their khaki uniforms as they rush up to us. The guards try to silence the prisoners' calls while they usher us to a concrete cottage off to the side of the cells, and the door slams shut behind us.

Silence.

We enter GP's version of the Luzira library: a computer lab. About twenty-two men spend four hours a day here, five days a week. They cease typing to smile at me; some look no older than sixteen. "Education Is the Way to the Future" reads one poster on the bright green wall.

"Come, let me show you something," Carla says. She opens a small door off to the side and voilà! It's a closet—no, a radio station: Free 88.9 FM. At the mike, surrounded by posters of Gregory Isaacs, Michael Bolton, Shaggy, and Kenny Rogers, is Serano, one of the musicians featured in *Songs of Redemption*, a recent documentary about the music program. He reminds me of Wilson, an uncanny combination of old man and little boy: tiny in stature, his dreadlocks tied up under a peach-colored bandanna and Yankee cap, he sports crisp white Nike Air Force Ones and a shimmering watch that seems twice his size. Twice, even, the size of his outsized smile, which saturates the room.

"Hello!"

"I'm a fan," I tell him. Indeed, when I watched the film his voice mystified me. Like Jah Cure's, every note wrings out soulful pain.

"See, my people," he says into the mike, "we're here talking about *The Secret*—and suddenly *I-and-I* am an example of how this manifests, seen? *I-and-I* want to reach people with my music and here, this lovely lady appears right before me. Will it to happen, my people!"

He segues into the sound track from the film. We make small talk, but I'm distracted by the reggae music, parachuting my spirit out of this dead zone. It's just the opposite of what Daughtry, who designed GP, would have wanted. "No sounds but of the hammer, the axe or the saw," he wrote in an 1844 report envisioning Jamaica's first modern prison.

Carla leads me to the neighboring "cultural center," another concrete hut next door to the computer room. I stand before a stage decorated with a mural of Bob Marley and contemporary reggae songstress Queen Ifrica. Massive speaker boxes hulk in the room, guitars hang on the walls, and a man plays the bongos. Prisoners in the music program record and release songs, and Carla had earlier told me that she is vigilant about getting them royalties, but the Jamaican music industry is a vexed, complex beast. Who actually profits remains consistently vague, and hand-to-mouth economics prevails.

An officer takes me into the recording studio off to the side of the stage, where an old *Vibe* magazine rests on the mixing board.

"We want to build it much bigger," he explains. "I am a musician, too. I am all in favor of this rehabilitation. Love working with the inmates."

On the way out, we pass the school area—"Almost-sorta high-school level," the officer tells me. Colonial-style rules and regulations hang on the door: No Sagging Pants, No Indecent Language, Maintain Proper Hygiene, Pants Must Be Worn at Waist. Just before Carla leads me to freedom, a final sign catches my eye. None Shall Escape, it reads.

——

A friend waits for me in the parking lot to drive me back to New Kingston. "So much trouble in the world," croons Bob Marley, from her car stereo. Singing along, I come to the depressing conclusion that music in prisons is the sweet sound of a salve. Because ultimately Uganda's prison library and Jamaica's prison music studio add up to the same thing: a Band-Aid on an amputated limb. Only a tiny minority of prisoners is lucky enough to profit from them, and weighed against everything else that these incarcerated people suffer, their fundamental impact remains minuscule.

But isn't some impact better than none? Band-Aids can't cure but they can stop the bleeding. So it is with writing and music and other arts-behind-bars programs, as study after study has indicated. A 1983 one, for instance, revealed a 74 percent favorable parole outcome rate for prisoners who participated in a California arts-based education program. Youth who were part of a Diversion in Music Education program in South Africa had a 9 percent recidivism rate six months after participation, which dropped to zero percent after a year. A study of New York's Rehabilitation Through the Arts program reported numerous positive impacts on participants, including a higher level of positive coping, declining anger levels, and fewer infractions; ultimately, participants were assessed as being more dependable, socially mature, and willing to sacrifice individual needs for the welfare of a group. Music educator Willem Van de Wall wrote extensively about the power of music behind bars to promote feelings of belonging and loyalty; Israeli music professor Laya Silber reported on an Israeli choir that helped female prisoners listen, form new bonds, and accept criticism.

Envisioning Serano's outsized smile, I recall a scene in the film *Songs of Redemption* during which he delivers a breathtaking performance in the cultural center, then runs offstage amid rousing applause, locks himself in the studio booth and begins to sob irrepressibly. "It's too much," he cries. "Jah knows...the music started to create a soul, being someone again, *feeling like a person.*"

The arts are cathartic. Humanizing. But the arts are also beautiful. Prisons are not beautiful, whatever gorgeous music or prose might emerge from them. And at the end of the music or writing or art class, the instructor—me—gets to exit to freedom, reflecting on the wonderful class and brilliant, grateful, adoring students—the same students who, meanwhile, must return to the treacherous realities of their cell blocks. Isn't it all a cruel tease, giving someone a taste of personhood again, but only for a few hours a week?

The problem exists on a grand scale, too, and this is the real catch-22 when it comes to prison arts. Band-Aids can make one forget that a nasty wound festers underneath; worse, they can make one pat oneself on the back for having taken care of the wound. Would it be better, maybe—especially in the dramatic prison hells of Uganda and Jamaica—to let the blood flow and have the gash on full display, so the root problem is addressed and true healing can begin? Because that root problem runs deep: thousands of poor people warehoused for small infractions or because they can't afford a bribe; atrocious conditions that belie even utterance of the word "rehabilitation"; corrupt criminal justice systems and stultifying wealth gaps that produce poverty and crime.

The list goes on, from Uganda to Jamaica and beyond. Even Jonathan's outstanding restorative justice program in South Africa is in many ways a mere Band-Aid, too—although it does represent the possibility of an alternative paradigm, capable of transforming justice from a retributive system to a restoration- and restitution-oriented one. And surely there's room, in this brand new paradigm, for arts programs to work their healing magic. But they can't stand alone.

I leave Jamaica as I left Uganda: immensely frustrated. Prison arts programs are certainly well-meaning efforts but they're also crumbs tossed at a system starved for radical overhaul. They're smoke screens, obstructing our view of the big picture, which is that when it comes to justice and safety and humane treatment, prisons simply don't make sense. Big-picture change is not about tinkering with or enhancing what is, but conjuring up bold imaginings of what could be. For all that I love and believe in it, art can be an obstacle to such imaginings because of the very thing it does so well: dazzle us, and then distract us, with beauty.

4.
Women and Drama | *Thailand*

We are caught in an inescapable network of mutuality,
tied in a single garment of destiny. —Martin Luther King Jr.

As soon as I am back from Jamaica, I check in on my students who've come home from prison. Then I make several trips upstate to Otisville to touch base with the ones still inside. I'm joined by a colleague, Lorraine Moller, a theater professor who's produced plays in American prisons for years, particularly with incarcerated women. As we wait for security to carry us to the classroom, where she'll guest-teach, we shake our heads over the fact that women now represent the world's fastest-growing prisoner demographic.

"You really should go to Thailand, and see what the princess is doing about that," she declares, after hearing about my project.

The princess, Lorraine explains, is Her Royal Highness Princess Bajrakitiyabha, the thirty-five-year-old granddaughter of King Bhumibol and Queen Sinkit. She's a former prosecutor, Thai icon—and a leading advocate for the rights of women in prison. The story of how this came to be is rather amazing. While studying law at Cornell, HRH returned home to visit a prison in Bangkok. In the midst of her tour a prisoner stepped out of line, prostrated herself before the royal visitor, and begged her, *Come back and help us.* Before stunned onlookers, the princess vowed that she would. Five years and three degrees later she launched the Kamlangji Project, Thai for "divine influence or action," which establishes "model" women's prisons around the country.

HRH also spent several months at John Jay, studying criminal justice, which is how Lorraine came to know her, and during that stay visited a New York women's prison.

"I'll reach out to her people," Lorraine says.

Shortly after she does, we're offered an invitation to visit Thailand as official guests of the Kamlangji team. We don't have many details, but we gather that the agenda involves touring prisons and leading some sort of drama workshop in the flagship facility. It will be an opportunity to consider a grim triad that is having catastrophic consequences in Thailand and all over the world: women, drugs, and prison.

More than 625,000 women and girls are incarcerated globally. The number of American women in prison has risen by 823 percent since 1977; 70 percent of the 80,000 women currently behind bars in the States are in for nonviolent offenses, a reality echoed in many countries, where women, generally speaking, serve time for theft, fraud, and drugs, all crimes closely correlated with poverty. In Thailand about 21,000 of the 25,231 convicted women in prison are in for drug charges and a mere 550 or so for violent offenses. About 18,000 of these women are serving at least twenty years, and forty-one are on death row. The numbers, in other words, are dramatic and bleak—surely the reason why the princess simply could not look away.

———

The morning after landing in Bangkok, I await my ride in the lobby. Buddhist monks in sandals and robes are arriving en masse for a conference, landing me submerged in a sea of orange. My pickup rushes in, late and out of breath. Her name is Pattirya, and she introduces herself with a gentle handshake and profuse apologies for the traffic. Then she guides me to a van marked Department of Justice, where I'm introduced to her other half, Pannaya. Pan and Pat, young, fresh-faced government recruits, will be my escorts through the "land of smiles."

"How far is Sukhumvit?" I ask, trying to get a handle on this sprawling city's size.

"Very close," says Pat. "Maybe more than one hour?"

At the Sukosol Hotel we pick up Lorraine, who'd elected to have the government team arrange her accommodations. Doors are opened by towering Thai ladies in purple robes, hotel hostesses. *Sawade-ka*, comes their singsong greeting, palms pressed together as if in prayer, heads bowed.

"Welcome John Jay Delegation" reads the sign at the Office of Justice Affairs, our first stop today. The office is a government think tank, and everything about the place connotes progress and efficiency. The decor is IKEA-chic, with crayon-yellow chairs and cheery plastic flowers. Portraits of corrections officers and HRH adorn the walls, along with inspirational slogans and the agency's mantra, "Engineered for Good Justice." In a bright-white conference room, neat lunch trays containing fried chicken, coconut pudding, and shrimp soup are served; Lorraine and I get a crash course in Thai justice.

The country's 114 prisons are divided between Central Prisons, housing those serving over fifteen years; Correctional Institutions, housing drug-related prisoners; and a House of Relegation for those considered "habitual offenders." Six classes of prisoners are classified like misbehaving children: excellent, very good, good, moderate, bad, and very bad. The system is filled to nearly three times its capacity; as in the United States, this is due, quite simply, to a war on drugs. In 2003 the Thai government changed its policy on methamphetamine overnight, classifying it as a first-degree narcotic. This sent the prison system to its highest levels ever, and to near bankruptcy. The government drew up suspect lists of alleged dealers and used financial incentives to encourage arrests. Informants would get 15 percent of the value of seized assets, arresting officials up to 40 percent. Crackdowns resulted in thousands being killed in the streets; officials claimed these killings were the result of gang warfare but international human rights watchdogs exposed them to be extrajudicial killings by an agitated police force.

Slowly the government managed to trim its prison population, mainly via use of good-time allowance systems, early parole, and royal pardons, which commemorate royal marriages, birthdays, and so on. One year 37,400 prisoners were released in honor of the king's birthday. Death penalties can be relaxed via royal pardon as well, and most "lifers" in Thailand in reality serve about a dozen years.

I struggle to take in the barrage of information, and to process the show-and-tell style in which it's presented. Government officials tend to toss out prison statistics as if they're not talking about human life. How can I casually nod my head in approval as slides of the latest in "humane restraint equipment" are presented for our perusal? Charts and graphs depicting royal pardons and sentence-reduction equations especially boggle my mind. Why concoct elaborate sentences only to find pretext after pretext for reducing them?

I say little, though, in an effort to be polite to our gracious hosts. And for the rest of the day, through torrential rain, the grand welcome tour continues. I bow, receive gifts, and rehearse *sawade-ka*. Cameras flash as government paparazzi transform each meet-and-greet into a photo op. Lorraine, who'd armed herself with Thai etiquette books prior to our trip, whispers in my ear throughout. *Crossing your legs is rude—no one shall see the bottoms of your feet! Accept business cards with two hands! Study them carefully when politely received!* Returning to the hotel, I'm exhausted and unsure what to think about what we've seen and heard so far, but also tremendously curious about what's to come.

————

The next morning we arrive at Bangkok Central Women's Correctional Institution, located in the high-security Klong Prem complex and housing some twenty thousand people. The massive white structure, with icinglike yellow accents, looks like a grand wedding cake, decked out in Thai flags and crowned by a giant, gold-framed photo of the king.

At the helm of the Kamlangji team escorting us is earnest, ever-smiling Dr. Napaporn, a professor recruited by HRH herself to run the initiative. Immediately I can see why. Napaporn is a wealth of information about all things related to Thai women and incarceration, but also a fountain of passion and compassion— an antidote to the cool government bureaucracy I witnessed yesterday. In her hands, statistics take life and become human lives again.

During the ride she briefs us on the global convention that the princess initiated, which resulted in 2010's UN Rules for the Treatment of Women Prisoners and Non-custodial Measures for Women Offenders, better known as the Bangkok Rules. One of its achievements was to identify women as a group that has distinct needs and is uniquely vulnerable. It's estimated that in Europe, 80 percent of women in prison have an identifiable mental illness, one in ten have attempted suicide before being imprisoned, and 75 percent struggle with drugs and alcohol; in America, the percentage of incarcerated women who are mentally ill is about 73 percent. As a result, safeguards ought to govern women's prisons across the world. There should be screenings for mental health issues, drug dependency, and sexual abuse. Nutritional advice ought to be given to detainees who are pregnant, breast-feeding, or menstruating, and staff should be trained in "gender sensitivity." The Bangkok Rules also advocate a ban on the shackling of women during childbirth—incidentally, only eighteen US states have any laws restricting this practice—and propose that a "gender-sensitive risk assessment" should take into account a woman's history of domestic violence, mental illness, and substance abuse problems during sentence allocation.

We drive into the prison complex, down back roads and through a slumlike area where, Napaporn explains, corrections officers live. A welcome line of officers sporting khaki uniforms greets us and we're ushered upstairs, into a plush conference room with red velvet chairs and sunshine-yellow drapes. Mango juice and warm banana muffins are served—made by prisoners, we're told. The lights are dimmed and a computer-generated voice narrates a video tour of the prison library and vocational training classes in food catering, sports, beauty arts. The list goes on, cheerily. Sewing! Meditating! Massaging! Yoga, salons, bakeries!

Is it a marketing campaign? For some retreat?

This perplexed feeling mounts as we're led through gates and a metal detector, paparazzi trailing us. An officer in salute stance announces the roll count of 4,500 prisoners today, 53 at court. And right inside the metal gates is the main prison area: a tidily arranged complex with a lush lawn, a small Buddhist shrine, several decrepit-looking buildings, and a line of women seated on a bench.

They wear baggy tops and long skirts, baby and royal blue for the sentenced prisoners, rusty brown for those on remand. Spying us, they steeple their hands and bow. They're awaiting visitors; those in on drug charges can receive them once a week and all others, every day. Visits are just fifteen minutes long, though, and mostly conducted through glass. Contact visits are granted just once a year, usually to children and mothers. It's generally known that throughout the world, women visit their husbands in prison with far more consistency than husbands visit their partners.

As I'm shepherded through sliding doors and into an air-conditioned room, a bundle is placed in my arms. It's a baby. One of two dozen adorable beings in a pristine white nursery. A photo of the princess in a gilded frame hangs on the wall and toys are stacked neatly in a corner, where three mothers breast-feed. It smells, deliciously, of baby—powder and lotion. Swaddled in blankets, the babies rest on an island of colorful pillows in the middle of the room, tended to by barefoot prisoners who are trained caretakers. My heart melts by the second.

"I have never seen babies so silent," I marvel.

"They are happy!" exclaims Napaporn. "If they were outside, they are poor. In here is better than outside. Meal, diaper. All free."

Lorraine, cooing, takes the baby I'm holding and Joseph lands in my arms.

"From Africa. Mother from Sudan," a corrections officer explains. Joseph gives me a toothless grin and a droplet of drool lands on my collar.

"I wish my daughter would have one already!" Lorraine exclaims, between coos.

This prison is home to about one hundred mothers, Napaporn goes on, who live together in a dorm. "Babies stay until age one," she says, as Joseph is extracted from my embrace. "Until age three, house provided by the department and weekly visit to mother. After that, family must provide. Or orphanage." Goodbyes, after that first year of maternal bonding, are heart-wrenching, she adds.

Universally speaking, broken homes are acute collateral consequences of incarceration, shattering a family's foundation emotionally and economically. On American shores, some 75 percent of women in prison are mothers and more than 2.7 million children have incarcerated parents. A 2014 study found significant health problems and behavioral issues in such children, indicating that in some respects, parental incarceration can be more harmful to a child's health than divorce or even the death of a parent. Only ten states in America allow incarcerated mothers to spend more than two or three days with their newborns. Here in Thailand the Kamlangji team determined that 43 percent of women in prison were, upon arrest, primary breadwinners. Thailand actually boasts one of the highest labor participation rates for women of any country in the region, in part because Buddhism designates women, who cannot be monks, as "this-worldly" and men as "otherworldly," thereby placing the onus of everyday economic matters primarily on women.

Rain thunders down and the air is dense with heat. I'm handed a Burberry-plaid umbrella. Prisoners, rushing to and fro, shield their heads with cardboard and garbage bags. Some trail us down a concrete walkway to a library, built in 2006 with HRH's support. The air conditioning is a welcome relief, as is the glimmer of normalcy that the library provides. Ladies sit serenely at the tables, reading magazines, giggling and whispering, checking out books.

"Very little," our host officer asserts, when asked by Lorraine about prison violence. "Some fighting over, maybe, people talk too much, too little space. Female prisoners are—how do you say?—more sensitive than males, so when something happen they become moody. Lots of moody."

The dormitories, as they're called, are immaculate, with linoleum floors and troughlike sinks flanked by Winnie the Pooh towels. Blue sleeping mats are stacked in a corner of the room, which holds forty-five women and is about the size of a studio apartment. A flat-screen TV hangs on the wall, beside two fans, meager weapons in the battle against the Bangkok June heat. Many hours are passed here. Daily bath and breakfast are at 6:00 a.m., workshop or library time at 8:00, dinner at 3:00 p.m., and lockup until morning at 4:30.

Outside the dormitory, a corkboard posts the number of people inside, their offenses, and their time until release. I ask Napaporn about the longest sentence listed. Twenty-five years and eleven months, she says, scanning the board. For possession. Of what? *Yaba*. Literally "madness drug"—caffeine-infused meth, in high demand. A Kamlangji study found that 90 percent of women behind bars faced *yaba*-related charges; in 35 percent of these cases the women possessed less than fourteen tablets. Looking visibly pained, Napaporn explains that fifteen pills can mean a life sentence or death.

Prisoners, I notice from the list, are identified by name, not number.

"No, no. Must know their name and face," the officer explains. "Sensitive women. Must know name and face."

Outside, puddles have become lakes. Guided into rubber boots, we slosh through wet heat and gray fog to the work area. Hot-pink mosquito nets swathe the room like clouds of cotton candy; those fashioning them hunch over sewing machines. A bright floral housedress is carried to us for inspection. The women smile and bow before rushing back to their stations.

I try to see beyond the smiles, but it's not easy. I'm learning the dismal facts and figures, but as human beings, the women here remain blank slates to me. I've not exchanged a word with them, and barely made eye contact—heads are too often bowed. Lorraine and I have been promised the chance to interview women during tomorrow's visit to another prison, and next week's work calls for plenty of interaction, but I wonder about my ability to connect with people here, as I have in the other countries. Given that it's a royal visit, plus the colossal cultural barriers, how sincere an interface can I expect?

The sewing machines keep humming. I could be in any global factory. Which notion is more distressing, I muse, the idea that prisons are an improvement on the outside world, as in the baby nursery, or the possibility, inspired by this vista of capitalism, that they're essentially on par with it? Both realities suggest that poverty is itself a kind of prison. Which is why many of my students in New York come home to freedom only to tell me, months later, that the daily grind of life can sometimes make freedom feel not so different from being behind bars.

The tour concludes as strangely as it began, with food and souvenirs. The prison restaurant, just outside the barbed wire, is a big local draw, both for the built-in gimmick of being staffed by prisoners, as part of their culinary training, and for the quality of the food. Today there's a popular local TV show filming here, interviewing officers stationed by the ladies' room and hungry patrons devouring noodles. At the table, doily place mats, quilted pink menus, and matching pink chopstick holders mark each seat. Waitresses in pink dresses, sporting those same affectless looks I'd faced all day, take our order and place spicy papaya salad and pad thai before us.

Next door the gift shop sells prisoner-made goods and also doubles as a massage parlor. Rifling through pillows, place mats, and purses embroidered with little Thai girls at the playground, trying to determine if making purchases would constitute supporting the prison system or, instead, the efforts to reform it, I spy one more framed royal photo. There's the king's nephew, pants rolled up, enjoying a foot massage from an incarcerated trainee.

———

"I know you tell me not to worry, but I am. I'm worrying," Lorraine sighs during dinner that night at Vertigo, the rooftop restaurant that makes good on its name. Like many Asian megalopolises, their skylines swarming with postmodern edifices, Bangkok lives in the heavens. Next week is the drama workshop Lorraine and I will run, but we still don't know the parameters of our access and haven't quite figured out how the whole thing will work. For weeks before our departure, Lorraine had sent me e-mails. *How about this drama exercise? You ought to read this book about Thai gender roles. And maybe this one on women and prostitution in Thailand?*

I'd told her to relax; overplanning is counterproductive.

"It'll be fine," I assure her, with an extra gulp of wine.

After dinner I go for a walk on Khao San Road, Bangkok's definitive tourist strip. It's all knickknack vendors, cheap skewered meat, and thumping bars flooded with Germans in Bob Marley T-shirts. One sign reads Laughing Gas and TOEFL For Sale; another, Very Strong Liquor: No ID Check. I dub it night of the living stereotypes, essence of "backpacker" come to life. Including, of course, one very critical backpacker ingredient: drugs.

The party and the prison are thus hardly far apart. Meth and, beginning in the early nineties, ecstasy, have local markets, especially among hedonistic travelers, and these customers demand suppliers, mostly recruited from the incarcerated women I met today. Thailand is a major transshipment point for heroin from neighboring Myanmar, the world's second-biggest producer of opium, after Afghanistan. Organized crime groups and border-residing minority groups like the Hill People are at the forefront of this complex trade, and in 1979 the country's Narcotics Act spelled out draconian punishments for sundry categories of drugs. "Tough-on-drugs" policies and rhetoric were inspired by America's own drug war around the same time. And as in the States, the whole thing is motivated by politics, serving to boost government popularity while diverting attention from its policy failures.

Bleary-eyed, I hail a tuk-tuk and sputter back to the hotel.

———

Inside another Thai women's prison later that week, we watch four women with short haircuts craft Hello Kitty bookshelves.

Napaporn, speaking kindly to them, introduces us; they restfully steeple their hands.

Pim, wearing pink lipstick and a matching pink clothespin in her hair, is nineteen and serving an eight-year sentence. She carried her boyfriend's *yaba* because, well, he asked her to, and he was her boyfriend; given Thai gender roles, Napaporn explains, questioning male authority figures is not an option. One of her studies found that more than half of incarcerated women with drug cases had codefendants, 44 percent of whom were husbands or lovers.

Wanee meticulously applies glue to pastel-colored shelves. She smiles as she tells us that she's a mother of three serving life, for two *yaba* pills. Life, because she crossed a national border to visit her family in Laos, and carried pills with her.

I try to muster up more questions but I'm arrested by the quiet anguish of the scene. And the women's answers are brief and unrevealing; civility and power dynamics hang like cobwebs over our conversation. Smiles and *sawade-ka*s are all that feel appropriate.

In the kitchen fifteen women in prison uniforms, cooking staff, are seated mermaid style on the floor. Massive silver woks rest beside heaps of produce. A menu on the wall informs us that chicken soup, cucumber with Chinese sausage, and curry with pork rind are for dinner. Dollhouse-size samples are presented for our inspection. *Kapoon-ka!* comes the choruslike call, as we move on to the heaven-scented bakery.

"Is it difficult to bake in this heat?" Lorraine asks one of the prisoners there, crouching to look her in the eye.

"Yes, but I like it. It is like home, baking." She brandishes her chiffon brownie.

Fifty-eight-year-old Grace, to be released in two months after serving eleven years, tells us she will go north to open a bakery, and this work has been helpful training. A third woman explains that she's served a year for possession of *kratom*—a plant in the same narcotics category as marijuana, even though it's grown for medicinal purposes in rural Thai villages.

I'm reminded of the fact that in America in the 1990s, some 80 percent of drug arrests were for marijuana. And in 2013, 3,278 people in the States—65 percent of them black—were serving life sentences for nonviolent offenses. These include one man sentenced to life for serving as a middleman in the sale of ten dollars' worth of marijuana, and a trucker who tried to earn the money for his two-year-old son's bone-marrow transplant by carrying meth in his vehicle, now nearing twenty years behind bars. Because America, like most countries, including Thailand, privileges the weight of narcotics above the role a defendant plays in a drug deal, a kingpin who imports fifteen kilos of cocaine potentially faces the same sentence as the trucker paid a hundred dollars to carry it. A more just gauge of guilt would be the profit taken from the operation—prosecuting an operation's masterminds, in other words, over and above its hapless street soldiers. But that would mean almost all of the women I'm meeting today would be free. Seventy-nine percent of incarcerated Thai women were arrested during sting operations netting small fish in the big drug pond.

"Before here I was waitress. At hotel," Grace tells us. "I have not worries about release." She offers a sample of her fruitcake.

Inside the programs building, prisoners massage each other's feet during a training course; a dozen others sit in a glassed-off room taking a computer class. On the porch is "art therapy," as Napaporn calls it. Five prisoners are creating paintings—a diary with a manga-inspired cover, portraits of the princess and the king, a massive one of Ganesha, the elephant-headed Hindu god of success. A dozen women are engaged in a flower-arranging course, and Lorraine is presented with an ornate display of white roses. An officer points toward one of the women, knee-deep in carnations.

"They put on makeup before they sleep," she laughs. "So when they dream, they pretend they are beautiful."

Lorraine asks how they treat misbehavior.

"They run up and down courtyard," the officer answers. "Or sit separate from everyone, maybe for up to one week. Or clean the prison."

Like naughty children, I think. Both of these so-called model prisons—utterly unique, all-female miniworlds adopted by Kamlangji—hinge on a kind of maternal authority structure. They're a cross between a military camp and a women's retreat, at which every prisoner is at all times engaged in some program. They call to mind America's Progressive-Era reformatory movement, which reflected changing conceptions of offenders: not depraved but wayward, led astray and thus ripe for being led back to the right path by way of supposedly scientific methods like probation, parole, and placement in precisely classified prisons, from minimum to maximum. Many of our women's prisons were born as reformatories, like New York's Bedford Hills, in 1907, and its House of Refuge for Women, in 1887. Far less severe than male prisons, these reformatories were lorded over by house mothers and an all-female staff. Prisoners there were often paroled to work as domestic servants, and there were gymnastics lessons, reading and writing, health care classes, nature walks, and choirs. At Indiana Reformatory, the women even sported gingham frocks and ate at tables dressed with tablecloths and flowers. This movement lost its steam around 1930, in part because the Depression made them financially unsustainable.

"I try not to look women in eye," the foreign affairs officer tells me on our way out. "It will be too sad for me. I am glad I don't go to the prison every day, only sometimes. Because I know. Even though they have programs, they are cared for, they are not happy. They want to be with their children and their mothers."

In the traditional Thai value system, *bunkhun*, loosely translated as "duty," implies that women must care for their children and their mothers, because they have one debt to pay and another to generate. A man can pay this debt in the highest way possible by becoming a monk, but since women cannot be monks, they pay in a more literal sense, as primary caretakers.

Later that afternoon at the sumptuous, surreal Temple of Dawn, which rises like a colorful Candyland from the drab city streets, I ogle ornate Buddhas, dodge tourist cameras, and contemplate *bunkhun*. I immediately think of Moon, the supermodel-looking manager at my hotel.

"I am Tiger," she'd said, as we chatted one evening. "You?"

Dragon, I tell her, and Virgo. She explains that she lives with her mother and nephew, and used to be engaged to a man but then he came out as gay and is now a woman. She models wedding dresses but plans to never marry.

"I have temple. And Mom. Men hurt you. Mom—never."

I, meanwhile, have no children and see my mother every few months. Lorraine had told me that she sacrificed her sabbatical year so she could nurse her mother back to health; I'm spending mine traveling around the world, and my primary ties, the ones I'm at pains to check e-mail for, the ones I call before heading off to another flight, are my students who've come home from prison in New York.

Pan picks me up for the ride home and asks me what I'll do tonight.

"Me, I will go home to my parents, my family," she says, before I can answer. "Maybe you think—boring."

I say nothing. What I feel, though, is envy. Traditional family has not been part of my orbit for decades; for the time being, I've cobbled together a beautiful version of "family" from friends, students, and causes. But the allure of the conventional never quite recedes. This trip, saturated in the ache of fragmented families, has brought my own home-life struggles with rootlessness into sharp focus.

"My mom had me very late in her life," Pan adds. "She is glad I came out, you see, healthy. She is my best friend."

How lucky you are, I think, turning to peer out the window.

———

The week's proceedings have a name: "We Shall Find Our Way Home."

Over breakfast at the hotel, I scan the advice column in the *Bangkok Post.*

Dear Annie, I read to Lorraine. She's fretting again. After today's powwow with the Kamlangji team, we'll be heading south to Ratchaburi to begin our drama workshop behind bars, and we still don't have a concrete agenda. We'd spent the weekend apart, Lorraine remaining in Bangkok and I heading up to Chiang Mai before moving over to her hotel.

My brother just got engaged, I continue reading. *I've just found out that the woman he will marry has been secretly texting the man she once had an affair with. Do I say something, or keep my mouth shut and plaster on a fake smile?*

"Now isn't that the dilemma," Lorraine muses, halfheartedly.

"Indeed," I say. "Family loyalty versus gender norms. The woman is meant to smile and stay silent."

With a jolt, Lorraine sets down her coffee and looks up.

"That's it! Let's act it out," she declares. "Enactments—this will be our role-playing exercise in the prison. This will work. The women will get it."

We hash out a game plan. Then we make our way to the conference room for a morning of speeches, formalities, and photo ops before heading to the prison. Our visit has morphed into a Kamlangji miniconference, themed around forms of prison therapy and attended by delegates from all over the world. There's Dr. Brian Steels, a sixty-seven-year-old professor of Aboriginal studies from Western Australia, where he engages in "narrative therapy" with prisoners; Sanyasa, a yoga therapist from India swathed in an orange robe, white turban, and beads, who says little but smiles often, yogically; and theater-therapy guru Kru Chang—his father was the first Thai student to graduate from UCLA and the first Thai to play Hamlet—who looks very much the prototypical "elder sage," with his harem pants, sandals, long gray hair, and bountiful beard.

"I was once the Johnny Depp of Thailand," Chang had declared days earlier, when Lorraine and I visited his home base. The drive from urban sprawl into a land of canals and a clearing in the bush delivered us to Moradokmai, his communelike school where forty Buddhist students, most from poor rural homes, learn their entire curriculum through theater. I wondered aloud, is there a relationship between Buddhism and theater?

"There is no relationship. It is one and the same," came Chang's cryptic answer, leaving me scratching my head.

At the prison today and tomorrow Lorraine will teach drama therapy and I will assist her, while also promoting behind-bars higher education and the Prison-to-College Pipeline model. Napaporn ushers us into the van, a VIP-style chariot with gold rims and leather seats, for the ride south to the prison. Her energy is palpable. I'd learned that she first got involved in this work after the princess came to her university to interview professors for the launch of Kamlangji. Napaporn had worked with other disadvantaged groups, including Thai ethnic minorities and the differently abled, but from the moment she set foot behind bars and met the women there, it became not a job but an obsession. I know this obsession well, I'd told her.

"I don't know how long it will last," she'd said. "Every day I worry: the project will end. Funding dry up. So I just try, impact as many people as possible. Yes?" She went on to tell me of a prison, up near the Myanmar border, where the team is now starting to work.

"It is dark, overcrowded. What do I do, Baz? Where do I begin to make it better? Staff sensitivity training? Yoga? This will help the girls to not be with anxiety, to sleep better. Not easy to sleep in those cells. But the project feels so big, so little a change in so big a problem."

I responded by telling her about Martin, one of my formerly incarcerated students who came dangerously close to going back inside, right after coming home. He showed up at my office with a black eye from a bar brawl; he was going to forget about school and make money, he'd shrugged. But after nagging, assurances, months of tough love, literally dragging him through registration—he grudgingly started college. Now he's a star philosophy student, prelaw, a paid intern at a top firm.

"A single life stands alone," was my response to her sighs.

In the van, headed south, I chat with Brian, seated next to me.

"How did you get involved in prison work?" I ask.

"I went to prison," he responds.

Brian spent three years behind bars on a charge for which he maintains his innocence. Then he went back inside, dedicating his life to impacting the system that traumatized him. With a background in sociology and criminology, he's one of a growing number of so-called convict criminologists, scholars whose work is informed by personal experience with the criminal justice system.

"And," I speak softly now, as Brian and I get lost in an intense discussion about his years inside, "how did your wife take it?"

"She divorced me," Brian says. "I learned quickly that family is fragile. And family is relative."

I nod vigorously. "Friends are family you choose," I proclaim. It's one of my mantras.

"Yes," agrees Brian.

The scene outside the window steals my attention, its lush green mountains and rice paddies opening their arms to eternity. Why is the road to hell, around the world, paved with magical vistas? It makes their dramatic disruption by concrete towers and shimmering barbed wire that much more unsettling, a startling marriage of ugliness and beauty.

Ratchaburi Central Prison, home to about nine hundred women, is expecting us. As we enter the buzzing courtyard, tinny music plays on a petite mobile library cart, and a cake and coffee stand is staffed by two prisoners in white aprons. The "Welcome to Ratchaburi" sign is made from color-cardboard cutouts.

In one corner are a dozen women buried in origami weave baskets, baby animals, and a massive portrait of the prison superintendent in full military regalia. Napaporn slings an origami basket on my arm—"Fashion!" laughs an officer—and two prisoners deposit a paper puppy and mouse inside it.

"Quick, quick—they are going to start the yoga now," Napaporn calls to Lorraine and me. We're shepherded to a pavilion with a luminous white floor, on which hundreds of women sit patiently. We're served water and sweet tapioca cakes and handed scented towels while some twenty-five incarcerated women file out, dressed in black tops and leggings; many have elaborately braided their hair and sport vivid pink lipstick.

Singing commences. It sounds like a sorrowful lullaby, chanted by prisoners in high-pitched tones. Chang, next to me, translates.

"The highs and lows of life," he says. "Keep dream lit at all times. Life is ups and downs but hope remains. Faith. Love. Hope."

The song stretches on and the women in black begin their yoga poses. It's a majestic dance, all circular configurations and pyramids and graceful splits and downward dogs. A climactic conclusion has them in a lotus-flower formation, which they hold for a strong two minutes as we offer thunderous applause. The lovely sight, set against its context of barbed wire, makes me cry.

There isn't time for tears, though. Napaporn shuttles Chang, Lorraine, Brian, Sanyasi, and me to various corners of the prison to get to work.

Our twenty-five students stand in a semicircle, fidgeting.

"This is a space for drama, which means it is a space to be free!" an animated Lorraine declares. Her confident, commanding classroom self emerges.

"Who enjoys performing?"

All of the women gingerly raise their hands and grin, as if eager to please. Our icebreaker, the mirror exercise, kicks things off. The class pairs up and is instructed to engage in movements. Partners must imitate every move made, without laughing.

Lorraine and I do the exercise along with them, her juddering movements and oddball faces nearly making me crack too broad a smile. The women, meanwhile, begin giggling, jumping, waving, trying to contain laugher. Two corrections officers are mirroring away, too, making googly eyes and goofy faces at their prisoner partners. One has a moon face so endearing, it distracts me.

Warmed up, we're ready for introductions. Stand in a semi-circle, Lorraine commands. Some ladies have their arms slung around their neighbors' waists; others lean on each other, shoulder to shoulder. Declare your name and an epithet to go with it—an adjective that captures you.

"Lovely Lorraine," she begins.

"Busy Baz."

Happy Ploy.

Joyous Plaem.

Playful Joy.

Mother Nan.

Daughter Pim.

Funny Wandee.

The women grow more at ease by the minute, and their giggles slowly taper off.

I take out the newspaper clipping and read it; our translator doesn't miss a beat. Meet Annie, I tell the class. And brother John. Fiancée Lisa, potential lover Robert, Tom the boss.

A student raises her hand.

"But who is Robert? His job?"

"He has a good job. He is rich."

Napaporn, standing on the sidelines, signals to me for a quick consultation in the corner. Robert, he should be a drug dealer, she says. A drug dealer who is trying to entice Lisa away from her hard-working fiancé with money and flashy things.

"This way," Napaporn explains, "it can be a lesson for the women. About not going with bad men. They know about this well—this is their lives."

"Robert," I return and tell the class, "is a drug dealer. He has lots of money." The prisoners' eyes grow wide. Yoga *"ooooohms"* from Sanyasi's class in the pavilion behind us seep in to form our background music.

"But John works many hours," I go on. "Where does he work?"

"Sells cars!" one woman calls out.

"Good," I say. "And he works very late, and very hard. And Lisa is often alone and frustrated."

As a class, we outline what the various scenes will look like.

"We need actors!" Lorraine commands. "Who would like to be Lisa?"

A slim young woman with a long ponytail tied with a red ribbon leaps up, her hand raised. And John? The ladies unanimously point to a thick, short-haired, broad-faced woman who lumbers toward the front of the class, barefoot and blushing.

"We need a stage!"

The women scurry into action, moving chairs around with alacrity. Here's the office space and the imaginary computers, where John works. These tulips are for the restaurant where Lisa is stood up and then meets Robert.

Scene one: improvise, ladies!

John types away in the office. The boss enters, demanding more work and more hours. John keeps typing, fingers in the air, eyes with deadly focus. Lisa, meanwhile, twirls her ponytail and checks her imaginary cell phone, then pulls out an imaginary mirror and applies lipstick. John is still typing away.

"*Cut!*" Lorraine calls. Time is up, to be continued tomorrow.

"Awwwwww," groan the women, in unison, showering us with goodbye waves.

"That went well, didn't it?" Lorraine says. Napaporn hands me my origami basket.

"I am surprised," says our translator. She was a teacher before becoming a probation officer. "In my classroom, the women would be so silent—they never wanted to express themselves. Good Thai women, see. But here they are different."

I'm reminded of a scene in Chang's school during our visit last week, as we sat in the outdoor amphitheater, devouring plates of lychee and mangosteen. "Theater is more than the truth," a student named Champion had said. "It makes it possible to tell things you cannot tell otherwise." The girl next to him chimed in: "Theater gives me the space to tell untold stories."

Lorraine had spoken of something called role deprivation, the stultifying way in which prison limits human beings, accustomed to playing multiple roles in our complex lives—at once mothers, daughters, professionals, wives, students—to a single hard-and-fast role: *prisoner.* The power of drama in prison is that it allows participants to perform a kind of resurrection; it's an opportunity to enact other roles, to have manifold selves again, for a few hours. I did see glimmers of this today as the women luxuriated in their performances, and even as they took leave of their "obedient prisoner" demeanors during the icebreakers.

The delegation files out of the prison, past the ornate shrine and through the security gates. Riding away from a vista bathed in moonlight, I ask Brian about his narrative therapy session, which amounts, from the sound of it, to the sharing of life narratives in an effort to alter them for the better. One woman, he says, sobbed the whole time because she hasn't seen her children in seven years.

"What do you say to that?" I ask.

"I shared my story," he says, steadily. "My children rejected me. It pains me. Many nights I sit and drink wine, too much wine, even though it eats at my esophagus. I have stomach cancer, you see." I grow wide-eyed.

"And my second wife, she has been terminally ill for years. This is the fact of our lives. We are victims of these things, but we can also choose not to be, to reject reading our role in our own narratives as that of victims. Once we do that, we've won."

We pull up at the night's hotel, where the Kamlangji team awaits our arrival. Rooms are basic but dinner is another sumptuous Thai buffet. Chang the theater guru, changed into jeans and an Abbey Road T-shirt, offers me a serving of chili fish.

"I don't know what you call this kind of fish in America. It's white fish. Boneless and childless," he says.

"How sad," Lorraine says, raising her spoon.

That night the team arranges an evening outing. We end up in what feels like a Midwestern saloon, complete with a man on guitar singing "How Deep Is Your Love?" To everyone's delight I drink a frothy pink concoction in a champagne glass—"Don't get drunk, professor," the team laughs. I don't. But I do, with Brian, shut the place down in an attempt to banish the sadness of today from our minds. We sip local rum and chat about prison and family and, sometimes, the prison that traditional family can be. And somewhere in the midst of the bonding and talking and gracious hospitality, I get a taste of that elusive feeling called *home*.

———

"They say they have been practicing," Jaidee announces, as Lorraine and I greet our students the next morning. They're scurrying to arrange the set and assume their roles.

John diligently types away in his office; the irate boss delivers her role with the authority of a corrections officer. Lisa waits longingly for John at the restaurant, waving her ponytail to and fro. Robert, at the table next to her, makes his move on the lonely lady; soon he is showering her with gifts in the form of an origami basket and yellow felt tulips, while John, despondent, scrolls through suspicious text messages on a flip-flop doubling as a cell phone. The audience, our class, is mesmerized.

"How should the proposal scene happen?" we pause to ask them. "Where?"

"Phuket!" comes the call, in unison.

Two women leap up from their seats to perform the role of palm trees swaying in the sun. Two more imitate the sounds of the waves in the background, and John gets down on one knee before Lisa, who visibly grapples with her answer. Choose the well-meaning, hardworking, yet financially struggling man or the wealthy drug dealer who beckons with all the pleasures of the high life? Divided into four groups, the students perform their version of an ending.

Group one takes center stage. Lisa opts for John, running into his dramatic embrace; the two soon have a child and live happily ever after. Robert, meanwhile, is arrested and led off the stage, bawling, in imaginary cuffs.

Applause!

Group two: Lisa tearfully rejects John's proposal, but also spurns Robert's advances. "I choose me!" declares the prisoner, exiting stage left with arms raised in triumph.

Group three: Lisa runs off with Robert, swathes herself in imaginary fur, and, lost in the high life, becomes addicted to *yaba*. Huddling in a corner of the stage, her end is anything but triumphant.

Finally, group four: Lisa runs off with Robert the drug dealer, after which both are arrested and imprisoned. Lisa, ponytail hanging low, tearfully gazes out her cell window and faintly calls John's name.

The women take their bows, and the class cannot stop applauding.

Our final exercise is "the gift." We stand in a circle, hold hands, and present the person next to us with something we feel they'd benefit from. Lorraine begins by handing her neighbor one thing: hope.

"I give you the gift to go home soon," says one prisoner to another.

I give you...to see your family soon. To forget about this hard time. To see your children. To care for your mother again.

The moon-faced officer stands in the circle with us. Her gift, to the prisoner who grips her hand tightly, is love.

My neighbor bestows her gift on me. "I give you success in your career," she smiles. How sadly ironic, I think, clasping her hand. Everyone else gets love and family; I get work. "And to come visit us again very soon," she adds, perhaps reading my mind.

What happens next is a new experience for me. Hugs. Long, gripping, family-style hugs, all around.

Many times in Otisville I have wanted to hug my students. The time Ron was denied parole for the fifth time, or the time Julio broke into sobs talking about the murder he committed twenty years ago, as an abused teenager filled with rage. Or the time Marc earned his first A and said he'd never believed he was good at anything until now. But of course there is no such thing as a hug from a female in a male prison. Hugs are postponed until homecomings.

The ladies grasp me tightly, one by one. Inevitably, tears come, from me, Lorraine, all of the women. I'm not quite certain why we're crying—it's only been two days, and I haven't even learned all of these women's names. It feels less like a tearful goodbye than a catharsis. Or perhaps a physical manifestation of the emotional bonding cultivated by our workshop. As a total-group experience, theater generates community in a remarkable way. And the experience of performing in a public space, being on display and witnessed by one's peers and by outsiders—it's a profound statement for an incarcerated person. *I am seen. I exist.*

Suddenly Chang's enigmatic statement last week, about theater and Buddhism being one and the same, makes sense. Acting is reacting; to perform one's own role one must feel another's role. This, too, is a tenet of Buddhism, the notion that the connective fabric of humanity bonds "you" and "me" together. It's a truth symbolized by the form of greeting here, not a waving-one-hand "hi" that is an "I" but a pressing together of palms that signifies you and me as an integrated entity, others as "extensions of ourselves—fellow facets of the same reality," to cite one Buddhist scholar. The opposite of this looks like Ibsen's potent description of a lunatic asylum: "Each shuts himself in a cask of self, the cask stopped with a bung of self and seasoned in a well of self."

People in prison are part of our human network—they're us and we're them. To treat them badly is to treat ourselves badly. In three terse lines, Buddha articulated a criminal justice and prisoner reentry system that just about says it all: "See yourself in others. Then whom can you hurt? What harm can you do?"

On our way out, Lorraine sighs.

"I could live here," she says. It's a ridiculous statement and she knows it, yet I understand what she means. This place is at its core a horror show, a warehousing of women, mothers, and daughters, torn from kin. Yet from the rubble of shattered families, Kamlangji has in some ways managed to piece together a sisterhood—a commune and community. It's a fragmented family, rife with cracks and haphazardly glued together, but a kind of family nonetheless. And it's exactly the opposite of the violent, animalistic, utterly unhuman portraits of prisoners promoted by pop culture, sensationalized portraits that make it easy to dismiss people behind bars as deserving of the cages in which they live.

"How was the yoga therapy?" Napaporn asks Sanyasa as we climb into the van. He beams.

That term again. "Therapy."

It's the week's buzzword, clearly, but like its prison catchword twin, "rehabilitation," it grates. I don't know what all of the women I've been working with have been charged with or convicted of; I don't know how many of them struggle with addiction, or carried their husband's drugs. But I do know the statistics, thanks to Napaporn and team. Odds are that about a quarter of our students today were victims; 23 percent of women in Bangkok and 34 percent of women in rural Thailand have been abused by their partners, with 39 percent specifying it as sexual abuse. Odds are they come from economic, educational, and social disadvantage; they didn't know the law when they broke it, then felt the impact of harsh laws in a society where even if they did fully grasp crimes and punishments, they can't afford lawyers—just like the 80 percent of

Americans accused of crimes who lack funds for representation. In one study, 74 percent of incarcerated Thai women had no lawyers during questioning; 40 percent of them said the police intimidated them with threats and 12 percent were physically assaulted.

Do these women need healing and therapy or does the law that governs them? Across the globe, draconian drug policy is packing prisons. Drug users and traffickers represent more than half of those in federal prison in the United States and Mexico, a quarter of all those in prison in Spain, and one-fifth entering prison in Japan; in Malaysia they constitute more than half of the nine hundred incarcerated people awaiting execution. And these are mainly small-time users, more than 83 percent of them, worldwide, convicted of possession.

All the yoga and drama in the world won't heal away those harsh realities.

My mind runs back to the pretty empowerment mottoes that wallpaper prisons, from South Africa to America, twelve-step slogans about *your* power to change *your* life through positive thinking, and how the future is wide open in *your* hands—free yourself from the prison of the mind! Such slogans remove the onus from unfair social systems and structures and place it squarely and unfairly on the individual, who must be superhuman to overcome the odds and systems and structures stacked against her.

Together the team rides back to Bangkok. At the hotel bar that evening, smiling Thai women who serve Brian and me could be twins of the prisoners I'd said goodbye to earlier. It's those hotel uniforms, the long purple dresses, just like the prisoners' but crafted from expensive silk. I'm haunted by the ghost of "Lisa" sitting at the "restaurant," demurely playing with her hair, or "John" typing away on that imaginary computer in the air. In the end I know these women only from their performances. But sometimes the performance can be just as authentic as the self, because it is more free than the self, especially when that self is locked away, buried behind bars.

———

Weeks later, when I'm back in New York, the invitation arrives in my e-mail. Will I return to Thailand in August, this time to meet the princess herself?

During our final meeting as a group, Napaporn had talked about bringing the whole "We Shall Find Our Way Home" team back over the summer, when HRH will visit and look in on Ratchaburi. I'd said yes at the time, but with some guilt, wondering why Thai professors weren't the ones being tapped for this work.

I honor my commitment, at least in part because I'm avidly curious to meet HRH herself. And so as the end of summer draws near I find myself on the road to Ratchaburi and again in a sea of orange, as HRH's color adorns banners, ribbons, tablecloths, and tents all over the prison. Hundreds of reporters, government figures, and official-looking folks in suits and ties mill about. The incarcerated women are, literally, marginalized, patiently seated in neat rows on the sidelines. I scan their faces, looking for some of my former students, but don't recognize any demure smiles. I do, however, spy the moon-faced officer, seated with us in the royal tent, where a cushioned throne and a small podium have been erected.

Humidity descends with vicious tenacity. Beads of sweat trail down my arm, dampening my baby-blue dress—no wearing of dark colors around Her Royal Highness, an e-mail from her team had instructed.

We wait for the princess. And wait.

As we're primed for the highly choreographed proceedings, the day turns fantastic. At once I'm playing a starring role in a play I've not rehearsed for, with stage directions called to me in a language I don't fully understand. *Turn here! Bow there! Walk down this aisle, right foot first! Crawl to your seat!* Yes, when the princess is seated you must crawl toward her—nonroyals can never be on a higher plane than she. Practice your curtsies, Lorraine and I are instructed. First upon standing, then put one hand out to receive the princess's gift. No eye contact! Then, yes eye contact, as you curtsy a second time. Prisoners sweep the red carpet with homespun brooms; the minister of justice arrives and paparazzi snap away.

Finally, HRH appears. She walks with a humble gait, wearing a shy smile to match her powder-blue suit, designer pumps, and Chanel purse. During gift time, I miraculously get my curtsy right and resume my seat.

Lorraine and I eventually take our turns at the golden microphone, she giving a talk about the importance of theater in prison and I promoting the value of education behind bars. Napaporn speaks of honoring human dignity and calls for radical reform of Thailand's judiciary and penal systems. The ladies in Sanyasi's yoga class perform a mesmerizing routine, and line up to receive certificates from the princess; one by one come their elegant curtsies. Finally, from her gilded seat, the princess leans into the microphone.

"Prisons should not be dark corners of the earth," she says steadily. The rest of her talk is, to me, lost in translation—except for what she says directly to the prisoners: "I wish you great happiness." And with that she is gone.

Then the imprisoned women appear, as if from thin air, singing that haunting lullaby again, the one I've yet to banish from my mind. This time Chang's translation is different, though. "Do good things and your reward will come to you," he whispers to me. "Give hope. Do good. Do good."

The day is done.

On our way out, Napaporn is ecstatic. Members of the university were present and are eager to pursue Prison-to-College Pipeline possibilities; the princess was vastly impressed. Before my flight home, we sit down for dinner at Lin Fa, a Chinese restaurant.

"You realize that we did put on a show for you, yes?" Napaporn says, rolling a Peking duck pancake.

"During all three prison visits? I imagined so," I confess.

Indeed, Kamlangji has done excellent work in these prisons, she explains; the programs were no stunt. But this is the rare exception—most Thai women's prisons are, alas, nothing like what we've seen. She grins.

"Have you seen the news clips? We are all over the media!" She whips out her phone and there we are, with Thai subtitles, on every TV news show in the country, on the newspapers' front pages. It turns out this is a celebratory dinner. The headline of the week is "The Princess and the Prison."

A revelation hits me. The real theater in my Thai experience has been not our workshops but the entirety of both visits. Kamlangji's prisons are not so much representative of reality as performances of a *possible* reality, not what is but what might be. This does not diminish them. On the contrary, performance has power. A fake laugh can turn real, and a model prison can become all prisons.

Yesterday at Ratchaburi was a grand performance, too. And it also paves a path from the possible to the actual. Why did the Thai public suddenly pay attention to prisoners, and fix its gaze upon the dark, forgotten place where they reside? Because their beloved princess stood, Chanel bag in hand, right in the heart of it. And so did we, respected foreign scholars. Behold royal privilege—and white privilege—in its best possible incarnation, at work in the name of a greater cause, just as I'd seen it work wonders in Rwanda, when I obtained permission for Santos to launch his prison program. I now understand the real reason Lorraine and I were needed here. Not for our expertise or experience but solely for our foreignness and our whiteness, vital ingredients in one of the biggest public relations coups Thai prison activism has ever staged.

What is PR but elaborately crafted theater? And when it comes to prisons and the people inside them, what is more critical than PR? Politicians created the drug laws that incarcerated these women, and their policy moves are dictated by public opinion. Change public opinion about crime and justice, about the so-called criminals in prison—they're not the evil monsters you think they are; they're hapless victims of unforgiving drug laws; they're ardent yogis, devoted subjects of Her Royal Highness—and the politicians will have to cater to their hearts and minds. America has proven this. In the seminal 1988 presidential race between George H. W. Bush and Michael Dukakis, a racially charged TV ad labeling Dukakis as "soft on crime" for his support of a weekend furlough program that allowed Willie Horton, a prisoner, to slip through the hands of prison officials and eventually rape and rob new victims is said to have propelled Bush's victory and deeply impacted political discourse such that "soft on crime" became instant political death.

But if the public decries prison, the politicians will. If prison can be marketed to the public, so can antiprison. In other words, changing the performance, the presentation, is far from superficial. Quite the contrary, it has the power to radically alter the crux of the system itself.

5.
Solitary and Supermaxes | *Brazil*

In order to reform them, they had been submitted to complete
isolation; but this absolute solitude, if nothing interrupts it,
is beyond the strength of man; it destroys the criminal without
intermission and without pity; it does not reform, it kills.
—Alexis de Tocqueville

It is not good for man to be alone. —Genesis 2:18

Cascavel is Portuguese for "rattlesnake."

Cascavel is also a small city in the Brazilian state of Paraná, close to the Argentine border. It's two short plane rides away from São Paulo, and the hour-long drive from the mini-airport to my destination, an even littler town named Catanduvas, is flooded by charmed vistas. A fingernail of a leftover moon dangles in the morning sky. Opulent greenery is disrupted by odd-looking pine trees shaped like upside-down rainbows on matchsticks—Dalí paintings come to life.

My sabbatical is over, but I've managed to steal away for a few days from teaching English 101 to a newly enrolled cohort of students in the Prison-to-College Pipeline. Pulling up to my destination, I see something disturbingly familiar, from almost all my prison travels. The Penitenciária Federal de Catanduvas, Brazil's first federal supermaximum prison, looks like a slice of the United States plunked down on foreign shores. I've come to learn more about this home to the so-called worst of the worst prisoners in a country making dramatic strides in mass incarceration.

Brazil's 550,000-strong prison population is the fastest-growing in the Americas, having nearly quadrupled in the last twenty years or so. I want to take a hard look at the practice of solitary confinement in top-security "supermax" prisons, which in the last twenty-five years began proliferating all over the world but are still relatively new to Brazil. In America alone, it's estimated that some 80,000 individuals live in solitary. If you include jails, immigrant detention centers, and juvenile and military facilities in the count, the total is more like 100,000. Parents who created solitary confinement cells in their homes would likely be prosecuted for child abuse, yet thousands of American juveniles spend time in solitary confinement. It's a reality I find almost impossible to wrap my head around.

André, a white-collar-crime lawyer who volunteers in Brazilian prisons, has accompanied me here. "Strange," he says as he unbuckles his seatbelt. "Last time two men with big guns were waiting for me." Today there's only a sea of metal and wire; the place seems sucked dry of humanity. A red sign on the fence indicates in Portuguese something about "attention" and "warning."

André steps out of the car and speaks loudly into a standing intercom.

"Bon dia!"

I'd met André this morning, in a São Paulo taxi. Though technically we'd met months ago, online, after I read about him in the context of a unique program taking place here. "Rehabilitation Through Reading" enables people to strike four days off their prison sentences, up to forty-eight days a year, for every preapproved work of literature, philosophy, or science they read and write a summary of. Over the course of our e-mail exchanges, André had organized my visit and agreed to join me as translator. My stay wouldn't be long enough to allow for work in the prison, but I was promised two full days inside and the opportunity to engage with the men, in their cells and in classrooms, about both their experience in a supermax and with the books program, which struck me as an intriguing, and unexpected, progressive intervention.

I'd flown to São Paulo and spent a weekend there, absorbing the metropolis's three prominent features: magnificent street art, divine samba tunes—and the omnipresent military police force, notorious for murder. According to the Brazilian Forum on Public Safety, police officers nationwide killed 11,197 people between 2009 and 2014—as compared to some 11,090 killed by US police in the last thirty years. The secretary for public security in Rio once referred to police killings of innocent bystanders as the breaking of eggs to make an omelet.

———

Outside the prison gate in Catanduvas, a minivan finally appears, with the DEPEN logo on it. For a moment I imagine the word is missing its final *D*, but no—it's an acronym for Brazil's national prisons department. The van is escorting out a black Ford SUV containing the top brass at the prison, on their way to early lunch. A tinted window is rolled down and we're invited to join them.

We follow the Ford to the dusty strip of paint-peeling store-fronts that is the town center. The sun is blazing. Inside what feels like a Wild West–style saloon, we weigh plates of meat stews at the buffet and join our hosts. The prison director wears a black suit, and his piercing green eyes smile behind thin glasses; Mara, the head pedagogue, flicks her dirty-blond hair to one side and extends a manicured hand to me.

"Over sixty people from Paraná state are employed by my prison," explains the director, puffing out his chest and explaining its history, as André translates.

The idea of the supermax took hold as a solution to gangs, an infamous staple of Latin American prison life. Their reach extends from Mexico, where in 2012, imprisoned members of the Zetas murdered forty-four prisoners at a jail in Apodaca, to Venezuela, where gangs control almost all prisons and guards are merely responsible for perimeter security, head count, and court transfers. In Brazil, the story really begins in 1991, at São Paulo's notorious Carandiru Prison, now closed. That year military police killed 111 incarcerated people, including pretrial detainees, most via machine guns at point-blank range from the doors of their cells. Surviving men were stripped naked and many were attacked by dogs trained to bite genitals; some were stabbed, others forced to watch exe-cutions, carry bodies, and clean up blood because police feared contracting AIDS. To avenge the prisoners' deaths, the Primeiro Comando da Capital gang was formed, and since then the PCC— often compared to South Africa's Numbers gang—has flowered into a mammoth entity that all but runs prison life throughout the country. Since its formation the gang has been behind hundreds of deaths and dozens of prison uprisings. One example that can stand in for numerous similar incidents took place in 2014, here at the state prison in Catanduvas, when a thirty-hour rebellion involved dozens of masked prisoners on the prison roof, unfurling PCC banners, tying the hands of other prisoners behind their backs, beating them, and dangling them over the roof's edge.

The Catanduvas supermax, opened in 2006, was the government's answer to gang violence. In a booklet distributed to the town's population, the Department of Corrections explained that this first-ever Brazilian federal prison would house those deemed highly dangerous in an effort to reduce gang activity. About 25 percent of its population would be PCC leaders from across the country, removed from the state system and temporarily deposited in this supermax, home to 208 solitary-confinement cells. The structure cost some $18 million to build, thus representing an unprecedented financial investment in incarceration, and four more identical supermaxes soon followed. The annual cost per prisoner in this supermax is a whopping $120,000 a year, compared to what can average $36 per prisoner in Brazil's impoverished state system, where prisoners often must feed and clothe themselves.

Back at the prison after lunch, Mara guides us through laborious security. There are two sets of sensitive metal detectors, electronic thumbprints, X-ray belts, wands, and thorough pat-downs. Surveillance cameras broadcast all angles of our search and this prison direct to Brasília, the country's capital.

An agent in a navy-blue uniform, one of dozens circulating about the place, has been assigned to escort Mara, André, and me. He carries hulking keys that clink and clatter. Apparently the gates were initially electronic, but after a virus locked everyone in, the old lock-and-key system was instated. We pass a barbed-wire

courtyard carpeted by gravel, where men and women in green uniforms wield buckets and sling garbage bags over their shoulders.
I take them for prisoners but in fact they're cleaning staff. We're
enveloped by the stinging smell of disinfectant.

It's dead quiet.

Where are the prisoners?

"Your school teaches law, yes? I have a law degree," our guide
declares proudly. Agents in the federal system, which boasts higher
salaries and better benefits than state prison jobs, generally have
university degrees and are tasked not only with security but with
intelligence gathering, mostly about gang activity. There are two
agents for every man imprisoned here, as opposed to an appalling
350 prisoners for every one agent in the state system.

"Wear this," Mara says, handing me a cover-up that resembles
a white lab coat. She dons one, too. It feels bizarre, as if we're sci-
entists or clinicians. But it's also a fitting uniform for so neutered
a setting.

Down the hallway, through a door flanked by clear garbage bags
filled with stale-looking bread, we enter a ward that evokes a meat
locker. Perhaps it's a morgue?

No, this narrow cell block is the prison-within-a-prison—
solitary-within-solitary. The Regime Disciplinar Diferenciado,
or RDD, is an extreme isolation regime used for exceptional disciplinary measures. The men in this unit, which many Brazilians
have decried as violating the constitution's ban on torture and
inhumane treatment, are denied any contact whatsoever with
other prisoners. Everyone at Catanduvas spends his first twenty
days here.

Our agent swings open the metal door to an empty cell, which
looks like a life-size dollhouse—or the nightmare version of one.

It's immaculate, about as big as a parking space, with a square desk, circular seat, and rectangular bed: blocks of conjoined concrete shapes under long fluorescent bulbs. Soft sunlight sneaks in through the slats of cathedral windows high above, dancing on yellow walls and creating neat orange shadows: four squares of sky. The sliver of a "sunbed," which substitutes for a yard and provides a gasp of outdoors, is the size of a shower and has a tiny observation window, so guards can keep watch. Lines marking days counted have been etched into the cell's metal door, the lone sign that human life was once here.

Human beings live behind two of the closed doors on this block, though I can't see or hear them. I know they're here only because their names are listed on paperwork affixed to the doors, along with their dates of admission. Both have been here, in extreme solitary, for two weeks now.

"You're getting a good report, yes?" the agent says, smiling at my notebook. "You have many supermaxes in America. Many trips there to make this one and now you are come to see ours. Funny."

America invented solitary and the supermax. Beginning in 1787, the Quakers experimented with solitary cells at the Walnut Street Jail in Philadelphia and then in 1829 Eastern State Penitentiary, opened as an all-solitary facility, modeled after monasteries, where prisoners covered their heads with monklike hoods and Bibles were their only possessions. By the late nineteenth century, New York's Auburn Prison model, involving daily hard labor and lockstep cohorts, had begun to take precedence. But solitary was resurrected during the 1930s in Alcatraz's "D Block" and other storied "big houses" like San Quentin, Folsom, and Attica—colossal institutions designed for thousands and specializing in monotonous routines and extreme prisoner isolation.

Solitary made a full-on comeback in 1983, when a prison in Marion, Illinois, became America's first to adopt a twenty-three-hour-a-day cell isolation policy. As the US prison population soared and tough-on-crime rhetoric intensified, other states followed suit. In 1989 California, where today the average term in solitary is 6.8 years, built Pelican Bay, considered the first supermax and characterized by extreme solitary, a total lack of activities or communal spaces, and a powerful administration not subject to outside review or grievance systems. In 1994 Colorado erected the so-called Alcatraz of the Rockies, ADX Florence, where the longest isolated federal prisoner has spent thirty-two years under a "no human contact" order. By 1999 there were fifty-seven supermaxes in thirty-four states; at Pelican Bay, 227 prisoners have been in solitary for over a decade.

Latin America, meanwhile, constructed its modern prisons between 1830 and 1940 and modeled several on Eastern State and a few on Auburn. Now, more than a century later, official visits to America and other countries boasting US-style supermaxes—in Australia, Canada, Mexico, Colombia, Ireland, Denmark, South Africa, and Russia—have brought us to Catanduvas.

En route to Cellblock Charlie, as the agent calls it, I finally hear a sound of life: muffled calls from the double-tiered wards, echoing through labyrinthine hallways.

Prisoners exist in the heart of this maze—and that term is apt, since its vestibules and courtyards have been designed to disorient. "Though he live to be in the same cell ten weary years," Alexis de Tocqueville once wrote of the American prisoner in solitary, "he has no means of knowing, down to the very last hour, in what part of the building it is situated."

I am steered to a cell where a hinged slat on the dense metal door creaks open. I peer through.

Eyes greet me. They belong to Carlos.

He stands at attention in his pristine, pint-sized cell, as if in a lineup.

"*Bon dia!*" André says.

Those eyes. Windows to a grief-stricken soul.

It's the most bizarre, unsettling conversation—interview?—I've ever conducted. I speak through a hole in a safelike door, André whispering hasty translation for me, and I'm surrounded by eaves-dropping ears, interred behind neighboring iron doors.

Carlos, forty-one, is from a notorious Rio favela. These are essentially self-contained slums erected on vacant land by a growing class of urban poor during the 1980s, often compared to the garrison communities of Kingston, Jamaica, or the townships of South Africa. They lack basic social services and are lorded over by gangs. Carlos has spent sixteen years in prison on homicide, gun possession, forg-ery, and hijacking charges, and has lived in Catanduvas for two years and eight months, after being transferred from the state system.

"But Mara," I ask, spinning around, "isn't there a 360-day limit to a prisoner's stay in solitary here, after which he's meant to be transferred back to the state?" I could've sworn the director told me as much.

"Most cases, yes," she says. "But not always. It depends. This rule has changed."

Carlos straightens out a wrinkle in his sky-blue T-shirt, which has "Interno Sistema Penetenciaro Federal" printed across it. He explains that he has a ninety-eight-year sentence, but no one actu-ally serves more than thirty years in Brazil.

"Good that our country is not like the USA," he quips.

Carlos unfastens three photos from his wall and proudly displays his five children, aged five to twenty-three, and a seven-year-old grandson. Like most of the men at Catanduvas he's had no in-person visits since his arrival. His family cannot afford to fly here—they can barely afford the bus fare from the favela to the virtual prison visit center in Rio, where families, using a Skype-like system, log on to see their incarcerated loved ones. Once, after Carlos painted the entire prison, the director paid his family's transportation fees to the virtual visit center—it cost about twenty dollars—but they've made just three more trips there since.

"How can I rehabilitate without family?" he asks.

"I dream, nightmares. Of being abandoned by my family, by my children. I wake up in panic with this kind of dream, anxious with fear. I want the chance to give them an example of how I made a mistake, yes, but I learned from my own mistakes, from the mistakes of others. I learned human beings deserve a second chance, an opportunity to show themselves so everybody will see that person has changed." Carlos pauses and swallows hard.

"Twenty-two hours inside this cell. It is just hell. My days are hell, to tell you the truth. I am suffocating. I am dead. There is nothing else to say. Buried but alive, still."

There is more to say, of course. But we talk Dostoyevsky instead. Carlos participates in Rehabilitation Through Reading, which Mara had explained to me. It was started in 2009 by a controversial federal judge who essentially told prison officials that, since there was no money for programs, let the prisoners read books! Like the supermax, it has American precedents such as Changing Lives Through Literature, a Massachusetts-based "bibliotherapy" program offering alternative probation options via literature classes. Good stories, the program's Web site explains, provoke us to feel compassion for fictional characters, each other, and ourselves. By stepping into another's shoes, it goes on, people in prison can process their emotional struggles without confessing.

Lifting a well-worn copy of *Crime e Castigo, Crime and Punishment*, from his shelf, Carlos delivers his analysis.

"Crime brings consequences to family. Think before you act. This is the novel's essence. The main character, too—he confesses. Guilt eats him alive. He murdered and stole and he cannot go on. He is tortured in his mind. Impossible to do wrong and not feel guilt."

"Do you feel guilt, Carlos?" I ask.

"Every day of my life. I am a living error—a walking mistake. Do you imagine how this feels? To be a living error? And only an error? But even in hell, I am hopeful. I am almost forty-two now, but my life is not ended. I want to go to university. Study theology and psychology. I am writing a book, too; it is titled *The Hikers of the Deep Fall*. The hikers are you and me who look inside and see that as human beings, our job is to grab the rope and climb. Upward. Never seeing the long fall."

Two men in white wheel a metal cart down the hallway, passing small plates of pills through the slats in each cell. Eighty percent of the men locked up here are on medication.

"I only took them when I first came here, yes…," Carlos says. "To sleep, pills. And for anxiety. Depression. To be alone all of these hours—impossible. I am afraid."

The agent seals the slat on Carlos's door and, without a good-bye, he vanishes. Time is up.

Through muted echoes, we follow another metal cart carrying magazines to the library. It looks more like a closet, encumbered by books. They're strewn about, especially the ones on the Rehabilitation Through Reading approved list, titles by José Saramago, Clarice Lispector, the Dalai Lama, J. D. Salinger. There's a Bible, a dictionary, a book of evangelical songs, and stack after stack of celebrity magazines.

"Lots of Sidney Sheldon," Mara says with disdain. At Otisville, too, the tiny library has a sliver of a history section, a few Latin American studies titles—and an outsized "fantasy" section.

"Prisoners are begging for more books, begging the government. Instead"—she rifles through a mound of glossy pages—"silly magazines."

Outside the gates, the air is suddenly fresh and the landscape a blanket of emerald. André and I drop Mara at her condo in Cascavel, a gated complex that is, like the prison she works in, a striking simulacrum of US housing.

"Thanks, America, for exporting this housing style to us, too," André quips.

Our hotel, meanwhile, seems like Miami circa 1952. The whole town might well exist in another time and place. It feels like 1980s America, from the big-hair styles on the women strolling about, snacking on *pão de queijo*, to the hard-rock soundtrack emanating from Irish pubs on the road. André and I sit at one of them, eating fried fish with *farofa*, a dish made with manioc flour, and unraveling our day. Wringing his hands, he bemoans his country's devotion to incarceration. The FIFA World Cup is around the corner and folks are joking, he tells me, that those pricey new stadiums will, once the crowds go home, become prisons. He grabs his temples.

"Even my family, my brother and father—they all say lock up the criminals and throw away the key. But how is this an answer?"

———

The next morning when we arrive, spots of fluorescent color in the form of women visitors animate the drab barbed wire. Dress-code rules ban almost every hue except yellow and pink, because Big Brother in Brasília must easily differentiate, on camera, between prisoners, staff, and visitors. The result is bizarrely cinematic. All of these women have come from worlds away, some have had their travel paid for by the PCC because their husbands are prominent gang members. Many have slept outside the gates in hopes of being first in line and all are about to endure marathons of waiting, security procedures, and body-cavity checks, only to land a few hours with loved ones. But here they are swathed in the most cheery, exuberant tints imaginable.

As we pass them and go through security, we are handed shots of *cafezinho*. Discarded plastic cups leave a trail through the prison; with agents working overnight shifts, this strong, black, sweet stuff is the oil that keeps the machine running.

Today is cold and rainy. Snaking through dark, concrete hallways, the chill seeps into my bones.

As we turn a corner, narrow rays of light illuminate a massive field behind bars, with a barbed-wire skylight. Cohorts of thirteen prisoners are granted two hours a day in this sun bed, which I'd spied earlier, and during this time they are forbidden to speak to more than three men at any given time.

The soccer ball slams against the wall. Bodies tear through the space with ferocious alacrity, leaping and kicking and calling to each other. Bodies gasp for air; bare-chested, barefoot bodies smile, laugh, leap, live.

Then: *Pare!*

Silence.

The soccer ball rolls to a slow halt. Prisoners freeze, line up against the wall and bow their heads. Smiles dissolve.

"*Número um!*" calls the agent.

The richly choreographed perp walk begins. One by one, head hanging down, march to the agent. About-face, kneel, present hands to be cuffed through the bars. Spin around and approach the next agent. About face again, as the door opens and slams shut, and the body is once more interred in a cell for twenty-two hours.

"*Número dois!*" calls the agent.

The ritual repeats until all that remains in the sun bed is a half-deflated soccer ball. Agents walk the perimeter with plastic gloves, checking for objects left behind.

Then, minutes later, the door opens and thirteen men march silently, single file with head bowed. They stand facing the wall and are uncuffed, one by one.

"*Liberal!*" calls the agent. *You are free!*

Instantly there are hugs and embraces, laughter and smiles, heads held high. They talk with each other, with the guards. Haircuts are given, with an electric razor plugged in near the bars. Puffs of hair sail to the ground; the soccer ball soars skyward. The whole thing is a death-and-resurrection rite of the most profound order.

I spy Carlos, looking even more boyish now that more than just his eyes are visible. Interno says his T-shirt, but I misread it as Inferno.

"Come, let me show you their cells," our agent says.

"Are you sure that's OK?" I ask, hesitating to trespass on private spaces.

"Of course. This prison is *ours*, not theirs," the agent insists proudly, guiding us inside *Cela Ola* on Cellblock Charlie.

A worn copy of *Dear John* by Nicholas Sparks rests on the urine-yellow concrete shelf, near a shower that automatically sprays water at the same hour every day. Four faded photographs of children are tacked above the bed. On the desk is a pen removed from its plastic casing, beside stenciled drawings of dalmatians, praying hands, and birds in cages.

Layers of gentle pink light stream through lofty cathedral windows. The muffled echoes of metal doors creaking open and the muted voices crying to each other from cellblocks faraway reach us like calls to prayer. For the first time I viscerally grasp the word "penitentiary," from "penitence." This place has the feel of an eerie, haunted monastery. It's as if I'm in a chilling cross between a church and a concentration camp.

Cells have no mirrors, the agent explains. In fact, one news crew filming here left a camera outside the slat of a cell overnight, and returned to find the man who lives in the cell staring at the camera lens, enchanted by his own reflection.

"Neat and clean and efficient, this cell," says the agent, as if he had built it himself. "Nothing like the state prison. Clean, safe."

Indeed Catanduvas is worlds away from Brazil's state prisons, which is clearly why I'm here. The government is eager to show off its pristine, pricey investment. In 2014—the year a video surfaced showing Brazilian prisoners beheading three fellow prisoners—a UN human-rights body expressed concern over the "dire state" of Brazil's savagely overcrowded, violent prisons, where more than 80 percent of incarcerated people cannot afford a lawyer. Many states do not provide separate facilities for women, and male officers in women's prisons are known to extort sexual favors; adolescents can be jailed with adults in units without bathrooms. In 2009, 16,466 people were found to be imprisoned irregularly; many had spent far longer in pretrial detention than they would have served as sentenced prisoners—in one case, a man spent eleven years on remand. In the state of Espírito Santo, amid accusations of torture and abuse between 2009 and 2011, the government barred entry to prison cells even to the officially mandated body monitoring the system.

It's mealtime. Through another hallway, more metal carts are steered by agents wearing wraparound shades. The ritual begins. One by one, drinks are poured into plastic cups, metal trays are inserted through door slats into eager hands, then the slats are slammed shut.

Visiting women in pink pass us on their way out, their cheeks puffy and damp. I make out the cries of a baby.

"So sad," Mara says, rubbing her eyes. "He is visiting family. Saying 'Daddy!'"

————

We spend the remainder of my time at Catanduvas in its two havens. Qualifying prisoners can escape their cells for a few hours several days a week, if they attend class or work jobs. Job options are limited and unusual. The men can make baskets from discarded magazines or craft children's toys from paper and Popsicle sticks; both are sold at local craft fairs. I'm presented with one of each product, inside a small room where a dozen men sit at collective tables behind bars. An origami duck, Mara says. And here are Moses, Jesus, and John the Baptist, crafted from matchsticks and googly eyes.

"Talk to them," Mara urges, introducing the *professora* to the prisoners. Again swallowing the obnoxious, disquieting feeling of being a visitor in a human zoo, I turn to the men behind bars.

Carlos Augustus, whose black-rimmed glasses hide a weary face, tells me he'd like to go to college one day and become a biologist. He explains that according to Brazil's Penal Execution Law, every five days a prisoner works, one day is deducted from his sentence, but only about one-quarter of prisoners are given employment.

"Working makes me calm," he tells me. "Anything not to be in a cell. I will do *anything* to escape being so alone. All those hours. I believe in love—in love as redemption. There is no love here."

Next to him is a sad-looking duo who Mara explains are father and son. I look hard at the father but what I see, transposed onto his face, is Anthony in South Africa, his daughter in another wing of Pollsmoor, his son buying drugs from the same dealer. And I see, too, a student back in New York, whose homecoming was dampened by the reality that though he was finally free, his eighteen-year-old son remained behind bars. The painfulness of this sight of a father and son, side by side in a supermax, makes my eyes well up. With all the absent fathers running like a nightmarish narrative thread through global stories of prison and poverty, the one present father in a prisoner's life is right beside him. The depth of failure one must feel, not only to be in prison but to look beside you and see your son here, too, this is hard to fathom.

I hold back my tears to chat with the men about their lives and what they've been reading. Carlos Augustus delivers a moving sermon about *Anna Karenina* and the power of true love, but soon the conversation turns on its head and they begin to interview me. What is the recidivism rate in America? Is there a difference between this prison and the one you work in? Should America adopt our Rehabilitation Through Reading program? Is it true that in America you still have the death penalty? *Really, the death penalty?* And life sentences?

Is it true that America is responsible for this prison? For the supermax?

For the hours we rot in our cells?

Growing light-headed, I exit the work area and numbly follow Mara. What about the twenty-one-year-old prisoner whose charge is bank robbery? I ask her. Can he really represent the "worst of the worst"?

"That is nothing," she says. "Last month we had a nineteen-year-old. I wondered—who is this little boy, so skinny? It turns out he was sent here because he spit in the prosecutor's face."

In America, banishment to the Solitary Housing Unit (SHU) can also happen for random reasons. In New York, for instance, 84 percent of SHU sentences are for such nonviolent conduct as failure to get out of the shower quickly, not obeying an order promptly, refusing to return a food tray, possessing excess postage stamps or "reckless eyeballing"—looking at an officer the wrong way. In 2013, a South Carolina man received a penalty of 37.5 years in solitary for posting on Facebook.

We pass the sun bed again, where the soccer ball thumps to a halt and prisoners rush to the bars, lobbing vehement questions at me. They wear contorted smiles.

Do you have the Internet in your American prison?

Could you survive twenty-two hours in a cell?

Tell Barack Obama we say hello!

The feverish energy is so overwhelming, it assaults me with an unnerving blend of sorrow and terror. Trembling, I break out in chills. I have never before witnessed humanity so flagrantly on the brink of going completely mad.

"These men have no work, no school, no program—just twenty-two hours in the cell," Mara explains. "Some for years now. So sad. So sad."

There are no gang murders at Catanduvas, as there are in Brazil's state prisons, and there is the opposite of overcrowding—nearly half the cells here are empty. Clearly, they suffer another kind of torture, a gradual psychological genocide. "A considerable number of the prisoners fell, after even a short confinement, into a semi-fatuous condition, from which it was next to impossible to arouse them, and others became violently insane; others still, committed suicide; while those who stood the ordeal better were not generally reformed, and in most cases did not recover sufficient mental activity to be of any subsequent service to the community," the US Supreme Court declared in 1890 after surveying the use of long-term solitary.

Over a century later Boston psychiatrist Stuart Grassian interviewed prisoners in solitary and found that a third developed acute psychosis and hallucinations, which he identified as symptoms of SHU Syndrome: social withdrawal, panic attacks, irrational rage, loss of impulse control, paranoia, severe and chronic depression, difficulties with concentration and memory, perceptual distortions. Self-mutilation is a common practice; those in solitary are known to bite into their own veins and cut off fingers and testicles. Suicide rates are five times higher in solitary; in California up to 70 percent of suicides take place there and teens are nineteen times more likely to commit suicide there. A 2009 *New Yorker* article by Atul Gawande, on the "hellhole" that is solitary, paints a visceral picture of the experience: "He talked to himself. He paced back and forth compulsively, shuffling along the same six-foot path for hours on end. Soon, he was having panic attacks, screaming for help. He hallucinated that the colors on the walls were changing. He became enraged by routine noises—the sound of doors opening as the guards made their hourly checks, the sounds of inmates in nearby cells. After a year or so, he was hearing voices on the television talking directly to him. He put the television under his bed, and rarely took it out again." In 1995 a federal judge found that conditions at Pelican Bay in California "may well hover on the edge of what is humanly tolerable."

Solitary units like Catanduvas represent a brutal amputation— cut off a problem in order to deter, punish, and keep others safe. But one cannot forget that this "problem" is also a *human being*, who may eventually return to the prison population and the world. How can it benefit him, or us, to return him there utterly mad?

And ultimately, can inducing insanity ever be morally justifiable?

Yet even if we push that concern aside, studies suggest that solitary confinement is not even effective. A 2006 study found that those who spent three months or more in solitary were more likely to reoffend and to commit a violent crime, while a 2003 study on supermaxes in Arizona, Illinois, and Minnesota found levels of prisoner violence unchanged. This is why the United Kingdom, for instance, has begun to turn away from the expensive, ineffective, inhumane practice; in the whole of England today, there are fewer people in solitary than there are in all the prisons of Maine. Instead, the British often house their most volatile in Close Supervision Centres, which are small, stable units of fewer than ten people. There they receive mental health treatment and education and earn rights for exercise, phone calls, contact visits, and cooking facilities. The idea is to give these men more control, not less, which minimizes the scenarios of humiliation and confrontation that, experts agree, form the root of prison violence.

———

Inside a small classroom manned by guards, ten students in blue sweats and flip-flops sit at their desks. They're separated from the teacher's bulky desk by bars. I cannot imagine teaching, literally, before bars; even in maximum security US prisons, I've seen nothing like this. Mara points to a red line on the teacher's side of the concrete floor, just before the bars.

"One time a prisoner was reading a dictionary, looking for a word," she tells me, "and he said he could not find the word, so the teacher approached the bars to show him in the book. And suddenly the guards charged in and drew their guns and shouted, 'Step back! Are you disrespecting teacher?' The prisoner's hands were trembling and he grew red in the face, humiliated. So, Baz, do not cross the red line."

Today's class, mixed-level, from fifth grade to high school, is led by a kindly teacher with frizzy blond hair and a colorful cartoon sewn onto the pocket of her white lab coat. She steps aside after she introduces me, and I say a few words about the Prison-to-College Pipeline and the value of education.

Then it's as if the horses are at the gate: ready, set—erupt!

"If you don't educate us we will be back on the street!" declares a dark-skinned man in the front row.

"I am fifty-one now. It is too late for me—but not for him." He points to a light-skinned young man beside him.

"I had no chance for education in my life. There was no school in my favela. I had nothing. Not even a birth certificate."

I'm meant to be interviewing the men about Rehabilitation Through Reading. After two days, though, it's clear that although the program means well—it's a potential sanity lifeline—it also, considering the dire circumstances here, borders on laughable. What is literature in the face of extreme solitary and proliferating supermaxes? What are a few days in the context of quarter-century sentences?

Instead, for hours this morning and then in the afternoon—when the teacher is absent and I am thrust before the class and told, "Teach!"—I let life narratives crash and burn all around me.

Fabio, forty: mother had him at age eleven, when she was raped; ran away from home at six because his alcoholic father was beating him to a pulp; landed in dozens of orphanages and became involved in crime at age seven; entered prison at eighteen and saw his mother only one other time, at twenty-six, behind bars.

Roberto, thirty-eight: born to a family of fourteen brothers; was recruited by the gangs and sold drugs so he could support his family; passed in and out of state prison, where he honed his criminal skills and grew addicted to meth; during a botched robbery of a small store, accidentally shot and killed a federal policeman. Has been in solitary here for five years.

Heads hang low and the room feels like a ticking time bomb.

Mi família, mi família. The words resound like a grief-stricken chorus. To be in solitary, this is torture. But to be thousands of miles away from wives, children, mothers—this, the men affirm, is the absolute abyss.

The prisoners talk on but André, exhausted and unable to keep up, stops translating. I continue nodding, anyway; I know what they're saying. Because I've heard it in America, in Jamaica, and especially back in Pollsmoor. The ghetto is the garrison is the township—and the favela. There are two elephants in the room, and the men are pointing right at them.

First, race.

A legacy of racial inequity produced these men, their favelas, and this prison. More than ten times as many African slaves were brought to Brazil than to the United States, and slavery continued well into the nineteenth century—Brazil was the last country in the Americas to abolish slavery, in 1888. After that, policing and punitive methods were used to secure a labor force for coffee and sugar production. Tens of thousands of poor blacks were arrested for misdemeanors—vagrancy, disorder, drunkenness, practicing of capoeira (a martial art that draws on African dance and music, and was illegal until the 1930s)—and put to work or sentenced to stints in the army. Brazil adopted a new federal constitution in 1988, but almost nothing was done to integrate the descendants of slaves into the economy or public life. Segregation here is a reality across all walks of life, from education and the labor market to land distribution, housing, and access to public services. As of 2009, for instance, just 17 percent of Brazil's black and mixed-race population was engaged in educational activity. Eighty percent have less than eight years of schooling, nearly two out of three nonwhite students fail to complete upper secondary school, and a paltry 6.6 percent attend university. More than 70 percent of Brazilians living below the poverty line are black or mixed-race, earning a wage less than half that of whites, and the life expectancy of nonwhite Brazilians is six years below whites'. Ninety-seven percent of executives and 83 percent of managers are white. If white and nonwhite Brazil were separate nations, the former would rank 44th in the UN World Human Development Index and the latter, 105th.

Is it any wonder that the homicide rates of nonwhite Brazilians are almost double those of whites—in some regions, more than three times higher? Or that nonwhite Brazilians, representing two-thirds of prisoners but half the country's population, are twice as likely as whites to be in jail? For centuries, the system was built to devastate them.

"Will you give up crime?" Mara is asking a bald prisoner with dense folds under his eyes.

"How can I give it up when I never had the chance to work?" he asks, looking as if he's going to burst out of his desk. "If I go to the street, who's going to get me work, who's going to help me?"

He turns to me with a glare. "How is it in America? Does the state help? Does the state give people jobs who have no opportunity? Take my name down. Remember it. Look me up and see if one day I finally get the job I deserve."

Minding the red line, I pass my notebook through the bars. *Pedro Henrique Procopio*, he writes, in elegant script. "Remember me," he says, returning it.

The other elephant in the room is class. Crime is driven by poverty and inequality, a fact realized in the United States, where income inequality is the highest it's been since 1928, and the richest fifth of families hold 88.9 percent of the country's wealth. But Brazil represents even more dramatic extremes of both poverty and inequality—income inequality exists at about 25 percent higher rates than it does in the States. The roots of this lie between 1870 and 1980, when Brazil's economy grew at a faster rate than nearly any other major country. During the 1950s it was on a path to overtake the United States, and some 20 million people migrated to the country's cities, one of the biggest such movements in history. But a sudden collapse in growth impoverished millions; between 1980 and 1990 the minimum wage decreased by 46 percent and per capita income dropped 7.6 percent. The proportion of income appropriated by the richest fifth of the population grew to 65 percent, while that of the poorest half dropped to 12 percent. Three percent of the country's GDP is spent on health and less than 5 percent on education, as compared to 12 percent on pensions— nearly two-thirds of which are enjoyed by the richest fifth of Brazil.

Those working in the informal economy, meanwhile, roughly 40 percent of the workforce, get no state benefits. There's a severe housing crisis, too. One in three families lives in inadequate housing, and the country has an estimated shortage of 5.8 million units.

Yet despite astounding poverty and widespread lack of social services, the Brazilian government dug deep into its pockets to spend hundreds of millions building the prison I'm standing in.

Why? I ask the students, my teachers.

They sum it up using an old Brazilian expression: "To make a show for an Englishman."

The government needs gangs, the prisoners tell me; they coordinate ghetto life and prison life. This is true of the Numbers gang in Pollsmoor, too. Yet politicians here also make regular public shows of eradicating these same gangs, to get reelected. Catanduvas and its four brother institutions represent very grand, very expensive *public shows*. Never mind that its use of solitary is clearly a form of torture. Never mind that it's not only not solving problems of crime, violence, and inequality, or even the "problem" of gangs, because a stint in federal can stigmatize prisoners as dangerous and ultimately promote gang leaders, who return to their states with infamous reputations. And never mind that this strategy failed in the United States, as explained by David Skarbek in his 2014 book *The Social Order of the Underworld*, which delves into California prison gangs and argues that they, like the PCC gang here, "end up providing governance in a brutal but effective way." California first tried to contain gangs by breaking them up and scattering their members to distant prisons so as to dilute their influence, but that ultimately allowed gangs to spread their influence and reach across states and into the federal system.

Never mind all of these realities. The whole of Catanduvas is a grand exercise in political theater, and human lives are its principal actors.

"The media say I am a monster," says Fabio. "I'm not a monster. The people who created this evil place are monsters."

The bars grow blurry and my headache intensifies. I try to serve up words of inspiration. Hear about one of my best friends, Kirk, I say, who earned a college degree behind bars in America and then a doctorate in social work from an Ivy League university. And my other students, who are guaranteed a slot in university upon release from prison. The prisoners' eyes flicker.

"Let us share something with your students," they say. "From one prisoner to another, across the world."

What they share overflows with hope, emerging full force from the inferno.

Education frees us. The only bars are in my head and I have removed them through learning. Capitalism will destroy you, because life is not what you have but what you are. Learn. Don't give up.

"You are blessed from Brazil," Carlos Augustus calls to me as I gather my things and prepare to go. "Thank you for remembering us."

Thank you for remembering us. What a peculiar thing to say while still alive. Then again, are they? Solitary, wrote Dostoyevsky, "drains the man's vital sap, enervates his soul, cows and enfeebles it, and then holds up the morally withered mummy, half imbecile, as a model of penitence and reformation." For these men, being seen and being captured by my pen represents a momentary disinterring: being unforgotten.

In Mara's office, where we return at the end of the day, the staff is gathered around a computer screen, smiling. They turn the screen to me and reveal a phrase on Google Translate: "The men were moved." Moved? Where? To another prison?

"No, no," explains Mara. "The prisoners were moved by your presence. They said they were inspired by the stories of your students in prison. They were *moved*."

I'm moved, too, though it's small comfort.

André and I ride to the airport in total silence. André, because he's inflamed with anger at his country's grotesque investment. He has been here before and volunteers in the state system; his fiancée, too, is a public defender who works in women's prisons. But knowing the system well cannot temper the horror of witnessing it at its worst. I am silent because between sobs I feel the emotional equivalent of the color sucked out of my face.

Back in America, weeks later, I'd ask my students at Otisville to write back to the Brazilian ones I'd told them about. They do, beautifully.

"I hope you are in good health and learning from whatever it is that you've done," writes Richard. "The reason I call you my brother in arms is because even though we may be worlds apart, you are still a man, and spiritually you are my brother. I believe that education is the key to success. Just to give you a little about myself, I am a simple, loving person who likes to learn."

Robert waxes reflective:

We are both physically incarcerated. However, despite the governments' best attempts to keep us stagnated, they can never incarcerate us mentally; that is only something we can do to ourselves. I'm twenty-three years old today and I have been in prison since I was sixteen years old. I did not realize how important education was for me when I first came to prison, and as a result, I found myself in a lot of unnecessary trouble. Once I picked up a book, I was honestly amazed at how "free" reading made me feel. Even when I was on lockdown for twenty-three hours a day, I lost track of where I was at times because I was so caught up in my readings. I felt it was important to share that little detail because I heard you are in school and I want this letter to be a motivational tool to keep you going.

Moving words, hopeful words, gorgeous words—they are all these. But still it's the first time I return from a prison odyssey without even a shred of hope.

For one, the candle in the dark here, the literature program, is so infinitesimal as to be irrelevant—it even feels like part of the grand public relations charade that is Catanduvas as a whole. And second, even as a number of American states have recently begun to rethink their use of solitary—in 2014 ten states adopted measures aimed at curtailing solitary, abolishing it for juveniles or the mentally ill, improving its conditions, or reintegrating isolated prisoners into the general population—Catanduvas tells a very different story. America's baby has once again taken on new life beyond its shores. Supermaxes and solitary are not only a global reality, they're a *growing* global reality: an American nightmare from which the world has chosen not to wake.

6.
Private Prisons | *Australia*

"Have you ever been convicted of a crime?" scrolls across the screen
of a snazzy electronic immigration kiosk at Sydney Airport, welcoming me to Australia. I think it must be the third time Australia
has asked me this in the last two days. I seem to remember it coming
up twice on the electronic visa form I completed before flying.

Such a line of inquiry in the land of Oz feels both fitting and
ironic. After all, the country was born as a penal colony, which
means two centuries ago almost everyone arriving here had a
criminal history. During the pre-prison era, when banishment
was Europe's preferred punishment system, colonizing countries
shipped more than a quarter million people dubbed "convicts" to
far-flung places like Singapore, French Guiana, Gibraltar, Ber-
muda, and Mauritius. Australia was added to the list after the
American Revolution, when Britain could no longer dump its
human refuse on US soil. Between 1788 and 1868, 166,000 men,
women, and children were shipped from Britain to Australia, and
by 1830 they and their children constituted 90 percent of the new

colony's population. It was about more than just punishment, because after the abolition of the slave trade in 1833, these colonial prisoners became Europe's labor force, building infrastructures and economies. And well after the transportation of prisoners ceased, their economic value persisted. Following the US Civil War, for instance, local convict labor reconstructed the country, from railroads to plantations, with Alabama leasing its prisoners to the federal government until as late as 1928.

These are the roots of the prison industrial complex, a tangle of legal, business, and government interests that has existed for centuries.

I've journeyed to Oz during my winter break to grapple with this muddle: the modern-day conflation of capitalism and "convict" in the form of the $22.7 billion private prison industry. It dates back to 1985, when the first private prison opened in Marion County, Kentucky. The model and its profits soon proliferated, to the point that revenue for America's biggest private prison company, Corrections Corporation of America (CCA), recently capped $1.7 billion. Private prisons have cropped up in a dozen countries, from Britain and France to New Zealand, the Caribbean, and South Africa.

They've also taken hold in Australia, a country so physically far from America, yet when it comes to criminal justice policy, very close. Since the 1970s Australia has copycatted our tough-on-crime rhetoric and punitive policies. Despite its already low homicide and robbery rates—in 2011 these rates were one and four in 100,000, respectively, having decreased in the past two decades—its prison population is growing at 9 percent a year. The country holds the world's largest proportion of prisoners in private facilities—about 19 percent of its 33,000 prisoners. It has a wholly private immigrant detention system, too, run by Serco, a British company that also operates two private prisons in Western Australia and has eight thousand people in its care.

"Serco? Is that an operating system? Like, the Matrix?" So I'd joked to Brian, the criminologist I'd befriended in Thailand, back when he first told me about the prisons he works in via Curtin University in Perth. Then I launched into a tirade against the private prison industry.

I was preaching to the choir. Because to anyone even a tad progressive, private prisons are anathema. Driven by bottom lines, they go to dramatic lengths to maintain control of taxpayer dollars and human lives. Because their business model depends on keeping beds filled, they spend millions on lobbying and campaign contributions to ensure that policies remain punitive. CCA, for instance, spent $18 million on US federal lobbying between 1999 and 2009. It's also heavily linked to the American Legislative Exchange Council, which promotes templates for tougher immigration and sentencing laws and has made offers to forty-eight states to purchase state-owned prisons and jails in exchange for mandatory 90 percent occupancy rates.

"I know, I know," Brian had said. "Believe me, I was up in arms when this whole movement started here. I stood on the steps of city hall for days, protesting privatization. But then I realized the situation is more complicated than I'd imagined."

"Really?" I'd asked, still skeptical.

"Come see for yourself," Brian replied. Several months later, here I am.

———

"Looks like Phoenix," remarks the American sitting next to me on the plane, peering down at Perth as we approach.

Today is Saturday afternoon, 112 degrees of arid summer sunshine. Where is everyone? The capital of Western Australia feels like a ghost town. After checking into my hotel, I hop on a free city bus, pass a pristine riverside park, transfer to a pristine subway, and finally reach a pristine beach. Ah, here's everyone. The sand at Scarborough is jammed. Smiling blond women with deep tans dole out free lemonade; more blond people giddily jump waves so big, they seem to be giving clouds a high five.

Sitting in the midst of this clean, beautiful city, surrounded by surfers and beachgoers, it's hard to imagine prison even existing here.

Yet Australia's prison population has doubled in the past decade or so. And this state, Western Australia, boasts the country's highest number of prisoners per capita. Nearly half of them are in for nonviolent offenses. And as in America, Brazil, and South Africa, they're overwhelmingly poor minorities. Indigenous people make up around 2 percent of Australia's population, but they're 27.5 percent of its prison population. Western Australia has the country's highest indigenous imprisonment rate, with ratios of Aboriginal people jailed that are, depressingly, even more astronomical than those for African Americans in the United States. They're close to twenty times more likely to be jailed here—one in twenty-four is behind bars. An indigenous young person is fifty times more likely than any other Australian to be in sentenced detention.

"Welcome to Oz!" Brian says with a hug, picking me up at my hotel the next morning. It's a joyous reunion, even if it'll be spent mostly in prison settings. I'd bonded with Brian in Thailand, in part because we share an identical mission in life, and also because his zealous optimism intensely stirs me. It's an optimism I share, but encountering it in someone in whom it ought not to exist, someone who's been dealt extraordinarily bad cards in life, is especially inspiring. I try to keep such people close to me as reminders of just how deep and eternal hope can spring.

En route to Wandoo Reintegration Facility, a minimum security prison for males aged eighteen to twenty-four, Brian explains that the facility used to be a run-down juvenile remand center. He was part of the team behind its transformation into a facility for this vulnerable age group, legally old enough to be housed with adults, but also young enough to be victimized and dangerously impacted by them. Serco took over Wandoo's management in 2012.

"You should see how it looked before the conversion. Simply awful," Brian explains. "And smelled—unreal. Not for human beings. Rotten garbage."

What I smell, as soon as we arrive, is lunch. Sans security check we're ushered into the cafeteria, despite my jetlag-induced memory lapse.

"Forgot your ID? No worries, mate. Just hurry on in for some cut lunch," says the smiling woman at the front desk.

At once I imagine I've landed in a TV ad: that recurring late-night one for a rehab center in Malibu, all green hills and cool breezes—is it Passages? Promises? Nausea begins to creep in; I'm conditioned to feel sick at the smell of food behind bars, mainly by virtue of association with wrenching memories. But my queasiness abruptly pauses and reconsiders. This food actually smells delicious.

"Artisanal Pizza" reads the sign at the buffet. "Organic squash and goat cheese." We're in a glass gazebo, and I'm seated beside a woman wearing slacks and a dark-blue polo shirt branded with Serco in red letters, by the collar.

"Where are the prisoners?" I ask her.

"You mean residents?" She waves her hand—they're milling about freely. Since no one is wearing traditional uniforms, I can't tell who's staff and who isn't.

"Many are at work, though, and won't be back until later."

"I'm confused," I confess.

"So are many of the boys who get transferred here," she laughs. "They expect traditional punishment. They're used to the prison regime. Being passive, controlled. Here they essentially run the place." She's not a corrections officer; that term isn't used at Wandoo. She's a staff member. Her background isn't in criminal justice, either, but psychology, and Serco may soon finance her PhD.

"Cuppa?" she asks, pouring my tea. I sip quietly.

"Wendy!" The residents call to the sprightly Scottish superintendent—no, "contract director"—as she leads us from lunch to the conference room. Vivid Aboriginal art wallpapers the bright, airy building.

"The focus at Wandoo," Wendy explains, as lemon chiffon cake is served, "is on preparing residents for release. Providing them with life skills, education and training, and employment opportunities. The young men stay here for up to three years before release, and we give them intensive case management and a strong reintegration focus. They go to NA and AA meetings in the community— mostly we're talking about drug and property crimes—and we have regular art and music workshops.

"But they"—Wendy gestures toward three young white men sitting at the table with us—"can tell you better than I can. Right, boys?"

They nod, all serenity and smiles. Their uniforms resemble soccer jerseys, in South African Springbok colors.

"I keep busy, is what I do, mate," says James, nineteen. He has ginger-red hair and paint specks dot his green shirt. "I'm in the computer lab, the cardio-fitness suite, the library. Busy. When I'm here, that is. Mostly I work off-site, at the food bank. Until three-thirty every day. It's our reparations, to the community," he explains.

Wandoo, Wendy interjects, operates on restorative justice principles, which she calls "the relationship model."

"It's like a campus," explains Mac, showing off the EER Support Team printed on his yellow T-shirt. He's part of the prisoner cohort that coordinates volunteer work throughout the facility. "When there's conflict, we work it out, like a city council. We are responsible for running things. You get asked, not told, to do things here."

"I do think I tell, occasionally," one staff member laughs. "But we're all works in progress, eh?"

"I'm at the food bank, too," Mac goes on. All the young men here are scheduled to work in the community on a daily basis, then return to Wandoo after the workday. "And when I go home, in four months, I'll come back in to give talks and to visit here. I'm only just down the road. Do you have people do that, ma'am, in your prison?" I'd told them about the Prison-to-College Pipeline; they'd especially loved hearing about the learning exchanges, the interactions between incarcerated and outside students in a normal-classroom context.

"When the folks in the food bank, the customers, when they treat us normally, like mates—that's what's nice. To feel regular, normal, again," Mac had said. What the three prisoners don't grasp is my program's name, a play on America's "school-to-prison pipeline," or the way in which dysfunctional schools become training grounds for and direct feeders into the criminal justice system. *Metal detectors in schools?* All three prisoners repeat my words, with blank stares. *School-to-prison pipeline?*

"I go out all the time, to check the surf, mate. During breaks from work," says one of the prisoners. Indeed he looks like a surfer, tall and lean, with blond hair and green eyes, arms blanketed with tattoos.

On the way out of Wandoo, after goodbyes and good lucks, there's a momentary scare. A small crowd of residents and staff have gathered on a grassy knoll, pointing and waving.

Snake!

"Never mind that," says Wendy. "They'll catch it."

Clearly it's the most dangerous thing here.

For the first time I leave a prison holding back tears of joy. There is *humanity* at Wandoo.

But thoughts of my students back in New York rain on my emotional parade. It pains me that many of them might have spent their time in a prison like Wandoo, had such a thing existed in America. Instead, because New York is one of only two states sentencing even sixteen- and seventeen-year-olds to adult facilities, they landed in adult prisons, many of them for crimes that add up to little more than adolescent foolery or coming from deeply dysfunctional family settings. There they lose vital years, plus additional years spent reversing the psychological damage done behind bars at a hyper-vulnerable age.

"Wandoo shouldn't exist at all," Brian says as we get in his car. "These young men should be in community, full time. When I was on work-release in prison, I didn't need to come back inside; I'd never have violated. Neither would've my peers."

It's funny, just as I'm wishing Wandoo on my students, Brian is wishing it away. Progress is relative.

"The only reason these boys aren't in the community, with their families, is because we as a society are risk-averse," Brian goes on. "But we'll never have a risk-free society. There's liable to be a crime tonight—there's nothing we can do about it. Risk is built into life. A life ruled by fear is not living. Fear builds prisons."

He's right, of course. I let forth a rant about the local papers I've been poring over every morning with my coffee.

"There's basically four topics covered, all fears. Sharks, bushfires, drunken pub brawls, prisoner escapes. OK, I get that last one"—Serco has been garnering bad press of late for a series of escapes during prisoner transport. "But damn, Perth is the cleanest, safest, most chipper place I've ever been, so what's all this anxiety about?"

"Welcome to the Rupert Murdoch press," Brian grunts.

Ah, yes. I'd forgotten that the media mogul behind Fox News and the *New York Post*, renowned for peddling exclamation-point hype and passing hysteria off as news, launched his empire here. It's an empire I hold partly responsible for mass incarceration in my own country. Beginning in the 1980s, the era when President Reagan famously spoke of the criminal as "a human predator"— "nothing in nature is more cruel or more dangerous," he said— local news became crime-saturated, fear-mongering spectacles, even as crime declined. Between 1993 and 1996 the US murder rate dropped by 20 percent, yet the number of murders reported on ABC, NBC, and CBS rose by 721 percent. Such anxious public rhetoric about the wickedness of the criminal and the vulnerability of the victim shored up America's increasingly punitive policies.

By the time I reach my hotel, I'm fixated on fear, progress, and Wandoo. And I'm drowning in self-reproach.

The private prison wasn't evil.

It's supposed to be. I know the statistics. Here in Oz, all immigration detention centers are private, and Serco's revenues from such contracts add up to more than $1.8 billion. This, again, mirrors America, where Immigration and Customs Enforcement, an agency spending over $1.9 billion annually on custody operations, is creating a network of massive immigration detention centers managed largely by private companies. They're rapidly transforming these detainees into a labor force—a *slave* labor force. In 2013 at least sixty thousand immigrants worked in the federal government's nationwide detention centers, more than worked for any other single employer in the country. Paying these detainees thirteen cents an hour, sometimes merely in candy bars, saves at least $40 million a year.

I open my laptop and browse Serco's Web site. It calls itself an "international service company" with a nifty catchall motto, Bringing Service to Life. With 100,000 staff worldwide and a $10 billion portfolio, it has security, defense, health, and transport contracts in some thirty countries. I scroll down to the Ethos section, which speaks in lofty terms about allowing staff responsibility and the opportunity to make a real difference for their clients. Flipping through the company's annual report, with its generic corporate-speak and photos of jaunty staff retreats, one could altogether overlook the fact that Serco deals in prisons.

Further research bolsters my confusion. Serco facilities are less expensive to run, and unlike government prisons, Serco's contracts involve recidivism-based measures. The cost-effectiveness bit doesn't surprise me; it's a selling point of privatization. But whereas

American private prisons are often accused of saving via less train-ing, substandard services, and lower staff salaries and benefits, this hardly seems the culture I'd witnessed at Wandoo. Serco's London-based think-tank arm presents a series of seemingly attractive arguments. Treating people in prison more humanely ultimately costs less, and private prisons are more accountable than government-run prisons because contracts specify financial penal-ties for not meeting standards of health and educational services. Private prisons are cheaper, Serco claims, because of sound man-agement, efficient staff levels, and flexible practices.

―――――

But does it take a private company to run a humane prison? I shudder at that oxymoronic phrase as it emerges from my mouth days later, when Brian takes me to Boronia Pre-release Centre. It's home to eighty-two women within five years of release. As in the United States, women are Australia's fastest-rising group of prisoners, the bulk of them serving time for drug and property offenses.

I meet Brian in his office at Curtin University. He gives me a tour of the Centre for Aboriginal Studies and a crash course in Aboriginal art, its intricate dots, loops, and circles serving as codes for complex narratives, known as yarning. We stroll from the leafy campus walkway past cheery students eating kale salad and organic sandwiches at the cafeteria, to a brick building with a small sign and—wait, am I still on campus or is this prison? There's no barbed wire and no metal detector. No uniforms, no indications of rank, no loudspeaker systems blasting eardrums with "Brown to the mailroom, stat!" The prison and the college are neighbors, and it's near impossible to tell where one begins and the other ends.

A woman wearing a bloodred pantsuit is kissing her son good-bye and sending him off in a taxi. Is she a prisoner or a college student? The sunny outdoor deck, where staff and visitors snack on fruit platters and tiramisu, is adorned with bright flower pots and charming lampposts and surrounded by manicured lawns. A vegetable garden, education and health center, computer lab, and copies of a colorful newsletter, *The Grapevine*, round out our tour.

"The idea is to simulate real life as much as possible," Brian explains. "And to foster agency and responsibility, not passivity." Like Wandoo, Boronia is an open space in which the women work in the morning and go to classes during the afternoon.

"Meaningful work," the powerhouse of a superintendent explains. "We are not in the business of offering slave labor. We want supportive employers. As soon as an employer asks me, 'What's she in for?' I know they're not for us."

When the women go on home leave to visit their families, they're given two directives: don't access the Internet and don't get pregnant. Housing is designed such that every few weeks the prisoners' children can spend a night at the facility, and a full-fledged parenting program ensures that it's quality time, not time spent parked before the TV.

I pick up a bottle of brand-name moisturizer in the well-stocked supermarket, where a giant food pyramid hangs on the wall and the shelves are color-coded according to nutritional content. Green means healthy and red not so healthy, thus more expensive. The women get prepaid credit cards and shop at their will, but they must buy within the healthy pyramid or their money runs out in a snap.

"You want to buy three tubs of margarine?" explains the super-intendent. "Go ahead. But not on my money!"

The "catering coordinator" tells us, in his French accent, that he oversees menus and cooking classes for the women, many of whom have large families and too often lean on McDonald's to feed them.

"Boronia is all about breaking down the institutionalized mentality of our women. They need to think for themselves," the superintendent concludes. "This is what prison does to you: You line up and hold your food tray and there's food. You leave your clothes out and they're washed. You lose your basic life skills. Here, if you don't cook you don't eat. This whole way of thinking is a shock at first, but it's critical."

What she's describing is deinstitutionalization at its best. But then again, what if institutionalization never had to happen in the first place? What if the whole of one's corrections experience could be spent this way, not simply the last lap? And could the model be replicated in higher-security prisons?

"Of course," declares the superintendent. "It all comes down to size and management. Max is just a fence. I spent fifteen years running a max."

"It didn't shatter your optimism?"

"No, it showed me that it's all wrong—this approach doesn't work. Boronia is definitely not representative of Australia, but it's a very big, very small step in the right direction, see? Baby steps. It takes a while to turn the *Queen Mary* around."

———

The days march on, stubborn in their splendor: another perfect day in perfect Perth. The sun always seems to be just-right bright in the cloudless blue sky; one night I spend an hour trying to photograph the moon because no one, I'm sure, will believe it hung so gaudily close. What would it do to a person, to live in this genetically modified "cool city," where the economic boom of the last decade manifests itself not in big-and-bling but eco-fabulous? I'm worlds away from where this prison journey started, from the ur-townships of Pollsmoor and the Uzis of Uganda. This is the stultifyingly sunny land of Oz.

I say as much, one evening, to my new friend Craig. He's a reporter for the Indigenous News Network and also moonlights as a comedian. We'd met via Facebook through various connections, and he's fast becoming my favorite companion because he, like me, loves to poke holes in the perfect-Perth facade. His favorite topic to skewer, with incisive hilarity, is Australian racism.

"Because that's what's lurking beneath all the sunshine in sunny Perth," Craig says.

It's also on full display at the imperial-looking Fremantle Prison, which I visit one afternoon. Built in the 1850s by convict laborers, modeled after England's Pentonville Prison—itself mirroring American penitentiaries—Fremantle was the region's biggest colonial prison until it closed in 1991 and became a museum.

"Doing Time Tours" are advertised on the way in; I bypass them and go solo, entranced for hours by a gallery of prison murals and paintings. They're mostly Aboriginal art, because that's who has long filled the prisons here. For Aboriginal populations, Australia averages five times the incarceration rate even of black South Africans at the height of apartheid. Apartheid, I learn, was actually modeled after Australia's 1905 Aborigines Act, which limited movement, governed sex, set curfews, and more. In 1841 nearby Rottnest Island became the legal prison for Aboriginal men, and by 1952 they represented up to 40 percent of the nation's prison population. Same old story: another minority population ghettoized, stigmatized, incarcerated en masse;

another labor force manufactured by way of prisons, assigned to fill cells and then further criminalized by a system that remains stacked against them. I can feel the rage welling up within me.

"For Convicts Big and Small" reads the sign at the gift shop. Aprons, mugs, and wine racks are for sale, all featuring cute "jailbird" designs. Care to purchase an adorable little convict magnet? asks a shopkeeper.

This marriage of convict and commerce is even more disturbing to me than the prison gift shops in Thailand, because it epitomizes the rosy marketing of a penal-colony past. I'd grappled with it as soon as I arrived, when I spent a weekend in Sydney. Following the lead of a tourism brochure entitled "Convicts, Criminals and Culture," I'd trekked around the city visiting monuments and museums, absorbing the idea of a whole country founded on second chances. I did not have a "convict brekkie" at the Hyde Park Barracks Museum, or make my meal "truly memorable by dining in the former solitary confinement room," as the brochure beckoned. But I did visit the fascinating museum, a former prison for the transported. Until 1822, the narrative goes, all lived peacefully in "the land of convicts and kangaroos." But then a visiting British commissioner balked. They're living *too* peacefully, he decreed, accusing the local leader, Governor Macquarie, of that familiar political sin of being soft on crime, and demanding harsh conditions. No more pardons or parole for these criminals. Give them chain gangs, hard labor, and draconian discipline.

Touring the museum meant confronting this discipline. The "treadmill" was a terrible torture device, and floggings were administered for infractions as minor as insolence.

As I watched, tittering children ran about, hooting and hollering at the interactive exhibit, trying on "convict clothes," playing with cute little rats serving as cartoon guideposts. In the cramped chamber where prisoners slept, rows of hammocks evoked slave ships—and three little girls were joyfully swinging across them. It felt like prison-as-Disneyland. This place of sadness and suffering ought to have the solemnity of a concentration camp.

But wait, you say. The people here were hardly pitiable victims—they were "convicts." So explained the tourist beside me to his son, puzzled by the whips and chains: "These were very bad criminals and this was what they deserved, honey." It's the same thing we say today: These very bad people are getting what they deserve, behind bars.

But who are these "bad people," really?

The nefarious "convicts" of Oz were primarily poor people who, perhaps, stole a loaf of bread. By the eighteenth century, a series of such minor crimes could earn one the sentence of banishment—vanishment, as it's also aptly called. Eighty-three percent of Australian "convicts," their mean age a mere twenty-six, were guilty of crimes against property. They were overwhelmingly literate and skilled workers, a labor market, not a criminal class. But call them convicts and it's suddenly easy to dismiss, to justify, their enslavement and their suffering. This is still true. Call someone a "criminal" or "ex-con" or "offender" and you have, in one fell swoop, reduced them to their worst act and vindicated yourself for tolerating their lynching. You've also lumped all criminal acts, from marijuana smoking to mass murder, into one catchall category, though even the worst categories of crimes can be so broad as to be meaningless. "Sex offender" might denote the vile act of rape or the deplorable yet quite different act of brushing up against a woman inappropriately in a club. "Violent crime" can mean murder or intimidation.

Terms like "convict" and "offender" are scarlet letters, expediently trapping people in their worst selves forever. Such shameful stigmas are why language, when it comes to crime and punishment, deeply matters. Australia has only in the last decade or so begun to shed its shame over its early settlers. It was once a disgrace to find a "convict" in one's family tree, but now it's considered a badge of honor; eleven historic "convict"-related sites were recently added to the World Heritage list here. How could it be otherwise? One in ten Aussies is said to have a "convict" ancestor. This is a nation of the formerly incarcerated. They can't beat it, so they'd better commodify it.

This is yet another way in which Oz is the United States's far-flung twin. At the beginning of the millennium, 5.6 million Americans had served time. By age twenty-three, at least a third of them have been arrested; up to 100 million Americans have a criminal record, and in some major cities, 80 percent of young African-American men have one. What is this but the updated version of a penal colony, where an entire population sports the label which our country so adroitly, so abundantly manufactures?

The day of my third and final prison visit arrives, and the name intrigues. *Acacia.* It could be a writer's retreat, but it's a Serco-run prison, soon to be the largest in Australia and, with 1,387 men, sizable even by American standards. It's the last prison on my agenda here, and the dry, dusty drive there brings Brian and me through Swan Valley, where tourists indulge in wine-tasting tours, and, via memory lane, to Thailand, Uganda, Brazil—another road to hell paved in divine vistas. Lined with warning signs, too. *Beware the bushfires!* The color-coded fire-hazard rating system here makes me think of post-9/11 America, when orange and red terrorist "threat levels" appeared on every news screen, ensuring that our anxiety never abated.

We take a turn into Warloo Farm, where sheep roam in fields of gold. And then into barbed wire, low tin roofs, and cement blocks. Compared to the progressive Serco prisons I've visited up till now, Acacia has the feel of a standard prison; it actually strikes me as a more parched-looking version of Otisville, back home. At the Visitors' Center, with its bolted tables and phone booths, broom-wielding prisoners wear green uniforms. There is a caged-in gym, and cell blocks made from zinc and concrete, including the block known as "Bronx"—there's a "Queens" and "Brooklyn," too—where dozens of tattooed men smoke cigarettes and do push-ups in their cells. I visit behind-bars factories with full-on assembly lines, where hundreds of men are paid up to nine dollars a day to build bedframes, fireplaces, or car parts. In the chicken farm and greenhouse, I wave off the smell of manure, disinfect my shoes, and inspect pristine rows of spinach and arugula. Everything here is logged, monetized, and efficiently organized around skills training, the earning of trade certificates, and direct channels to corporations. My mind seesaws as I try to appraise the scene. Certainly productive, paid work and job training are better than idle, wasted time. But Acacia is also the prison industrial complex in its most intense incarnation. Right before my eyes is evidence of a prison turned into a mass money-making enterprise.

Around my waist I wear a "distress button," presented by the German guard who checked me in and explained that if I felt in danger, I should simply press it and help would arrive at once. This was new to me. So are the vivid streaks of progressive thinking here. It's evidenced by the Aboriginal art everywhere: serpents, lizards, and moons painted by incarcerated men and volunteering Curtin University students. Admittedly, it's a bit like mowing down the trees to build mansions and then naming suburban streets after the razed greenery, but I appreciate the gesture nonetheless. And the self-care units that mimic apartment or dorm living, with kitchens and common areas shared by several "poddies" — the only thing that screams prison in these units are dense iron doors on the bedrooms, locked every evening. On the way into the self-care units are computerized check-ins. Via thumbprint, men can receive messages, check their accounts, and coordinate their program schedules.

Under a knotty tree is a designated yarning circle for indigenous prisoners, a kind of town hall meeting area. And there's much planning for more enlightened programs and structures, including a family day fair, "greening" the place with gardens, biophilic walls, and therapeutic natural light, restorative justice week, and charity walks. Construction cranes are everywhere; soon a new education center and performing arts space will invigorate programs.

"I want a rock opera. And an actor's workshop, and an amphitheater," says Brent, Acacia's education manager and a bundle of enthusiasm. He and an on-site psychologist lead our tour. She sports funky tattoos down her forearm and, like Brent, wears a smart Serco uniform — button-down pinstripe shirt, pink-ribbon pin. They're both in their thirties.

We chat over a lunch of veggie wraps and Serco-branded water, tidily arranged on a glossy table.

"It's in my job description to be innovative," Brent tells me, passing a tray of seedless watermelon. "Before Serco recruited me, I worked in a state hospital. I got almost nothing accomplished there—too much red tape. Here, I can make things happen. I've got collaborations in the works with the state, with arts organizations. It's exciting. And it can happen quickly."

I witness this quickness for myself that afternoon in a classroom building, where sixteen members of the educational staff await my arrival. A slew of educational programs here range from business and accounting certifications to a mining course, university-level distance learning, and Aboriginal-style classrooms, privileging narrative-driven oral work over traditional pen-and-paper learning.

Like Brent, the whole staff is, for the most part, lively and young, younger than any prison staff I've ever met. I brief them about the Prison-to-College Pipeline and they ask all the right questions. How many have enrolled in university since coming home from prison? About one-third, I reply. Does the school worry about getting a bad rap for educating those so-called criminals? How do you make special accommodations for indigenous students?

We don't have many indigenous students, I explain; our version of that—our overincarcerated, underserved community—is African-American and Latino/a. Eyes widen; heads nod. The zeal is tangible, and it intensifies during my discussion session with four incarcerated men, all of whom are thrilled by the prospect of a university program at Acacia. They share near-identical educational histories. Whether from boredom or financial need, they dropped out of school at a young age and now deeply regret that decision.

"Time here, it's dead time," one of them tells me. "We need school so we stop killing time, mate."

"I'd be keen on studying sociology or psychology, but that's illegal for us," says another. Brent and Brian explain that certain subjects are entirely off limits to those with criminal records.

"Where's the logic in that?" I blurt. "Psychology? Who can be of better service to people impacted by the criminal justice system than people who've been there and done that?" I tell the men about my colleagues at various reentry organizations whose staff included formerly incarcerated individuals, many of them with master's degrees and PhDs. I also tell them about Martin, my pre-law Prison-to-College Pipeline student, who's definitely eligible for law school although he may be blocked from passing the bar because of a felony conviction at age twenty-two. Shouldn't those in the system benefit from being represented by those who have the wisdom of personal experience with it?

"We'd love to take your classes," the prisoners sigh.

"I'd love to teach here," I tell them.

"Why don't you?" says Brent.

It's that easy. I'm approved to come back to Acacia next week and lead a one-day autobiography workshop, the perfect opportunity to delve more deeply into the place and contribute a little something to it.

On the way out, Brian and I hand in our distress buttons. Many times today I felt distress, I think, but never once was this feeling connected to safety.

"See, Baz. The picture is a complicated one," Brian reflects. "No one hates the idea of a private prison more than me. But the reality is that the private sector is being monitored; the government is not. Look at how quickly they could schedule a program. When I was inside I went to every program available, every one. And there were barely any to go to. Here at least you have people innovating."

As I start prepping for next week's class, my friend Craig gives me a hand researching local private-prison politics. There's no shortage of scandals to deepen my dilemma around the issue, especially when it comes to detention centers, filled to the brim here on account of Australia's severe mandatory detention laws. All such centers are privately run, either by Serco—the value of their contract stands at more than $756 million—or G4S, an Anglo-Danish company whose name connotes a missile factory.

G4S has been faulted for lethal neglect and abusive use of solitary; in 2007, their drivers ignored the cries of detainees locked in a sweltering van, leaving them so dehydrated that one drank his own urine. The company was ordered to pay $500,000 for inhumane treatment, although three of the five victims had already been deported. Serco, meanwhile, is being threatened with a lawsuit by the workers' union, complaining about pay and conditions. Riots, fires, and suicidal protests left millions of dollars in damage at Serco-run centers across the country in recent years, and self-harm by detainees rose twelvefold. A government inspection reported on hazardous overcrowding, inadequate and ill-trained staff, inadequate crisis planning, and lack of a requirement for Serco to add employees when population exceeds capacity. At one detention center, immigrants griped about insanity-producing conditions like long, open-ended detentions; another, in the outback, was shut down amid riots and hunger strikes in 2002. Even Western Australia's former chief prison inspector has admitted, "These big global companies, in relation to specific activities, are more powerful than the governments they're dealing with."

Such horror stories abound in the United States, as well. At the GEO-controlled Reeves County Detention Center in Texas, for instance, residents rioted in 2009 and 2010 after several detainees died in solitary. But then again, abusive treatment of incarcerated people abounds all over the world—in government-run prisons, too. After one massive riot at Western Australia's only nonprivate juvenile detention center, for instance, over one hundred juveniles, the bulk of them with serious mental health problems, were transferred to an adult prison and locked in their cells for nineteen hours a day. Craig tells me about a state prison way up in the Northern Territory that's said to be almost entirely filled with Aboriginal people, with atrocious conditions that are barely monitored. Perhaps, I muse, it's not about private or public—it's about accountability and process overall.

I collect my readings for the autobiography class and send them to Brent, a bit haltingly. Will Malcolm X be approved by the powers that be? Will anything be approved in time? At Otisville, it can take weeks or even months before getting the OK on assigned texts for class.

But after I return from a jog along the Swan River, through a park filled with happy cyclers and marked by a statue titled Peace Grove, an e-mail from Brent arrives. All readings are approved, printed, Xeroxed, and awaiting me at Acacia.

———

"Tell me how it is that an American girl comes to have a German last name and a Bavarian first name?" The German guard at Acacia's front gate asks as he scans my ID with his piercing blue eyes.

"Actually, sir, the last name is Hungarian. And the first name, Hebrew. From the Bible."

"Hebrew? Hebrew?" He mutters under his breath. And to me: "No, ma'am, dis is German name. *Drei*: 'three,' *singer*: three singers, who vould sing every January 6, on Epiphany. That is you: *drei singer*. Epiphany."

"Well, actually, my great-grandfather—"

Waving me off, he hands me a distress button.

In the staff lounge, hipster-looking teachers pass around Cadbury's cookies. We chat about teaching in prison—one of the teachers' high school–level class is working on a project asking students to engineer perfect worlds. Then Brent carries me to my classroom, where I rearrange the seats in a grand circle. Instead of infantilizing posters peddling self-help slogans, the concrete walls here are covered with graduation photos and relevant newspaper articles. "Education Can Add Years to Your Life," reads one. A Serco water bottle rests on my desk.

Students trickle in slowly.

"Is this Business Management?" a head pokes in. Next door, I tell him.

The four men I met last week are here. With the exception of a Sri Lankan prisoner, the whole class is white, and Brent would later explain why. He selected only college-ready students and the Aboriginal prisoners are victims of massive educational disadvantage. This hardly surprises me.

So, Frederick Douglass and Malcolm X land in a room of white Australian incarcerated men.

As in Uganda, my students have never heard of a slave narrative. But unlike in Uganda, the more we read aloud from it, the more they're visibly moved.

"Segregation still exists today, mate," asserts Sam from Fremantle, his bulky arms carpeted in tattoos. "Australia is one of the most racist societies on earth."

"Worse than America?" his classmate challenges him. "America is easily the most racist place on earth. Slavery and all."

"Look at our white-dominated world, mate," Sam asserts. "The thing about Aussie racism, see, is that it's not easy to shake because people don't even see it. And for the Aboriginals, it becomes years of mental oppression."

I often wished myself a beast. Anything, no matter what, to get rid of thinking!

Frederick Douglass's words about learning to read ring out in the prison classroom.

"We know this feeling," sighs Andrei. He's chubby with black, spiky hair; the other day he'd told me he's a musician, and his mother was a renowned ballerina.

"Would you get rid of thinking?" I ask. "Is ignorance bliss?"

"Why should it be?" Sam challenges. "Knowledge is power."

"But intellectually knowing the circumstances of your oppression and being powerless to do anything about it—that's torture," Andrei argues, pointing vigorously at the handout. "Like the man says, education makes one unfit to be a slave."

A man in a Serco uniform arrives with a camera, snapping away. Andrei goes on. "In these circumstances, I'd prefer to be a beast than a thinking human being in a cell."

"This Malcolm X fella doesn't think so," his classmate chimes in, reading from the next handout:

I knew right there in prison that reading had changed forever the course of my life. As I see it today, the ability to read awoke inside me some long dormant craving to be mentally alive... Not long ago, an English writer telephoned me from London, asking questions. One was, "What's your alma mater?" I told him, "Books." You will never catch me with a free fifteen minutes in which I'm not studying something I feel might be able to help the black man.

"He's definitely got less humility than the Douglass guy," a fifty-something student wearing small round glasses says. "He's in your face with it. That last line starts 'you'—like he's challenging the reader."

"That's because a hundred years between 'em and not much has changed—there's still the same kind of slavery only now it's in the prison cell," Sam argues. "Mate's fed up. And the bar is set higher. It's not about nicely asking for freedom. It's about, 'Give us full rights already.'"

"He won't be an Uncle—what do you lot call it?" a student chimes in. "Uncle Tom, is it?"

It's miraculous; the class teaches itself. I couldn't have scripted it better, this attention to nuance, racial sensitivities, total immersion in the material and scrupulous note taking. When I return for part two in the afternoon—it wasn't initially part of the plan, but after the men insist, Brent swiftly accommodates—we analyze a short story by Chimamanda Ngozi Adichie about a middle-class teen who ends up in a Nigerian prison. Not only do the men adroitly unpack the complex race, class, and gender dynamics of an African country they've barely even heard of, they transform the analysis into a weighty moral discussion about lessons learned and unlearned behind bars, and utilitarianism versus moral absolutes. The room becomes an echo chamber of self-referential questions. What does it mean to live comfortably in a deeply corrupt society? Can one ever be fully free of hypocrisy? Is it moral to sacrifice a few in the name of the greater whole?

"We're those people, right here in Acacia. Sacrificed for the good of everyone else. An example, deterrents. Scapegoats," says Sam.

Later he reads the start of his autobiography. "I am twenty-eight years old but I was only born about two years ago," it begins. Two years ago is when he came to prison and lost his family's love.

> *It's funny how a whole life can be defined by one singular*
> *moment, whether the body of this life was wholesome*
> *and filled largely by good, a single lapse of judgment, a moment*
> *of poor decision, can leave even those closest to you with the*
> *opinion that your whole life has been one giant slippery slope to*
> *destruction, to death, to jail.*

Sam goes on about his memories of a joyous childhood, his siblings arguing about who loves him more. Not anymore, he continues:

> *As I sit in my cell and wonder what my family is up to, I can't help*
> *but picture them sitting around arguing over who loathes me*
> *the most, who "saw it coming," who was the most shocked, the*
> *most hurt. The irony is that if they could bring themselves*
> *to have some form of contact with me, they being my brother Ben*
> *and my two sisters Rebecca and Gabe, they would see that not*
> *only am I still their little brother that loves them, looks up to them*
> *and misses them, but that I have more to offer them as a person*
> *and a friend now than I ever would have had my life and lifestyle*
> *remained the way it was before prison.*

Like Sam's, all of the other men's essays are strikingly well written and thoughtful. Andrei details his childhood in England: he has seventeen years left in prison and was a renowned sound engineer until heroin led his life astray. "People don't realize how easy it is to become us," he declares.

Another student writes of killing his dear friend in a heat-of-the-moment burst of anger; yet another lingers on memories of his father, who worked in Oz's gold mines. "He was the quintessential miner and rail worker of historical Australia," he reads aloud. "Big build, tough as nails, jet-black hair always slicked back with a handful of Brylcreem, and loved a can or ten of the cheapest beer he could find."

The man stops reading because he starts sobbing. "This was hard," he says, burying a tear-streaked face in his tattooed hands. "I miss my dad. I really miss him."

The room stands still.

Last week, when I asked the four men if they enjoyed writing, only one said yes. Today they all beg me to return and say they're going to continue their autobiographies.

"We were so hungry for this," Andrei tells me.

His words remind me of Uganda, where I taught much the same class in a radically different context; Luzira is, literally and metaphorically, as different from Acacia as black is from white. Yet the reception to writing was the same. Both sets of men tapped into wells of interred pain. Both expressed profound hunger for more and deep delight in discovering that expressing themselves on paper provides a momentary breath of freedom.

Through the oven-dry heat, Brent walks me out of Acacia. It's one of my easiest prison exits because given the structure in place here, I leave confident that any tiny impact I've made will last long after I've gone. Brent is all fired up, ready to bring in more college-level instructors and use today as a master class.

"We'd better return this to the library," he says, picking up a worn copy of *The Art of War* abandoned on the ground. He goes on, detailing his vision.

"I can change the higher education here in under a year, and that's what I'm going to do. I'll keep you posted on it."

———

He does. As soon as I get back to America, Brent writes to let me know that he's tracking down the next guest lecturer for the Prisoner Brain Trust, the name he's given to the collective of university-level students I taught.

It's not Wandoo or Boronia, with their therapeutic settings and restorative justice foundations. But Acacia is testament to one simple thing capable of revolutionizing even a traditional prison setting: *people.* Reading Brent's e-mail makes me think of Mara in Brazil, laboring to make some sliver of a difference in a solitary confinement hell. I think of an officer in Thailand who told me that in his prison there is one officer per thousand prisoners and two officers have been stabbed in the past five months alone. And of some corrections officers at Otisville, who count down toward retirement in language that erases the line between the fences: five more years to serve, they tell me. "The guards are as locked in as you are as prisoners," said one of the students who participated in the famous 1971 Stanford prison experiment, during which some played the role of prisoners and others, their captors. "They just have the run of the cellblock, but they have a locked door behind them which they can't open, and so really you're all together and what you create, you create together."

For months, Brent keeps me abreast of the programs he's launching at Acacia: theater activities, a speaker series, a film festival. Band-Aids they may be, but as the director of Boronia had said, it takes a while to turn the *Queen Mary* around.

Back in New York, I continue to mull over the vexed relationship between capitalism and "convict." There's a new buzzword in the world of prison reform: the social impact bond (SIB). The government sets a precise, measurable outcome that it wants achieved in a particular population, then vows to pay an external organization—which wants a return on capital but also seeks to do good for the community—only if the organization accomplishes that outcome. Investors provide working capital for the organization to hire and manage service providers, and a third-party evaluator determines whether the outcome has been achieved. If the project succeeds, the government pays the external organization, which then repays the investors with interest. If the project fails, investors aren't repaid with public funds.

Making headlines is one such SIB launched on Riker's Island, right near my home—the largest penal colony in the world. The city of New York, I read, has contracted with a nonprofit, nonpartisan social research organization to reduce the rate of recidivism by at least 10 percent over four years among annual cohorts of about three thousand young men exiting Riker's. To do this, they will manage two nonprofit service providers; working capital for the intervention, $9.6 million over four years, is provided by Goldman Sachs as a loan. It's an exciting prospect, this union of progressiveness and practicality.

At John Jay College, I meet with a woman launching the Reset Foundation, gearing up to establish Wandoo-like prison settings in California and New York for court-involved youth, based on the charter school model in public education. They'll repurpose existing funding to build a campus instead of a prison, and are held accountable for improved outcomes like academic growth, lifetime earnings, and reduced recidivism.

It all hammers home the important point that not all capitalism is created equal. Private prisons are a very convenient, very salient villain—and indeed as it stands today, there's a terrifying amount that's villainous about them.

But there doesn't necessarily have to be. Perhaps there's such a thing as privatization with a conscience, implemented morally and progressively in the name of true corrections. Imagine it: agencies taking SIB-style approaches, barred from impact on policy and held to a high set of standards that involve recidivism and postrelease success rates, not beds filled and money saved at all costs. It's in line with the surge, these days, of B Corporations, for-profit companies that pledge to achieve social goals as well as business ones. There are over a thousand of them in the United States today—like Warby Parker, a chic eyeglasses company that has partnered with a nonprofit donating free glasses to those in need around the world. *New Yorker* columnist James Surowiecki argued that the B Corporation is a winning model because it protects businesses from pressure from investors and, on account of being attached to a higher cause, lures strong employees and committed consumers. Calling it a return to the business eras of Henry Ford or Johnson and Johnson, he dubs the growth of B Corporations "a reminder that the idea that corporations should be only lean, mean, profit-maximizing machines isn't dictated by the inherent nature of capitalism, let alone by human nature."

In the end, it's a muddle I'll continue to wade into as I visit another country whose culture, then and now, is steeped in both prisons and profit: Singapore.

7.
Reentry | *Singapore*

*The fetters fell off. I picked them up. I wanted to hold them in
my hand, to look at them for the last time. I seemed already to be
wondering that they could have been on my legs a minute before.*

*"Well, with God's blessing, with God's blessing!" said the
convicts in coarse, abrupt voices, in which, however, there was
a note of pleasure.*

*Yes, with God's blessing! Freedom, new life, resurrection
from the dead... what a glorious moment!*
—Fyodor Dostoyevsky, *House of the Dead*

Something resembling an oblong blimp is perched on a rooftop. Or
maybe it's a supersized surfboard, sprawled across three gleaming
skyscrapers. Trees sprout from it, grasping toward the heavens.

"What *is* that?" I blurt out, to no one in particular. I'm looking
at Marina Bay Sands, the most expensive building in the world.

Having recently arrived in Singapore, I am taking in the city-
state's futuristic skyline. Aside from the surfboard-in-the-sky

edifice, there's a white building shaped like a grand lotus flower, a glass Rubik's Cube–looking thing skating on water and branded by Louis Vuitton, and towering structures that resemble a cross between massive daisies and airport control towers—a passerby explains that these are Gardens by the Bay. Singapore looks a little like Disneyland.

Disneyland with a death penalty, that is. So one journalist notably dubbed it, alluding to the draconian criminal justice system for which the country is known. Free candies distributed at the airport are subtle reminders of this no-nonsense approach—chewing gum is illegal here. My landing card serves up a much less subtle prompt. "Warning: Death for drug traffickers under Singaporean law" is stamped in bold letters across the bottom.

"Singapore Is a Fine Country" reads the slogan on tourist trinkets peddled all over Chinatown, where I stroll the day after arriving. You can earn a hefty fine for many things in Singapore, from posting the wrong thing on Facebook to eating fetid durian fruit on the metro. You can be caned for thirty different crimes, including, most famously, graffiti; in 1994, when visiting American Michael Fay was caned for vandalism and theft, the brutal practice made international headlines. The daily paper reveals as much as any statistic. During my first few days here I read about teens accused of spray-painting expletives, discharging a fire extinguisher, trespassing, stealing, and damaging property. Their punishment? Fines, jail for up to three years, three to eight strokes of the cane. And a man convicted of robbery, drug consumption, and failing to show up for a drug test got ten years and twelve strokes of the cane.

This allegiance to punishment is part of why Singapore is the next-to-last stop on my prison journey. But the other reason I'm here goes back to a Singaporean ad I'd discovered on YouTube while in Thailand, when I was doing research on prisons, PR, and the princess. In it, a young, melancholy-looking man in shirt and tie goes about his daily business, a forlorn-sounding hum in the background. Here he is taking the crowded commute to a corporate job, perched meekly at the boardroom table, numbly pushing a grocery cart down the supermarket aisle. But all the while he's lugging around a cumbersome ball and chain, hindering him at every turn. A single statement appears: "Help ex-convicts lead a normal life." And then, "SCORE: Singapore Corporation of Rehabilitative Enterprises." Who are they, I'd wondered? Their formidable bit of marketing haunted me, exactly as it was meant to.

SCORE, it turns out, is part of the Singaporean government's effort to tackle that hitch in the prison solution to crime: the fact that such a "solution" is temporary. Most prisoners eventually leave prison. What does society do with them when they do?

This process, known as reentry, is a global criminal justice buzzword. It was invented in America and attained national standing in President George W. Bush's 2008 Second Chance Act, which included support for prisoners coming home. Mayors and governors across the country opened up reentry offices and launched committees, like New York's Council on Community Re-Entry and Reintegration, established by Governor Andrew Cuomo in 2014. Foundations sponsored studies on the subject and universities opened research institutes dedicated to it; my own Prison-to-College Pipeline, the country's first education program explicitly designed with reentry in mind, is housed at John Jay's Prisoner Reentry Institute.

Reentry. It sounds so seamlessly simple, as if you've temporarily left home and are now just returning, ready to pick up where you left off. But the process is anything but simple. It's a dramatic coming-back-to-life, a strenuous resurrection, a full-on crisis.

Imagine you spend five, ten, twenty-five years locked away in an alternate universe that plays by wholly different rules. You're doing time; time, halted, is doing things to you, doing things without you. Then one day you're set free. Where do you go? Where do you live? How do you adjust to the utterly *other* world you're suddenly in—socially, technologically, and otherwise? How do you find a job? Find your way around? Surely the country that locked you up will help you readjust after you've paid your debt?

No. Odds are that you, like most people coming home from prison, aren't eligible for welfare, food stamps, or public housing. Like 80 percent of those incarcerated in US prisons you're without health insurance; if you were ever enrolled in Medicaid it was terminated while you were in prison and the government hasn't reenrolled you. Employers don't want to hire you; in a sample of four large urban labor markets, 40 percent openly admitted they wouldn't hire someone with a criminal record. If you do have a job, you earn about 40 percent less than your peers who have not been formerly incarcerated, and if you live in any but four states you have no say about this reality, or any other government policy that devastates your life, because you can't vote; you're one of 5.85 million Americans—7.2 percent of our citizens—impacted by "felon disenfranchisement" laws. Of this total, over two million are African Americans, one of many factors named by law professor Michelle Alexander in her best-selling 2012 book *The New Jim Crow*, which describes what segregation looks like in the twenty-first century: a new racial caste system born of the invisible punishment that is reentry. The "lower caste of individuals who are permanently barred by law and custom from mainstream society," she writes, is designed to "warehouse a population deemed disposable," that is, blacks and Latinos, and to deepen social inequalities. Inequality produces crime, which means that ironically this "New Jim Crow" system ultimately diminishes safety; masses of people cycling in and out of the system are being denied the economic, social, and political resources that would help them stay out of prison. The result of all this is that America's recidivism rate hovers at 60 percent.

Singapore's recidivism rate, though, is only about 25 percent. Some nine thousand people here go home from prison every year, and the country has launched a host of ventures to handle this influx. I'm keen to get a look at these progressive movements in the land of penalties. As my journey draws to a close, I'm ready to turn to the subject of getting out of prison.

—

On the morning of my first meeting with prison authorities, though, I'm wondering about getting into prison. The question nagged me. *How did I get here?* Singapore is hardly known for transparency—the government all but runs the press, and the country is notoriously guarded about its justice system. The simple answer is that I met someone who knew someone, at a criminal justice conference last year. And being a professor at John Jay certainly helps open doors. But still, I wondered, why would they let an inquisitive outsider in?

My query is answered during an all-day orientation at the manicured SCORE offices.

Adorning the office wall, near the impressive library and the DIY health center, hangs a blown-up 2011 *Straits Times* article about grand revisions to the Singapore Prison Service, or SPS. "What a Difference a Decade Makes," the headline reads. Prisons were once old military barracks but now they're "purpose-built." Prison officers, once barred from even talking to prisoners—"in case the latter manipulate or corrupt them"—now boast degrees in economics, law, science, and the arts, and they *must* talk to prisoners in order to "learn what they need."

A vital word entered SPS's vocabulary in 1996: *rehabilitation.* In one fell swoop Singapore decided to speak of prison as about more than just punishment; the SPS operations philosophy and corporate statement were revised accordingly. New prisons, terminology, and dizzying acronyms were born, like MAS (Mandatory Aftercare Scheme), CBS (Community Based Sentences)—the list goes on. This new approach yielded results. The country's recidivism rate dropped from 40 percent in 2000 to 23.6 in 2010. I'm here because the government is eager to show off its born-again identity.

Learning this made me even more eager to see the system at work. Not only because it reflects such a dramatic shift in a short span of time, but because it's justice by choice and not by economic necessity. Plenty of countries, the United States included, have their prison conditions dictated at least in part by dollar signs. They simply can't afford better conditions or can't competently manage finances to produce them. Singapore, though, with its lucrative job market, governmental efficiency, and vast prosperity—it's one of the richest nations in the world, said to possess over $500 billion in sovereign wealth funds—can do as it chooses. For decades its choice was harsh punishment. What's the choice now? The whole thing seems a remarkable test-tube scenario, cutting to the heart of ideologies about retribution, reform, and justice.

———

The next day my destination is Changi, a rambling complex neighboring the airport that houses all but one of Singapore's fourteen prisons. It was a colonial prison built by the British administration of the Straits Settlements in 1936, and now it comfortably houses some 12,000 prisoners and 2,500 corrections officers. During World War II the Japanese military detained civilians there, and the former Seralang Barracks, where I'll spend today, was a prisoner-of-war camp for up to fifty thousand British and Australian soldiers. With the exception of these barracks and one lone crumbling wall, the complex was recently demolished and the prison rebuilt.

Military barracks, then, have been reborn as Seralang Park Community Supervision Center, a work-release facility for prisoners nearing the end of their sentences and for former prisoners checking in with postrelease supervisors. I make my way through the barbed wire into a vista of rusty green zinc.

More than half the country's prisoners pass through here at some point, most after release. They report to an area that feels like a public-school auditorium. Hundreds of formerly incarcerated people are checking into electronic self-registration kiosks, taking their seats in the waiting area and meeting with their supervisors to discuss life on the outside—their jobs as cleaners or telemarketers or cooks. Singapore has a 99 percent success rate in finding jobs for the formerly incarcerated, primarily in the food and beverage, retail, and tourism industries. Thanks to job coaches and consistent collaboration with human resources departments, they boast that 59 percent of those "emplaced," as they call it, retain their jobs for at least six months after release. This is radically different from the United States, where roughly half of the formerly incarcerated remain jobless up to a year after their release. Surveys show that employers are not shy about overtly discriminating against people with criminal records, baldly expressing negative views about them in ways they might hesitate to do with regard to other factors like gender, age, or race.

Dorms, where up to 120 men reside for their last few months in prison and a few serve their entire sentence, are gray and spare. The only decor is metal lockers and child-size bunk beds fitted with cartoon-covered sheets, a step up from the straw mats they sleep on in prison. "Optimism," reads a sign on the drab wall. Those in prison here do not wear uniforms and are placed in jobs on the outside; they're also granted home leaves and volunteer in community projects.

"There is no trouble; prisoners behave," an officer tells me. "They treasure this place. Don't want to mess up." Those who do are put on display, via a wall of mug shots. I scan the posters. "Failed to notify employer when sick," reads one. "Lied to officer in order to gain curfew extension." "Attempted to cheat the company by falsifying membership sign-ups."

The officer is a former engineer. "I used to build houses, but now I build people," he declares on our way out.

Work-release, which I'd also glimpsed at Wandoo in Australia, is something of a no-brainer. A study conducted in Minnesota, for instance, found that work-release reduced the likelihood of a prisoner returning for a new crime, significantly increased the odds that he or she found a job, and upped hours worked and wages earned. It saved the state government some $1.25 million, too. Yet it barely exists on American shores, mostly on account of our extreme aversion to risk. Letting people off the prison compound simply makes people too nervous.

After the visit to Seralang Park, I eat an early dinner at one of Singapore's famous hawker centers. They're tightly regulated by the government and boast the safest street food money can buy. And their array of offerings, a convergence of Malay, Chinese, and Indian cooking, is a delectable manifestation of local multiculturalism. It's said that Singaporeans enact ethnic tolerance simply by eating.

Back at my hotel, a message waits for me. "Baz!" comes the ecstatic-sounding voice mail. "It's Jonathan! I'm home! Call me!" My twenty-three-year-old student is free, after six years behind bars. Thrilled, I dial right back.

"Is Jonathan there? This is his professor." Pause. Then, on the other end, sobs.

"I never thought I'd hear anyone say that," cries Jonathan's sister, who'd answered the phone. I tell her how proud I am of her brother, and what a talented student he is. She passes the phone to him.

"I can't wait to come to college, Baz," Jonathan declares. I can practically see the grin on his face.

Hanging up, I'm still fighting tears. Prison homecomings never lose their emotional impact.

But for me prison homecomings have also grown bittersweet. Because they begin with almost childlike optimism—of the sort I just heard in Jonathan's voice. The sort that borders on magical thinking, that makes Richard, a week before release, tell my class back home that he's like that alchemist in the novel he loves, "because I can be transformed." Optimism buoys my students through the days, hours, weeks of blunting postprison bureaucracy: ID offices, parole officer meetings, anger management sessions, this program and that program, and more government offices than I can keep track of. Optimism keeps them patient and calm as they learn to use technology born while they were in banishment. "Hi Baz," one of my students texted me on his second day home. "Just practicing texting." "When did silverware get so heavy?" marveled another, lifting a metal fork for the first time in thirteen years.

But this optimism usually has an expiration date. The honeymoon period with freedom comes to an end as the realities of life in the New Jim Crow set in. Jobs are scarce, old neighborhoods are perilous obstacle courses, and families have been devastated by years of separation. The postprison trauma sets in, too. When you went to prison at seventeen, time froze. So even if you're thirty-eight, you're still seventeen when it comes to relationship-building and communication skills and more. There are no solid support systems in place to help you work through this developmental roadblock and the trauma of what happened to you, or didn't happen to you, behind bars. And since prison can thrust its inhabitants into a state of denial about their crimes, because surviving often demands the blocking out of anything too emotionally upending, there is no support, either, as you work through the process of grappling with your mistakes, which generally hit you with a painful thud as you return to the world.

Many of my students go through a missing-in-action period during this posthoneymoon phase. I wake up nights worried that something's gone terribly wrong; I check online to make sure they haven't gone back to prison. But I do my best to let them be. Then, one day, they resurface. And slowly pick up the pieces, salvaging slices of spent hope and patching together something that approximates a new beginning.

———

"Cluster A. And over there, Cluster B. Clusters C and D were never built because we did not have enough prisoners so did not need them." Fee Leng, my SCORE host and a former corrections officer, is leading me into the heart of the modern section of Changi Prison. We scan our fingerprints at the entrance to the newly built complex. In my hands is a copy of the *Panopticon*, SPS's magazine.

"Cluster A was built in 2009 and Cluster B in 2011. We are not"—Fee Leng laughs—"so creative with names."

Behind the prisons, just outside the barbed wire, is a sea of warehouses. The two sets of boxlike buildings—all with orange-and-blue facades and a neat, glassy appearance—seamlessly blend together. Nothing in this area can be taller than four stories because the airport is next door, which means much of the prison had to be built underground. This makes for terrible ventilation problems inside.

We follow a path lined by trees that look like wizened fingers. Cluster A, Fee Leng explains, is primarily home to death row and long-term prisoners, and Cluster B, our destination today, houses those on remand or serving time for drugs—60 to 70 percent of the total prison population.

"This way to the VIP Lounge," says the officer inside, steering us past paintings of pink flamingos and pulsating sunsets.

"*Visitors'* Lounge," Fee Leng interjects.

It looks VIP to me, with its plush red couches, bar, foosball table, and air hockey set. There's a massive model of Cluster B in the middle of the room; the facility has one-man, four-man, and eight-man cells. Never a two-man cell, Fee Leng explains, because if something goes wrong between them there'd be no third-party witness.

Be the type of person you want to meet.

If there's a will, there's a way.

Henry Ford, Confucius, Abraham Lincoln, Dale Carnegie: their you-can-do-it wisdom is scrawled across every surface en route from the lounge to our destination.

It doesn't matter where you are coming from. All that matters is where you are going.

The setup resembles a housing scheme, with metallic railings and trim walkways, and it's quiet to the point of sterility. There are paintings of colorful birds and starfish, a wall of inspiration serving up more sanguine quotes on heart-shaped cutouts, a mural of purple Singaporean orchids—nothing that suggests prison. Not even the smell. There is, in fact, no smell.

But as we get off an elevator, the sound of walkie-talkies intrudes and an electronic door is opened. Here are the blue bars, opened to let us through. The world inside them seems, at once, an odd mélange of prison and preschool.

"Good morning, sir-ma'am! Thank you, sir-ma'am!"

The greeting comes almost as an assault, from thirty-six prisoners wearing blue T-shirts and standing at attention. This is the Rehab unit, part one of a ten-month program here at Changi's new Pre-Release Center.

"It is an integrated criminogenic program, what we call a therapeutic environment, for prisoners going home soon," says today's guiding officer, a man of many smiles and fervent dynamism. This is Asia's first and only such center, modeled after similar ones in Canada, the United Kingdom, and Australia, where I'd seen it first-hand, at Boronia. "It has to start here, not the day we boot 'em out the door," the superintendent there had said, curtly summing up the model's ethos.

Living here are 343 men in ten cohorts. In the two years since the program's launch, 530 men have passed through and all but 30 have stayed out of prison.

"Every time someone comes back we get a report, and it's a stab in the heart," the spirited officer had said, all sincerity. "My bottom line is my numbers. Must reduce recidivism."

The program consists of three phases, incrementally allotting prisoners more and more personal responsibility. Each phase is color-coded; the Rehab housing block is blue. It's a double-tiered unit with a shared hallway and common area, where a dozen shirtless men sporting an array of colorful tattoos are assembled at metal picnic tables. Black Vans sneakers are tidily arranged outside the doors of their cells, alongside a box for feedback forms, its instructions in Singapore's four languages: English, Mandarin, Tamil, and Malay. A lone telephone sits at the end of the hallway—banned in all Singaporean prison units but this one, because encouraged family contact is part of the prerelease program.

Cohorts, deliberately diverse in age and ethnicity—"they must learn to tolerate each other's quirks and idiosyncrasies," the officer explains—are run like communities, with their own disciplinary boards, elected leaders, and rules. Trained officers known as case coordinators oversee the cohorts and use restorative practices when possible. Instead of throwing the book at rule-breaking men, they figure out why the offense was committed and what restitution options are available.

"In my previous situation, a max prison, we didn't talk to inmates, let alone run classes," the officer says.

I scan the never-ending stream of quotes on the wall.

I will make it. I will make it. I will make it.

"You can be a model prisoner but a terrible citizen," the officer goes on. "Soon they will be citizens in society again. This program is about bringing them back to that place. Unlearning behaviors and basic manners, from time in prison and before."

He points to a rust-and-blue-hued painting. "*Storming the Past*. It is a maelstrom, and you are a ship who must find your footing. That is the symbol for Rehab."

We move on to Renew, across the room.

Ready for his opportunity when it comes.

There is no such thing in anyone's life as an unimportant day.

"Good morning, sir-ma'am! Thank you, sir-ma'am!" The prisoners at attention here wear green.

"Here is the symbol of this unit." The officer points to another painting. "The tree, the hands—this is the next step in the growth process."

Much of this process involves renouncing gangs, which in Singapore have Chinese origins and revolve around drugs, primarily heroin. Staff estimate that 40 percent of the men here are active gang members, and another 20 percent, sleeper members; our guiding officer is especially excited about the peer-led antigang program, in which prisoners sit in a circle and share emotional issues that led to their involvement with drugs and gangs.

"Prison has a lot of P's—programs," he says. "And this one has a nickname, 'The Mother of all P's.' The prisoners hate it at first. It is hard to talk about life, harder for them than punishment or caning. These are hardened criminals and they cannot sit in a class and talk about feelings. They sweat; they beg for psychological drugs. At the end of it they have the option to renounce their gang. Many do."

At the minimart station, I scan the color codes. Rehab residents are permitted basic purchases, via points acquired for good conduct: Milo, Oreo cookies, cards for their families, all stamped in green. Renew residents, closer to release, can purchase toothbrushes or reading glasses. Restart residents, nearest to returning to the world, are eligible to buy things like yoga mats, to help them adjust to sleeping on beds again.

Nizam, an Indian prisoner who stands with hands behind his back, is the supervisor here. "You may talk to him," the officer goads, after introducing us. I hesitate; detailed instructions from SCORE staff included a firm directive about not addressing any prisoners during my visit. Nizam, unprompted, tells me he's served seven years and has been in and out of prison eleven times. He'll be home in five months.

"I am grateful for this program, ma'am. I am ex-gangster, ma'am, and it's very different this time, going home, because of this program. I know myself now. I will apply what I have learned about responsibility here, ma'am." He bows his head.

Nizam wears yellow, the color of Restart. Their symbol is a cliff at sunset, and the men in their unit are assembled around a laptop, preparing for the graduation ceremony later this week.

"Good morning, sir-ma'am! Thank you, sir-ma'am!" Again, the assailing greeting.

A prisoner wearing small glasses shows off the PowerPoint they're developing and explains that his cohort will sing two songs.

"One is a Chinese song. The other is Bon Jovi. 'Living on a Prayer.'"

When it's obvious that the goals cannot be reached, don't adjust the goals, adjust the steps.

As we walk on, the officer explains that all wall quotes must be approved by a committee, and many appear in Chinese and Malay, as well. There is also a prisoner quote competition.

"And here is the winner, in Mandarin." He reads the Chinese characters overhead. *Love is a light that continues to guide you home.*

The yard area, essentially a massive gym, is designed to function as a community center, complete with a well-stocked library featuring English and Chinese novels, along with Buddhist and Hindu texts. Some men sit, chatting casually, behind a barrier labeled Responsibility, one of the center's five core values; others play futsal, a popular game that's banned from other prisons because it's a contact sport, but permitted here as part of the reentry effort—they'll soon play it on the outside. On the opposite end of the room a line of men are getting haircuts, also regulated by cohort, as indicated by a diagram on the wall. Rehab residents must get cuts in one particular style, but men in Restart can be cut any way, as long as it's short and neat.

And with that, my tour is done. Fee Leng walks me through long corridors, toward an exit.

The darkest hour is just before the dawn.

———

Later that week, still processing what I've seen thus far, I take a walk in the clouds. Singapore actually affords visitors the opportunity to do this, having created a "cloud forest" at Gardens by the Bay. It turns out to be one of the most awesomely beautiful tourist attractions I've ever seen. Surely, I think, dodging hordes of Korean visitors taking selfies in the sky, a country that manufactured a climate zone can fashion a flawless criminal justice system.

Not that it has an especially dire need for one. The number of crime cases in Singapore recently fell by 4.3 percent to its lowest rate in thirty years. Strolling through dark, enchanting Chinatown alleyways at night, I relish this overall feeling of security. I also recall my first visit here, seven years ago. It was a brief trip, for a conference, but one particular experience at the mall stayed with me. I'd handed the cashier a twenty-dollar bill; taking it for a dollar bill, she offered no change. When I objected, she asked for my number and said she'd ring me if, at the end of the day, the register was over. *Yeah, right*, thought the cynical New Yorker.

At 11:01 my phone rang.

"Ma'am, we have your nineteen dollars," came the voice on the line. I was flabbergasted. What would it be like, I marveled, to live in a country so law-abiding? The locals I'd been chatting with this time around had explained that Singaporeans are spoiled by living in an "air-conditioned nation" of first-world problems. A weekend shopping trip to Malaysia, Fee Leng had remarked, is enough to make locals appreciate home. "Sometimes we have to be reminded not to take safety and economic security for granted," she'd said.

The government engages in plenty of reminding, promoting a national narrative in which Singapore is an exceptional miracle of a country. "An island city-state could not be ordinary if it was to survive," writes the late Lee Kuan Yew, who was elected in 1959 as the first prime minister of self-governing Singapore, in his book *From Third World to First*. I pick it up at a local bookstore—Lee's works seem to be on display at every shop I walk into—and spend an afternoon on a bench by the marina, engrossed in it. "We had to make extraordinary efforts to become a tightly knit, rugged and adaptable people who could do things better and cheaper than our neighbors. We had to be different."

The odds were against him. At the time of independence, first from Britain and then Malaysia, the country had virtually no domestic market and poor education levels, and it relied almost fully on British handouts. Sandwiched between Indonesia and Malaysia, two much larger powers, it also had to manage a potentially divisive ethnic mix—about 75 percent Chinese, 14 percent Malay, and 7 percent Indian. In 1964 there were race riots. But under Lee's guidance peace prevailed and the country climbed from a per capita GDP of $400 in 1959 to $52,052 in 2012.

Lee achieved this by plotting infrastructure, creating an economic development bank, building industrial parks to attract American and European investors, and paying government employees generously so as to reduce corruption; all were part of his effort to merge the competitive spirit of capitalism with the group solidarity bred by socialism. Home ownership gives everyone a stake in society, so Singaporeans can buy spacious public housing at affordable rates, with a wait that's rarely longer than six months; residential quotas promote racial integration. Foreign aid was anathema to Lee, as was welfare; instead, community centers and citizen service play the role of brother's keeper. He also beautified the airport and city to create strong first impressions for investors, launched a green movement and a government unit to care for the lush gardens and trees planted, banned cigarette ads and, yes, chewing gum, and even promoted the end of "Third World habits," like spitting in the street.

Reading Lee's book reminds me of a connection I had forgotten between Singapore and the place I began my journey: Rwanda. President Paul Kagame has publicly stated that he modeled postgenocide Rwanda after postcolonial Singapore, taking pages from Lee's book. He created an attractive investment environment, reduced corruption, built infrastructure for a high-tech economy, and so on. As is true of Singaporeans, almost all Rwandans have health insurance and access to education. They live in lands of proficiency and productivity, lands where corporate-speak acronyms reign. Rwanda and Singapore are both grand regional exceptions.

And I also know there are costs associated with being such exceptions, such "oases" of social and economic stability. These include a resounding lack of social liberties, big scale and small; bans on things like plastic bags, in Rwanda, and, here, chewing gum; and a government-controlled press and curtailed free speech. "If this is a 'nanny state,'" Lee writes, addressing his critics, "I am proud to have fostered one." Later I find a playful local Web site mocking this nannyism, with a list of Singaporean characteristics. Number 42 speaks to the country's efficiency: "You get irritated if you don't see a sign telling you how long your wait's going to be for a bus, a train, or the expressway." But plenty of others parody the price paid for it. Number 10: "You've lost your ability to criticize people in higher positions than you, even if they're wrong." Number 55: "You agree that what the government thinks of your personal habits and lifestyle should determine whether you get a condo and how much you pay for it." And number 27: "You justify every argument with the phrase 'in order for us to be competitive in the twenty-first century.'"

This last one is especially mighty. Because being a miraculous exception means you also exist in a state of perpetual anxiety, always *this close* to becoming just like the neighbors. Fragility makes it easy to justify anything. Do you want another genocide? More race riots? Economic and political upheaval, as in Indonesia, Malaysia, the Congo? Then trust your government and don't ask too many questions, which might upset the hard-won social order you enjoy daily.

That evening, at the *satay* stands outside my hotel, I'm still mulling over Lee and this grand social compromise. I'm joined by two progressive law students introduced to me via e-mail by a friend back home. They run an anti–death penalty campaign here and will soon launch one against caning.

"That one will be an even harder sell," Damien tells me. "Singaporeans are so attached to punishment as a whole, and especially corporal punishment. And also they think caning is like the spanking that every kid here gets, growing up. They don't realize what it really is. We will need to use photos. Have you seen a caning? Do you know that flesh literally flies?" He shakes his head in disgust.

"The government, see, they point to the United States, when there's a school shooting or something tragic. And they say, you want *that*? America is like, democracy gone wrong. So if you don't want all those tragedies and that crime, keep quiet and be content with the status quo."

Fear is the most powerful instrument of social control. This is true in Rwanda and Singapore but also Australia and America— where it fueled the birth of mass incarceration to begin with.

But still, I say to Damien, the safety, the ease, the lifestyle. In Singapore one never has to, say, haggle with a taxi man, Uganda-style; all meters are locked and monitored. Even simple, daily quality-of-life gifts like that are hard to scoff at. He nods, appreciating the dilemma. And for several moments we eat in silence.

"I'm surprised they even let you talk to prisoners," Damien remarks as we part. I explain that I barely have, actually, thus far. In fact during my journey, the countries where I've had the least amount of contact with people in prison have been Rwanda and right here. This makes sense; prisoners are warts on the national narrative of engineered social perfection. They're disruptions to the well-oiled political machine, so they must be quarantined, punished, corrected, silenced.

––––––

I'm so far from working closely with incarcerated people here that I spend one afternoon engaged with mock prisoners on TV. They're actors in ads, like the ball-and-chain ad I'd seen in Thailand, created by a group called the Yellow Ribbon Project. A decade-old, PR-driven venture devoted to assisting the formerly incarcerated, they boast a scholarship fund of more than $2 million, a job bank with more than 3,800 employers, and more than one thousand community partners. They campaign to promote the acceptance of the formerly incarcerated in mainstream culture by putting out ads and billboards and holding regular promotional events, mostly during September, which is Yellow Ribbon Month. Over the years the YRP has staged concerts, film screenings, and fashion shows, published poetry books and music albums, hosted prison art exhibits, developed a cell phone app, and distributed millions of yellow ribbons for people to wear on their lapels, signifying support for the formerly incarcerated.

"We weren't trying to join the ribbon bandwagon—pink ribbons and red ribbons and such," Jin, YRP's marketing manager, tells me. The name was born when the CEO of SCORE was in a karaoke lounge about a decade ago, ruminating about a name for this new project. An old Tony Orlando song came booming over the speakers.

I'm really still in prison and my love, she holds the key
A simple yellow ribbon's what I need to set me free
And I wrote and told her please
Whoa, tie a yellow ribbon round the ole oak tree
It's been three long years, do you still want me?

The song is about veterans coming home from war, and the parallel seemed perfect: returning veterans and returning prisoners, both of whom have survived trauma and thus need extra help to restart their lives as civilians.

"We have a new campaign every September," Jin says.

"Why not year round?" I ask.

"Money. We're not Coca-Cola, you know? But when the ads stop running, we feed stories to the press." One opportune thing about government-controlled media, I think to myself.

He cues up several ads on the projector. In most, men are identifiable as formerly incarcerated because they sport tattoos. Physical manifestation of a criminal past, tattoos are popular in prisons and gangs here, and thus represent Singapore's supreme scarlet letter. Jin shows me an earnest, three-part infomercial depicting the life of a returning prisoner through different perspectives, including the eyes of a proud prison officer, a devoted prison volunteer, and a gratified employer. Watching the ball-and-chain ad again, I get lost in the actor's intensely wistful eyes. I must've peered into versions of those eyes dozens of times now, behind bars around the world.

"He's already served his time. But will you still be passing judgment?" asks one of the YRP's print ads, across a photo of a man leaving the prison yard. "To stay out of prison, all he needs is a break" is printed below a forlorn-looking man awaiting a job interview.

"We need this campaign in America," I blurt out, excited. I'm reminded of the ultra-hip "Truth" campaign, which markets against smoking and tobacco companies by way of flash mobs and funky, youth-oriented ads. I tell Jin about it, and also about America's Ban the Box campaign, which promotes limiting employers' exposure to criminal background information until later in the hiring process. Thanks in part to this campaign, Ban the Box legislation has been passed in more than fifty cities and counties, and several big chains, like Walmart and Target, have eliminated criminal history questions from their application forms.

"Although in America, by the way," I tell Jin, unable to stop myself from slipping into professor mode, "progressive people don't use terms like 'ex-convict' or 'inmate' or 'offender.' It's offensive to label someone by their worst act."

He looks at me blankly.

"Language is so powerful, part of this same process of changing people's perceptions," I go on. "I use 'prisoner' in my research only rarely. I hate that term, too, but at least it refers to a place, not a condition or state of character."

"So what do you call ex-convicts?" Jin asks.

"We say 'formerly incarcerated.'"

Jin bursts into laughter.

"'Formerly incarcerated'? If you say that in Singapore, people will not understand you. *'Formerly incarcerated.'* They will think you are saying 'formerly in castle.'"

He's still laughing as he cues up another ad.

————

"Furniture," says the taxi driver, after I announce my destination in the morning. "Nice furniture. Lots of them."

"No, halfway house," I repeat. "Helping Hand Halfway House."

"Yes, furniture," he repeats, nodding. "Furniture. From prisoners."

I didn't know this. What I do know is that my visit today is to one of Singapore's twenty halfway houses, born in 1987 as a Christian organization for ex-addicts but now open to all faiths and types of formerly incarcerated people. It's a Volunteer Welfare Organization under the Ministry of Community, Youth, and Sports, with Public Character status, which means it's a for-profit social enterprise, a marriage of capitalism and charity. And it's home to up to one hundred men, some serving out the last six months of their sentence, some having just left prison, and some simply walk-ins.

"Men there move house, also," my driver goes on. "Last time I move house I use them. I see the skin"—he pinches his forearm—"tattoos. First when I see them, I see tattoo and big size, and they talk rough, and I feel scared. But they do good job. And I say, it is good, they are working. Used to be prisoners but now good work."

We reach our destination, some fifteen minutes from the city center, with ease. I've yet to encounter anything beyond minor traffic on Singaporean roads.

"Open to Public—Please Don't Mind Our Tattoos," reads the massive plastic sign draped over a three-tiered apartment complex. "Everything 50% Off (Some 70% Off)." The sweet smell of mahogany wafts through the air. In the back portion of a vast parking lot, men in maroon T-shirts are shrink-wrapping lovely Indonesian chests, majestic grandfather clocks, and benches hewed from driftwood. Behind them is a room filled with sparkling vases and egg-shaped lamps tiled in shimmering shells. The CEO, an engineer by training, explains that the goods are imported from

Indonesia and prepped for sale by the residents. The place operates on four million Singaporean dollars a year, half provided by the government and half generated by the furniture and moving businesses.

"I myself was on heroin, back in the seventies," Richard, the program manager, says flatly, guiding me up the concrete stairwell for a tour. "Came to a halfway house for treatment, but couldn't stay off drugs. I went to prison. I came back here. Now I work here."

"How did you beat the addiction?" I ask. Richard spins around to face me.

"You know what kept me off drugs? Jesus. Nothing else." I balk silently. What sort of rehab plan is that?

Spare, neat, drab dorm rooms look much like those at Seralang Park, the work-release center. An old fan battles the dense humidity. Eight petite bunk beds sport Mickey Mouse sheets; there's a Garfield rug on the floor and a Yellow Ribbon Project towel draped from the bottom bunk.

The infantilizing decor reminds me of the prerelease center. It speaks to a certain paternalistic, preschool approach to reentry. A well-meaning approach, but one that also insults and belittles—as if all it takes to solve someone's gang or drug problems are inspirational quotes on the wall and some *you-can-do-it* zeal.

"It's nice," I mumble. Indeed it is clean and seemingly safe, more than I can say about many of the postrelease housing options where my New York students land. At John Jay College my colleagues did a study on them in 2013, exposing the growing market of "three-quarter houses": privately operated, for-profit, unregulated residences—small buildings that rent bunks, really. The report uncovered widespread building code violations, perilous overcrowding, and scandalously illegal practices like unlawful evictions and ties to shady programs billing Medicaid.

"Rooms are OK," replies Richard, with a shrug. He explains that men here must work and participate in life skills classes, dinners, and drug rehab; religious services are encouraged but optional. And many do as Richard did, staying on longer and getting a job here. Eighty percent of the staff is formerly incarcerated.

Richard points toward the aluminum louvers on the windows.

"We added those after neighbors complained. The men would stand in their rooms with no shirt, with tattoos out, and people would see them through the window. One man went to government and complained, saying tattooed prisoners are taking over the neighborhood. So now, after five p.m. men must wear shirts outside."

The whoosh of traffic from the highway just outside the door drowns out all noise.

"What sort of neighborhood is this?" I ask.

"Just, well, normal people. We call it Heartland. Some rich houses now, but we're no Marina Bay, no Beverly Hills, as you say. We just try to keep low profile."

"In America we use the phrase 'NIMBY': not in my backyard. Everyone wants prisons, halfway houses, homeless shelters—just not in their precious neighborhoods."

"It's not easy," the CEO interjects, sighing. "No one wants to fund this sort of thing. Orphans, old folks, yes." He holds his hands toward the floor. "Prisoners and ex-prisoners, we're here, at the bottom. Asian culture says it's a waste of money to rehabilitate ex-offenders. 'Why don't you help yourselves?' people say. 'You shouldn't count on others to help you.'" It reminds me of the conservative approach to crime in America, deeply offensive because it eschews social structures in favor of that naive "pull-yourself-up-by-the-bootsraps" myth.

After the tour, inside an air-conditioned conference room, four men in maroon T-shirts are paraded in to speak with me. The CEO suggests I interview them in private — "they'll be more free to speak without all of us here," he says. My SCORE government escort, though, has other ideas. He stays put.

The four men, all convicted of drug charges, scan the room with heavy unease. Kimsing, I learn, has been home for three weeks, and he wears the same forlorn, anxious look as the actor in the Yellow Ribbon ads. Son Keong, home for just over two months, wears it, too, and both seem mildly shell-shocked, giving me one-word answers and clearly hoping this official interview will end quickly.

The other two men, former residents turned staff members, are more comfortable chatting. Shan spent six years inside and has been working at Helping Hand for two years. Gary, who's been in and out of prison six times, has been sober for nineteen years now. He's missing a row of front teeth, and the few hairs remaining on his head resemble rows of gray needles. I pose a question I often ask students: What's your dream job?

"Dream job?" Son Keong repeats, perplexed. "I'm old. There's nothing left for me, no dream job. Just drug-free life. That is the dream."

"Be my own boss. In anything," is Kimsing's curt response.

Shan nods. "Never thought about it. Dream job? I guess, be my own boss...I don't know," he says quietly.

And Gary? "Policeman. Or run for office." He breaks into a deep-throated chuckle. "But never. I can't get those jobs with a prison record."

"What would be your political platform?" I press him. He stares me down.

"Singapore, our problem is not crime," he declares. "Our problem is *drugs*. In your country, you have a drug problem, you go for rehab. But here, we don't have rehab. We have halfway house. So we come here or we go to prison."

My government escort shuffles nervously in his seat.

"I'm not a criminal," Gary continues. "I do harm to myself, so they put me away. Prison is not a solution."

"Does it help at all?" I ask.

"No. And then we come home and they won't hire us. Only for labor jobs. Kitchens, labor."

"Do you find this fair?" I turn to Shan.

"Well, this is the law. I did heroin. I broke the law." Shan folds his hands on the table.

"It's the law, yes, but is it *fair*?"

"It's just—the law. I carry stigma. I go back, I get seven to thirteen years. I won't go back."

The government escort leans toward me.

"Why don't you ask them why they were drawn to gangs and drugs?" he says firmly.

"Bad company," answers Shan. "I had negative peer influence when I was young and joined gang." Kimsing and Son Keong nod in agreement, murmuring something about peer pressure and the wrong crowd. It sounds lifted from an afterschool-special script.

Finally, Gary can't contain himself. "Why did I do drugs?" he blurts, exasperated. "Drugs are fantastic! Have you tried it? You feel fantastic!"

I wait for my government escort to stop him, but Gary rants on, a stream of truth-telling.

"I say, legalize drugs! Why not? Because in Singapore it's a joke. There's no treatment in prison. Punishment, yes, but treatment, no. 'Just say no,' they say. A joke! Thailand, Malaysia, they have proper rehab centers. America, rehab. Here: prison and halfway house. Nothing helped me but finally wanting to change. But by then, too late. My life wasted."

His torrent is a breath of fresh air. The drug laws here dwarf even Thailand's in their severity. They have their roots in the nineteenth century, when containing the "deviant" behavior of Chinese immigrants, especially their lucrative opium trade, was a colonial priority. Today, drug consumption carries a mandatory one-year sentence for a first offense. There's a presumption of trafficking for relatively small amounts, like thirty grams of cannabis, and for those carrying keys to premises containing drugs. Officers can arrest someone for simply being in the company of a user, search "suspicious" premises and individuals without warrants, and demand on-the-spot urinalysis. In 2012 the law was mitigated and the death penalty is no longer mandatory for drug traffickers who are mere couriers, who cooperate with the police, or who are considered to have mental disabilities.

But in light of Gary's words, the law here appears even more acutely unjust. How can one punish when treatment is barely available? Drug rehab can certainly be a shoddy and unaffordable process even in the States, but at least options exist; evidence-based behavioral treatments have been shown to work, especially when combined with pharmaceutical approaches—methods like cognitive-behavioral therapy, which helps addicts recognize addiction triggers, and contingency management, providing incentives and rewards to patients who stay clean. In Singapore, on the other hand, what minimal rehab options there are might as well be direct pipelines to prison. Should addicts seek help from a doctor, that doctor is legally obliged to submit their details to the Central Narcotics Bureau. Once this happens, they're targets, closely monitored and subject to random testing for years after rehab. What user would seek help under such circumstances?

Exasperated, Gary takes his leave, along with the three other men. But as I'm collecting my notes, alone in the conference room, Shan returns. He looks around apprehensively, then speaks softly to me.

"Cluster B, you know, is worse than the old building," he tells me. "No air, no light—we come out pale because we are never outside, for maybe five, ten years."

I ask him if he's been caned.

"Many times."

"Which is more traumatic, prison or caning?" I press him. Shan doesn't falter.

"Prison. Prison is worse than caning. The pain of prison, the terrible punishment that goes on and on. And then, the stigma. Stigma. It never goes away. I am going to be married soon, I am staying clean and starting a new life. But still, the stigma." He shakes his head and repeats the haunting mantra. *The stigma.*

With every iteration of the word, I hear my students and formerly incarcerated friends. Years after they serve time, anyone can still find their names in an online "inmate lookup" system. If they're sex offenders, it's far worse; the stigma makes life all but unlivable. When Shan speaks I hear Mike, one of my students with a sex offense. He stayed in prison a year past his conditional release date because he was not eligible to live almost anywhere, on account of sex-offense housing regulations. Even some of the least attractive halfway houses bar people with his brand of crime. Mike's struggle, in particular, underscores what's so evil about this stigma: it reveals our flagrant lack of faith in the one-size-fits-all justice system we've erected. Because if we truly believed that people were corrected in a so-called correctional institution, we would not have to keep them on such a viciously tight leash once they exit it.

As Richard walks me out of Helping Hand, the sweet smell of peanut sauce drowns out the scent of furniture. Lunch is being served in the outdoor cafeteria.

"This place does good work," he affirms as we say goodbye. "We try."

Good halfway houses do try and can do good work. They offer strong wraparound services: intensive, individualized assistance in all arenas, from counseling and family planning to job training. They provide fair labor conditions, safe housing, supportive staff, and relevant programming. Unfortunately, on American shores this hardly exists across the board, which is why one 2013 study showed that formerly incarcerated individuals at halfway houses have higher recidivism rates than those living elsewhere. A scathing *New Yorker* magazine article the following year exposed horrific labor conditions, sexual abuse, and rampant drug use at postrelease homes around the country. These homes have no incentive to reduce recidivism because they're for-profit, and they mandate substance abuse programs that often interfere with tenants' education and employment, all because landlords reportedly get kickbacks from such programs. I once had a student lose several job opportunities upon coming home because he had to attend drug treatment at his halfway house, lest he be evicted—even though he's never had a drug problem.

I pull up this *New Yorker* article when I reach my hotel. I read again about the growth of private probation companies and what's starting to be dubbed the Prisoner Reentry Industrial Complex. It's a lucrative industry, with hundreds of thousands of people ticketed for minor offenses like failing to pay parking tickets, then sentenced to probation managed by private companies—who make millions. Major banks such as JPMorgan Chase, too, are profiting from the correctional system's use of prepaid debit cards, or so-called release cards, containing the remaining funds left in a person's prison commissary; unregulated, these cards charge exorbitant transaction and maintenance fees. Here in Singapore, reentry industries clearly abound, whether Helping Hand or the other acronym-titled organizations giving me PowerPoint presentations during my time here. All, as the CEO said, are indeed trying.

But it's Gary's strident voice that resonates in my head. Because he's really asking the same thing I asked myself in Thailand, land of similarly draconian drug laws. What is good programming in the face of people who never really deserved to be locked up—who, if anything, need treatment and not punishment? What does it mean to create a superb reentry plan for those who ought never to have had to reenter in the first place? The schizophrenia at the heart of Singapore's criminal justice policies suddenly strikes a painful chord. Punish these so-called misfits—but then, don't. It's as if the country's drug laws manufacture offenders, not so they can have the pleasure of stoning them—this was the old, revenge-hungry way—but so they can have the self-righteous joy of *rehabilitating* them. It all adds up to one more way to enact Singaporean efficiency: *Look how productively, how humanely we do reentry.*

The problem is, this performance demands a sinner, and today I met four of them. Sinners who feel more like scapegoats.

———

I affix the yellow ribbon to my white collar. Some fifty people are doing the same, milling about in the prison's antiseptic central lobby and gearing up for brunch.

Yes, brunch. Today is Dining Behind Bars, a Yellow Ribbon Project fund-raising event held several times a year, and the final activity on my official itinerary.

"Buses are outside!" comes the signal. We file in to be shuttled over to Cluster A. To the lustrous Changi Tearoom, actually, which has its own entrance, so we barely have to penetrate the land of barbed wire. A seven-prisoner band shod in crisp, slate-gray oxfords, their heads closely shaved, greets us with instrumental music in a room elegantly set up with red tablecloths and walls of prisoner-made art for auction. *Life Was Slower Then* is the title of one painting for sale; it's a placid scene of humble fishing boats along the Singapore River, in the days before development took over. One of the powerhouses behind this development is at my table, the senior vice president of Marina Bay Sands.

On cue, the music swells. Three singers in lavish purple vests make their entrance, sashaying toward the stage with microphones in hand.

"Tie a yellow ribbon round the ole oak tree," they sing, all smiles and snapping fingers. My tablemates hum along, bopping their heads.

One might imagine that by this point in my journey, I'd be immune to such bizarre, disquieting prison scenes. But you never get used to them. So when we're directed to line up for a tour of Medium A, I'm relieved to enter the real thing.

Except the real prison tour proves only slightly less of a performance.

"Do not call us officers," says our grinning guide in uniform, adjusting the yellow ribbon beside his name tag and explaining the new penal terminology. "We are *Captains of Lives*."

The officer leads us into a model cell, unoccupied, where everything is labeled: toothbrush, uniform, "modesty wall" separating shower from sleeping area. And, of course, the straw mats for which Singaporean prisons are famous.

"But why not give them beds? Is it not cruel?" someone asks.

"This is punishment, still," our guide answers. "Rehab, yes, but punishment. We cannot give beds to people we are punishing. They must sleep on mats."

The yard is essentially a concrete cave with a volleyball net, devoid of natural light. I pester the officer with questions about scheduling, and he lets out that the first tenth of each prisoner's sentence is known as the deterrent phase, twenty-three hours per day spent in the cell "to reflect on their action." After that, prisoners can be eligible for programs.

But which programs? And for how many hours a day? So much time in the cell, even with cellmates, is beginning to strike me as solitary by another name. Jobs, counseling, he says, waving me off. I press him for details, but he utters something about 30 percent of prisoners having jobs, then steers us onward.

Just 30 percent? And the others languish in dank cells all day?

"Good morning, sir-ma'am! Thank you, sir-ma'am!"

The salutation strikes again, as we don masks and hairnets to enter the SCORE bakery. A prisoner wearing a microphone headpiece presents the place for our inspection. We are halal-certified, and we make European-style breads and pastries. Here is the assembly line, and here is the UV light capable of detecting any foreign object that may have slipped into the bread, and also any defects.

It's intensely hot, and the delicious scent of treats in the oven tantalizes. How do these men bear it? Unlike us, they don't finish their stint by enjoying the fruits of their labor: chocolate muffins, éclairs, French bread—the bread served on Singapore Airlines flights.

"Our bakery has many corporate clients. The prison is also home to the largest laundry in Southeast Asia," the officer pronounces. "We serve about 90 percent of all hospitals. Forty million per year in revenue." Incarcerated men are paid a stipend, he goes on, and the skills training they receive is invaluable.

It's time to return to the tearoom and take our seats for the grand meal. Doors swing open theatrically; the music surges and the singers parade in, now sporting striped aprons and chef hats. A line of officers follows them, and more prisoners in blazers and bow ties. The first course is radish summer truffle with "beurre morne," followed by leek soup, then a delectable fish soufflé. All overseen by local celebrity chef Ryan Hong, who makes an appearance after the meal to take a bow and heap praises on his incarcerated trainees.

My table is impressed, and they rave about it. The food is divine, the Yellow Ribbon Project does excellent work, the prisoners are getting job skills.

"And the companies can stop hiring foreign workers," mutters a voice to my right. My ears perk up.

In 2013, I learn, Singapore had its first labor riot in fifty years. It revolved around the more than one million low-skilled foreign workers in Singapore. Never mind that they do the jobs locals don't want to do, went the chorus. The foreigners are flooding our gates; they're taking over.

I have a "no-duh" moment. This great government push to get former prisoners hired is quite simply about economics and politics, driven far more by practical aims than moral ones. In an economically booming country where an abundance of low-level jobs need filling, and where there's a long history of xenophobia, the attitude is, better to fill them with our own, even if they're "ex-cons."

The result is a movement and, conveniently, a labor force. Prisoners have been the backbone of Singapore's labor force since the country's inception. Like Australia, this was a penal colony. Between 1825 and 1867, 15,000 "convicts" from India, Burma, and Ceylon were shipped here to become, essentially, the public works department, clearing jungle, filling in swamps, and building roads, seawalls, and most of the country's historical buildings. They managed stray dogs and tended to gardens and cemeteries; despite vicious floggings, their labor conditions were touted as much better than India's—prisoners were paid at two-thirds the rate of free labor—and after their sentences, they were smoothly integrated into the workforce to keep the colony running.

I might be sitting in Singapore's brand-new prison, but it's actually uncanny how little has changed here.

"*Peace* has been sold to the gentleman at table two," announces the superintendent, marking the end of today's silent auction. All of the prisoner-made paintings have been purchased.

"*Sweet Innocence* will go to the woman at table one." The prison band segues into a final rendition of "Tie a Yellow Ribbon Round the Ole Oak Tree."

As we know, across the globe prisons have long been about manufacturing and managing labor forces. In America, historians argue, the beginning of the prison boom in the late 1970s coincided with a dramatic cut in jobs for low and unskilled workers. Prison was one method for dealing with a sudden surge of unemployed workers, by simply taking them off the market.

But should it matter *why* Singapore is promoting reentry and reintegration, as long as they're doing it? Would that America had a PR campaign around mass incarceration with as much impact as the Yellow Ribbon Project's. Would that we could boast of more top-level executives, like the VP at my table, who contribute to prison-related causes, let alone step foot inside a prison and commit to hiring formerly incarcerated people. And would that my students had a nationwide SCORE-like entity to find them jobs after release.

But still, Gary's voice resonates in my head. *They won't hire us. Only for labor jobs. Kitchens, labor.*

Resonating, too, is the voice of Jaden, whom I'd met earlier in the week at Tanah Merah, a high-security prison transformed in 2011 to a prison school. My tour of the place had revealed more of the Singaporean same: engineered progressiveness and kindly yet patronizing supervision. Murals featured starfish and lighthouses— "This symbolizes the prison school as promise for the future. You are the creator of your own reality," the officer read from his script. Daily life involves assemblies, choir practice, harmonica lessons, and evening tutorials; teachers are recruited from the school system for two-year stints. I even visited a multimedia hub, where a robot crawled across a massive TV screen and a prisoner wearing a cordless mike delivered a polished, well-rehearsed, TED-style talk about the many offerings here, including production work and "News Behind Bars," made by and for people in prison.

This was all heartening. Even if Tanah Merah has just 182 students, it's a place to learn, aspire, plan futures, pursue dreams. But then came Jaden. He was paraded in for me to interview, sporting a red T-shirt and Converse sneakers and looking about twenty-five. He's been home for two years now, and, letting off the same unease as the men in the halfway house, was prompted to deliver his spiel. I was in a gang from secondary school, he explained, wringing his hands. Got in trouble with the law for sniffing glue, cigarettes, trying meth. Crime.

"In America we simply call that 'adolescence,'" I interposed. Here, though, it's enough to land a teenager in prison, followed by the further trauma of reentry.

The superintendent reported that Jaden is studying building and construction and works in a gym, and we should be so proud of how far he's come. I nodded.

But downstairs, as we all exited the complex, Jaden and I chatted more casually. He asked about my students and my English class.

"I really want to be a writer, you know," he confessed.

"Really? So why don't you go back to school?" I asked. "And try to get published?"

He all but burst into laughter. "The shorts won't fit," he said. He meant it literally. In Singapore, once you drop out of school you cannot go back and wear that uniform again; you must pay for private education, which most cannot afford. This makes Tanah Merah an important exception—the rare place where educational options, and the chance to pursue *careers* as opposed to jobs, are open to prisoners and former prisoners. No wonder the men at the halfway house could not wrap their heads around the notion of a "dream job."

The injustice of it had struck me when I chatted with Jaden, and it strikes me again as I take my leave from Cluster A today. Shuttling former prisoners into labor stints, into bakeries and laundries and retail outlets, instead of affording them the full range of opportunities. It's an injustice reminiscent of my own country, where prison university programs like mine are a rarity but mundane vocational training thrives. Where even public universities have the right to deny people admission on account of minor or juvenile offenses sealed by the courts years ago.

The message is clear. You're good enough to work with your hands, but not with your mind. I will never forget the look on my incarcerated student Jose's face when I told him he might consider getting a PhD. It was the same look Jaden had given me this week, a look that said everything about the message conveyed to incarcerated and formerly incarcerated individuals for much of their lives. Dream jobs, higher education, chasing aspirations—that's not for *your kind of people.*

"Prisoner reentry is like building an emergency room to solve cancer," one of my activist inspirations, Glenn Martin of JustLeadership USA, has said. Once again I've laid eyes on a global Band-Aid. A supremely engineered one, from which there is plenty to learn, but a Band-Aid still. Onward.

8.
Justice? | *Norway*

Sorrow is inevitable, but not hell created by man.
—Nils Christie

*Love is an unfinished relationship. In its state of being unfinished,
love is boundless. We do not know where it will lead us, we do
not know where it will stop; in these ways it is without boundaries.
It ceases, is finished, when it is tried out and when its
boundaries are clarified and determined—finally drawn.*
—Thomas Mathiesen

*A true revolution of values will soon cause us to question the
fairness and justice of many of our past and present policies.
On the one hand, we are called to play the Good Samaritan on
life's roadside, but that will be only an initial act. One day we must
come to see that the whole Jericho road must be transformed
so that men and women will not be constantly beaten and robbed
as they make their journey on life's highway. True compassion*

is more than flinging a coin to a beggar. It comes to see that an
edifice which produces beggars needs restructuring.
—Martin Luther King Jr.

The 7:00 a.m. wake-up call jolts me from sleep. Climbing out of bed, I tear open the curtains. *Darkness.* Is it morning, or still last night? Norway in November doesn't know the difference. The minimal light here makes me feel as if I've landed in a world where it's perpetually dusk. Cloud-heavy skies resemble a mammoth down blanket, muting all colors, every now and again peeling back a corner to tease us with a hint of luster. Life has been reduced to three tones: icy blue, slate gray, dried-blood red.

Bundling up, I make my way to the tram. As usual, no one checks my ticket; public transport here operates on a trust system. Outside, streetlights are low. Oslo may be the fastest-growing capital in Europe, but as a city it doesn't gaudily announce its presence. The place is soothingly quiet, humble in its beauty. Waiting for my train, I browse the station's bookstore, chockablock with crime fiction, which is hugely popular here. It's ironic for a country whose melancholy, noirlike landscape is tailor-made for crime, yet whose reality contains so little of it. Norway is one of the safest places in the world.

That's why I'm here. If ever there were a utopia, Norway has a reputation for being it. It's an oil-rich, welfare society—top-quality education, health and child care are provided almost entirely by the state—with a long-standing culture of equality, safety, and communitarianism. Instead of serfdoms or a feudal society, Norway's economic life was for centuries based on small village units and local democratic self-government; nobility was abolished over two hundred years ago and there's never been a distinct upper class. Norway's climate and geography limited immigration, and cohesion was fortified by the country's uniform population. When agitprop filmmaker Michael Moore wanted, in his documentary *Sicko*, to depict a world that's the polar opposite of ours—the antithesis of America's capitalist, every-man-for-himself ethos, a Disneyland of social services and profound parity—he filmed in Norway.

He filmed, especially, in Bastoy Prison, my destination today. Nothing represents the Norwegian way like its prison system, which has adopted a "Principle of Normality" according to which punishment is the restriction of liberty itself, and which mandates that no one shall serve their sentence under stricter circumstances than is required by the security of the community. Criminologist John Pratt sums up the Scandinavian approach using the term "penal exceptionalism," referring to these countries' low rates of imprisonment and humane prison conditions. Prisons here are small, most housing fewer than fifty people and some just a handful. They're spread all over the country, which keeps prisoners close to their families and communities, and are designed to resemble life on the outside as much as possible. An incarcerated person's community continues to handle his health care, education, and other social services while he's incarcerated; the Norwegian import model, as it is known, thus connects people in prison to the same welfare organizations as other citizens and creates what's called a seamless sentence—meaning a person belongs to the same municipality before and after prison. Sentences here are short, averaging eight months, as compared to America's three years. Almost no one serves all his time, and after one-third of it is complete, a person in prison can apply for home leave and spend up to half his sentence off the premises.

The most highly touted aspect of the humane Norwegian prison system is the fact that it seems to work. Crime rates are very low and the recidivism rate is a mere 20 percent. Where else could I conclude my journey? I know what to expect; I'm one of the many believers ogling this system. Whether it lives up to the hype is the real question. Can Norway at last take me to that elusive thing I've been searching for in full, flourishing form: justice?

———

"Prison?" I ask two deckhands, after the train has carried me to the ferry and now I've boarded a small vessel hopefully bound for Bastoy Island.

"Yes," says one of the men, rubbing his hands together for warmth. He looks me up and down with arrogant blue eyes. "But sorry, it is only for men." Then he laughs. "Come, come, you're in the right place."

I look up at the masthead and notice that it's crowned by a dead, stuffed swan.

"We found it frozen in a block of ice, years ago," says the other deckhand. He wears a black ski hat and has a wizened, kindly face.

"It's creepy-looking," I say.

"You think so? Our mascot. You are afraid of criminals?" he suddenly asks. And, before I can answer, "We are criminals." I look into his eyes; they're laughing. Is he kidding?

"Really, we are. Criminals. Are you afraid?"

"Why would I be?" I shrug. I'm still not sure if he's joking.

"I am Wiggo," he says, offering a handshake. He's indeed a prisoner, serving a twenty-one-year sentence, the maximum in Norway, but he'll likely be out next year.

Cato, the other deckhand, is serving one and a half years for intention to commit a criminal act, though he insists he's innocent. He and Wiggo bring me to a vestibule to show me their daily schedule, posted on the wall.

"We work the six-to-noon shift," Cato says. "Then we go back to the prison and relax. Some exercise, then relax in my room. Come, you want to meet the captain? He is not a prisoner. The only one who isn't, on this boat."

Upstairs, the sturdy captain shakes my hand.

"You talking to those criminals?" he says, with a laugh. I'm lapping up this playful mockery of the scary-criminals mentality. There's clearly nothing to be afraid of here and everyone seems to know it.

As the boat sets sail I spy Bastoy, a cluster of gangly pine trees in a gray sea, stretching toward a gray sky. Inside the boat's small seating area, Cato sits down next to me and turns on the TV, flipping to the History Channel.

"Are you on Facebook?" he asks.

"You're allowed Facebook? And Internet?" I counter.

"Not while over there." He points to the pine trees. "But yes, when we are on home leave." I jot down my name on a slip of paper. For the first time since my arrival, a thin line of blue sky appears overhead.

"They say it is a summer camp, Bastoy," says Wiggo, as I leave the cabin to disembark. He is almost reprimanding me. "You will maybe think so. But no, it is prison. Trust me. We have our life stopped. Frozen."

I point to the swan. "Like your mascot. Frozen. Even on a beautiful island."

Wiggo nods emphatically.

"Back to the mainland!" he calls to Cato, ready for another run. Modern-day Charons, I think. Ferrying new souls across the river to the underworld.

It hardly looks like the underworld, though. Wiggo was right, it does look like summer camp. Or, this time of year, a calendar painting for October. Mottled leaves are falling on cyclers—yes, they're prisoners—and a horse-and-carriage canters by. Ginger-bread houses dot the landscape; they're dull yellow, with green trim and red roofs. I spy sheep and cows but no fence or barbed wire; Bastoy, after all, is an open prison, a concept born in Finland during the 1930s and now part of the norm throughout Scandinavia, where prisoners can sometimes keep their jobs on the outside while serving time, commuting daily. Thirty percent of Norway's prisons are open, and Bastoy, a notorious reformatory for boys converted in 1984 to a prison, is considered the crown jewel of them all.

A small yellow van driven by a smiling officer carries me to a cabin where I check my phone in, the first thing that remotely suggests "prison." Tom the governor—not warden or superintendent but *governor*—looks like Kevin Costner. He offers me a cup of coffee and we take a seat in his office, which, with its floral drapes, aloe plants, and faintly perfumed, cinder scent, reminds me of a quaint bed-and-breakfast somewhere in New England.

"It doesn't work. We only do it because we're lazy," Tom says flatly. He's talking about the traditional prison system, where he was stationed for twenty-two years before running this open prison. A fly buzzes loudly by the window as Tom goes on.

"I started skeptical. That changed quickly. More prisons should be open—almost all should be. We take as many as we can here, but there isn't room for everyone." Prisoners from around the country can apply to move to an open prison like Bastoy when they're within three years of release. The island is home to 115 men overseen by 73 staff members, but there's a waiting list of about 30.

"There's a perception that, 'Oh, this is the lightweight prison; you just take the nice guys for the summer-camp prison.' But in fact no. Our guys are into, pardon my French, some heavy shit. Drugs and violence. And the truth is, some have been problematic in other prisons but then they come here and we find them easy. We say, 'Is that the same guy you called difficult?' It's really very simple: Treat people like dirt and they will be dirt. Treat them like human beings and they will act like human beings."

He opens the window to let the fly go free.

"Come, let's take a stroll."

We wander through the forest, past grazing horses, a breeding area for birds, a greenhouse, and a barbecue pit where men can cook lunch. Prisoners live in shared houses resembling log cabins. The delicious smell of burning firewood wafts through the air, and South Africa's Robben Island springs to mind. Bastoy is the opposite of its doppelgänger: not a dark, evil twin but the humane edition of that prison-island hellhole.

"It's not about running a prison but running an island," Tom explains. This is a nature reserve, growing about 25 percent of its food. Most vehicles are electric and everything is recycled.

"Agriculture is a big part of our philosophy. We are humane, ecological. Animals have a social function, too, teaching empathy. Everyone works the land."

"Do you live on the island?" I ask.

"I commute by boat every day. I love this. No more driving in traffic to Oslo." He shakes his head. "I knew nothing about any of this, you know. I was a city boy. Now my life is so much restored by this place, this lifestyle. Just like for the prisoners."

Tom shows me a wooden church ornamented by a brass chandelier — "Norway is secular so this is more of a cultural space; the chaplain is more of a therapist than an old-fashioned minister," he explains. He also takes me to a gleaming supermarket, which sells premium cacao chocolate and aloe-vera juice. There are red phone booths for unlimited use, although Tom thinks cell phones and Internet should be permitted in all prisons.

"What are we afraid of? You can't kill anyone by Internet or by phone," he mutters.

I ask about stigma and reentry.

"In Norway, when you're released, you're released," he replies. "No big stigma. One guy I know spent eighteen years in prison and is now living in my neighborhood, a normal old guy, no one cares. You find this a lot. I have many friends who've been to prison. Norwegians are very forgiving people." He pauses. "Strange because we weren't always like that."

That's an understatement. This is the land of the pillaging Vikings and of the Nordic sagas, depicted on wooden friezes outside Oslo's city hall, which I visited the other day. The sagas are long tales of violence, murder, jealousy, and revenge, and it's fascinating to think that somewhere deep in Norway's past, a social tide turned and, as in Rwanda, a culture of peace and forgiveness came to triumph.

Over lunch, Tom continues to impress me with his progressive thinking. He explains that although the "conservative" party here would be considered liberal anywhere else, and in general the left and the right agree on the main threads of correctional policy, an influx of immigrants, rising xenophobia, and conservative politics lately threaten to undermine the country's progressive system and soft-on-crime approach. An anti-immigration Progress Party, part of the conservative-led government, is promoting a backlash against what's known as "naving," or living off welfare—NAV is the Norwegian Labor and Welfare Administration. In recent years a local newspaper claimed that 80 percent of Norwegians want stricter punishments, and a 2010 survey showed that a majority felt punishments were generally too lenient.

"It's your media that's also responsible," Tom says, biting into a slice of whole-grain toast with brown cheese. "American TV shows about tough prisons and talk about being 'tough on crime.' It influences people here. But thankfully that's started to change. All the bad press in the past few years from you guys has started to make us not take you all so seriously anymore. Especially in elections. In the political speeches, those biblical references by a secular country? And Sarah Palin? People are laughing and also crying—*this* is a country we want to imitate?"

I sigh. It's disturbing, the way media can make and unmake the problem. I say as much, adding that the culture of fear is to blame. I tell him a little about my Australian experience and the Murdoch media.

"Yes," Tom concurs. "Talk to people at a party and every— pardon my French—*idiot* will insist there's more crime than there is. Statistics say there is nothing to fear."

A study of home leave in Germany, I say, found that the failure-to-return rate amounts to a mere 1 percent.

"Exactly," Tom nods. "Here there were instances where prisoners committed crime while on home leave, but so few of them. You can't construct a whole justice system around one or two exceptions.

"I tell people, we're releasing neighbors every year. Do you want to release them as ticking time bombs? Is that who you want living next to you? Hey"—he puts down his toast—"have you seen the film about the Attica warden?"

Apparently a recently released Finnish documentary depicts a former Attica superintendent's tour of Halden, a new prison I'll be visiting later this week. They make a laughingstock of him, because where the Norwegian officials see rehabilitation and correction, the American sees risk and danger.

"He even looks at staff playing cards with the prisoners, chatting about each other's lives and calling each other by first names, and he is disgusted. 'That is not safe,' he keeps saying. But where are the statistics to show that it's a danger? How can you help the prisoners if you are not sharing, about you and your life and your kids? The men here know my kids, my address, everything. Why should I be afraid?"

It's as if Governor Tom were reading my mind.

After my visit, as I'm waiting for the yellow van to carry me back to the boat and to Oslo, a man with a chipped front tooth stands beside me.

"You are from America?" he asks. "You must think this place is crazy, huh?" Without letting me answer, he goes on.

"But if you treat people like shit, they will be shit. Why doesn't America get it? Funny, because Tony Robbins is so smart, and he is from America." He's talking about the self-help guru known for infomercials and books like *Unleash the Power Within*. The man lets out a nervous laugh.

"What are you doing here?" I ask him. His blue parka says ENGINEERING, so I assume he must be repairing equipment.

"Me? I am sitting here. I am going to see the doctor, because I may have to be transferred to another open prison. I am developing allergies to horses."

Oh—*he's in prison here.* I had no idea.

I find my own cluelessness deeply moving, because it means things are as they should be. He and I are two human beings. Like my meeting with the deckhands Wiggo and Cato, our casual, normal interaction contrasts starkly with the many prison interviews I've done over the years; it's a total erasure of boundaries between "us" and "them." Chatting with me like an old friend on the ride back to the mainland, he tells me that he once worked in oil and traveled the world, and although home leaves have kept him close to family and community, when he goes home next year it won't be so easy to pick up the pieces.

"I am hopeful, though. In prison, you can choose to see the sky or choose to see the moss on the ground. I look at the sky."

I do, too. For a sliver of a beautiful moment, the sun has dramatically emerged from the clouds and the world, in full-on color, looks wholly new.

———

An imposing fourteenth-century fortress towers over the cobblestone streets of Halden, a town in southeast Norway near the Swedish border. The air here is frigid, so I snap a quick photo of the bastion, then hurry from the train station to the taxi stand, where a warm car carries me into the mountains. I arrive at a more modern sort of fortress: a closed prison. It's marked by a twenty-foot concrete wall—no barbed wire, just the wall, which actually isn't a mean-looking wall but, obscured by pine trees and featuring a sloping, rounded top, an almost kindly one. I've heard about this wall. And this place, nicknamed the IKEA Prison because its sleek, modish style is said to mimic that of the Swedish retailers. Opened in 2012 to house 259 men and about as many staff, it cost $252 million to build and has been called the "nicest prison in the world" — usually mockingly. It's pointed to as an example of how Norway's so-called criminals get to live in a five-star hotel.

But why shouldn't a country that can afford it bestow restorative conditions on the people who need it most? Aren't prisons supposed to be for *correction*? I've already seen the photos and footage of Halden, but I'm still excited to lay eyes on the place. My guide, Lasse Andresen, a jolly little man who's the prison's inspector for operations and community relations, seems almost disappointed when I'm neither surprised nor appalled by what he proudly presents. Not by the absence of prison uniforms and bars, nor the gorgeous shared housing units, with their stainless-steel countertops, wraparound sofas, chic coffee tables, and long vertical windows designed to admit optimum sunlight. Not by the stylish prison yard, adorned with funky graffiti-style murals courtesy of local artist Dolk Lundgren; the immaculate gym with its climbing wall; the friendly prison choir, practicing Woody Guthrie's "Peace"; the knitted art on the wall, featuring poems by Pablo Neruda and W. H. Auden. And the magnificent health unit, home to a thriving medical staff and a plethora of drug treatment options, and the well-stocked library, where the book club is deep in conversation about a Norwegian novel.

But the gorgeous, private visiting rooms, stocked with condoms and lubricants—these do surprise and impress me.

"Big visiting hall, like you have in your country, is no good," Lasse says with disgust. "I see it in Belgium. How can families connect with no privacy? So loud and crowded?" I know exactly what he means, from my many hours spent in just such loud, unwelcoming prison visiting rooms. He points to the toys neatly stacked in the corner. "We try to do the best for the children." Then he swings open the door to another visiting room. Saying, "Let me take you home!" he reveals a massive mural of the New York City skyline.

I have a flashback to a particular New York prison visiting room, and the photos I'd take with my friend after being permitted our one hug goodbye. Every prison visiting room has a photo area, where a prisoner with an archaic-looking Polaroid camera charges two dollars for a shot of you and your incarcerated loved one, before a backdrop that's more fit for a prom than a prison. The backdrops rotate from week to week; I dubbed one *The Plantation* because it looked like the porch of a slave master's house, and the other, with its vivid cityscape, *Night on the Town*. That one looked nearly identical to the mural I'm looking at here in Halden, except this one is bizarre not for its out-of-placeness but for its sheer humanity. If we have to send people away from the very people most capable of "correcting" them, the people who love them, then at the very least, allow them some true intimacy. It benefits everyone, as one Minnesota study found, after looking at those released from prison between 2003 and 2007 and concluding that visitation significantly decreased the risk of recidivism.

From the passionate education inspector, I learn that Halden's promotion of intimacy extends to staff-prisoner relations.

"*Relations.* This is the basis of our system," she emphasizes. "I train officers to be firm and realistic, yes—not everybody can be helped or wants to be helped. But they must be open and sharing with the prisoners. When I see new officers nervously hiding their name tags, I know: You're not right for this job."

Candidates for the job must obtain a two-year degree from a special staff academy, where they study a mix of criminology, law, welfare, applied ethics, and social work. I'd visited the academy yesterday and been blown away by the humanity and depth of its curriculum. How to establish relationships with prisoners, how to communicate with them and see the person behind the offense— this is the goal of officer training, I was told. Officers are paid while they study and the job is considered a very good one, akin to that of a nurse or a teacher, with solid pay and generous benefits. It's such a desirable job, in fact, that 1,300 people were now interviewing for 150 to 175 slots. Learning that Norway trains prison staff in other countries, from Poland and Russia to Somalia—the governor of Halden told me he'd just returned from Namibia—gave me great joy. Better you than us, I'd said to myself, thinking of all the countries scurrying to import America's bereft model.

"I once met a nurse who works in a US prison," the education inspector says. "She told me there are 1,400 people in her prison. I said, 'How do you possibly take care of all those men?' And she shrugged and said, 'My job is just to make sure they don't die.'" She looks at me intensely.

"What is it with the American obsessions with risk? Norway is becoming like that now. Always another risk-assessment study. We had a prison riot *once* in Norway's history—why do we have to assess the risk of that? And spend money on riot gear?

"One time the authorities were thinking about making an ice hockey rink here, for the prisoners to have activity during winter. I told them I thought it was dangerous. They said, 'Yes, you're right. They might use the blades to kill each other.' And I said, 'Kill each other? When has that ever happened? I meant dangerous because they might get hurt playing the sport!'"

Looking at the clock, I tell my two inspector hosts that I could sit and listen to their progressive wisdom all day, but I have a train to catch.

"No, no," Lasse insists. "There is more to see. I will drive you to take the later train." It's the first time I've ever clamored to get *out* of a prison; usually I'm negotiating for more access to get in.

The sun is beginning to set through the pine trees as Lasse, slipping me a DVD of *Freedom: The Musical*, last year's theater production, walks me around Halden's perimeter. He clearly wants to show me every square inch of this place: the restaurant school; the luminous studio where Criminal Records, the music label, is housed; the high-end landscaping class, making lovely calendars featuring photos of their work; the gift shop, where I'm presented with a Halden cookbook; the print shop, with its flat-screen Mac computers.

"So, how do you like?" Lasse sweetly nudges. "What do you feel?"

What I feel, actually, is tired. Literally and metaphorically. Tired of prison tours, which leave me in the horrible position of ogling human beings. Tired of prisons themselves, because they're always sites of woe. I don't say this to my affable host, though. Instead I ask him one question. *Why?* Why would Norway spend all this money on this grandiose, over-the-top palace of a prison, especially when the country's other prisons don't measure up?

"I don't know," he shrugs. "They wanted to try."

They succeeded, I think. It's almost as if Halden is a statement, meant to provoke the world, just as Lasse wants to provoke me: *Look how we treat our criminals. Shame on you for not doing the same.* It's the opposite of the deterrence approach, which tries to scare people with atrocious hellholes — an approach we know doesn't work, anyway. Instead, Halden is Norway's way of boldly proclaiming its commitment to corrections over punishment. Of declaring that if the measure of a civilization is the quality of its justice system, Norway can be proud.

"Maybe we will not be able to sustain the upkeep, though," Lasse says. "Look"—he points to the Mac computer. "These are already beginning to rust. How will it look in five years?"

"I don't think it really matters," I reply. The conditions are material, almost symbolic. The real innovation of Halden, of Norway's prisons altogether, is the humane ideology behind them. *Relations*, as the other inspector had underscored.

As we drive to the train station, Lasse says, "Come, let me show you the prison where I worked for twenty-six years, before here." He points to a village prison, containing twenty-five people.

"And here is just like the town where I live," he goes on. "Small town, quiet. Houses all look the same." Suddenly, at the round-about, a car almost cuts us off.

"People drive so fast nowadays," Lasse scoffs, pulling into the train station. "So selfish. Only think about themselves."

His words ring in my ears during the ride back to Oslo. For two and a half hours I gaze out the window, lost in the vista and my thoughts. Norway's loveliness is of such a radically different sort than that of the tropical places I'm accustomed to loving. It's not peacock beauty but a soft winter wonderland, still and unassuming. The world has turned black and white, and I realize that I don't miss the color. Maybe, in fact, the world doesn't need so much color. Sameness need not be stultifying; it can be soothing, humbling, embracing.

And perhaps the essence of Norway lies in the beautiful evenness of this landscape. I've learned the Norwegian term *likhet*, which means both equality and sameness; the magnificent reward of one is born of the other. It's *likhet*, too, that undergirds the principles of justice here: you are equal to and the same as everyone else, even if they have committed a crime and you haven't.

There's another rich term here, *Jantelloven*. I first heard it from a woman I'd chatted with in Oslo, in the lounge of a trendy new hotel. She'd been praising the hotel for being bold and different and flagrantly fabulous, something people often shy away from in this egalitarian society. There's this notion of *Jantelloven*, she'd explained: a condescending attitude toward individuality and personal success. You're not to think you're special or better than anyone else.

"That's a wonderful concept!" I'd exclaimed. The woman glared at me.

"What's wonderful about that? It's a way of keeping you down."

The next day, during my visit to the staff academy, I'd brought up the conversation with the head of research, Berit Johnsen. All morning she'd been quietly wowing me with her ideas and stories, even given me a copy of her book, *Sport, Masculinities and Power Relations in Prison*. I'd flipped through the volume in awe; with its Foucault citations, complex gender analysis, ethical considerations, and political commitments, could this book really have been written by someone in corrections? Like everyone else I'd met in the field here, she was clearly a true intellectual; our conversation thus extended well beyond the realm of facts and figures and into philosophical analysis.

"I know what that woman meant," Berit had said. "*Jantelloven* can be a way of saying, 'Just stay in your lane.'"

"But," I said, getting excited, "it's also the perfect antithesis of American individualism. The selfishness of capitalism. All about me, me, me."

"That's the optimistic way to see it," she'd acknowledged. "Here, a poor woman does go to the same hospital as a rich woman.

There are state-run banks lending us money for education so we can all achieve education. There is something called *dugnad*, which is the tradition of volunteerism, communitarianism. We have a culture of work and labor, because work is your entrée to a welfare society. If you're not working, you're alone, outside society. To want to be a housewife with a rich husband is a foreign notion to us here. Everyone wants to work, to belong to the community."

Lately, though, she'd gone on to say, a troubling cultural shift has taken place.

"Now we have a generation of people who want to be celebrities. Be special. But not everyone can be a celebrity. Who will do the cleaning? Teach in the schools? Where are the Norwegians nowadays? Sitting in offices thinking they're exceptional. What we need to teach children is that being an ordinary citizen is great—it makes you part of something that's bigger than you."

A healthy dose of *Jantelloven* might be not just what Norway needs, but what the world needs. *Jantelloven* has no room for mass incarceration. Rife, rampant individualism, the stuff of which capitalism is made, is what undergirds prisons—the idea that it's all about me, over and above my neighbor, over and above my society as a conjoined entity. But if instead I value my community, my society, over and above my *self*, then I cannot cruelly punish another; I innately know that he is me and I am she and we are all in this together. My triumphs are not mine but his; her failures, her crimes, are also mine. This is our sameness. *We* are bigger than *I*.

———

On my final day in Oslo the snow starts falling. I don't mind the wet chill; the flakes paint an exquisite picture, dusting old buildings and brightening up shadowy streets. I sit in a seminar room at the University of Oslo, surrounded by scholars. Norway has a rich tradition of critical criminology, more deeply philosophical than the scientific, evidence-based research prized in US academies. Most famous in this vein is Professor Nils Christie, who'd responded to the introductory e-mail I'd sent him with an invitation to give a talk to faculty. I'd jumped at the chance. Professor Christie is my criminal justice guru. His work on restorative justice guided me through Rwanda and South Africa; his oeuvre, with its philosophical, poetic reflections on the nature of a just society, stirs me immensely.

"Tell us, Baz," he prompts, passing me a plate of gravlax and egg sandwiches. "What are your reflections on what you've seen here? And around the world?"

I explain that the trajectory of my prison journey took me from the broad to the specific, from rethinking overall concepts about revenge, forgiveness, and what "corrections" might mean, to more particular concerns like women in prison and the horrors of solitary, to the very practical economics of prison, in Australia and Singapore. In all countries, I found that prisons were, to echo the famous Mandela quote that spurred my odyssey, spot-on mirrors of the society that creates them.

I look down at my notes. I'd planned a long meditative talk about what I think I've learned in two years of global journeys, and that talk begins with three premises.

One, our goal should be the very simple one identified by Professor Christie in his book *Limits to Pain*: "Inflict as little pain as possible." As he so eloquently says, life holds no shortage of sorrow. We need not add more by erecting hells.

Two, it's incumbent on us to zero in on social systems over and above individual actions. Since their inception, prisons have been political and economic tools manipulated by the greedy, power-hungry few; from country to country, I've witnessed this reality. As South Africa, Brazil, Australia, and the United States have especially hammered home, our choices are thus conditioned by social forces, structural racisms, historical inequalities, even biology. In response, we must cultivate what British philosopher Jonathan Glover calls intellectual binocularity, which means thinking of ourselves and others as simultaneously subjects who act and objects who are acted upon, whose successes and failures are the product of manifold forces that have nothing whatsoever to do with us. That we cannot claim full credit for either our successes or our failures should both humble us and make us kinder. It should foster more talk of reforming structures as opposed to people.

Three, the burden of proof is not on us but on them. It should not fall on those who oppose incarceration as a response to crime but those who support it. Because if any other system had a 60 percent failure rate—that's the US recidivism rate, and in much of the world the numbers don't look much better—we'd dismantle that system right away and go right back to the drawing board. So the conversation ought not to begin with *alternatives* to incarceration; incarceration should be the last resort, used only when more successful measures don't work. Consider the American professor Michael Tonry's likening of prison to a medicine that cures one ailment while causing another. Also consider what iconic activist-scholar Angela Davis calls "abolition democracy." Like emancipation, which called for both ending slavery and building new institutions to replace it, the end of prisons is not merely a process of tearing down but of building up. "Prison abolition," Davis writes, "requires us to recognize the extent that our present social order—in which are embedded a complex array of social problems—will have to be radically transformed." This process involves "re-imagining institutions, ideas, and strategies, and creating new institutions, ideas and strategies that will render prisons obsolete."

Surveying the countries I've visited, such "re-imaginings" might be classified under three headings: before prison, during prison, and after it. Before is most vital. We cannot use the penal system as an alternative to social welfare. All countries must do more to address conditions that lead to crime, to prevent the need for prison altogether. To do this, they must, for one, reduce unemployment and inequality; it's been proven that countries with high levels of income inequality have homicide rates nearly four times higher than more equal societies. Norway and its welfare state is obviously a model here, but so is a term that's gained currency in the United States lately and has been put into practice in more than half its states. "Justice reinvestment" means spending the 54 billion that America spends on prisons on rebuilding human resources and infrastructure in neighborhoods ravaged by mass incarceration.

Ultimately, it's about acknowledging, as we do in health care, that prevention is worth far more than cure. Community policing and smart policing should replace repressive tactics like those in Jamaica and Brazil, South Africa and America. And when it comes to drug addicts and the mentally ill, the two populations filling prisons worldwide, we need to take radically different approaches in order to freeze the flow. Repeal the kind of mandatory penalties and harsh "one size fits all" punishments in effect from the United States to Singapore and Thailand—and even here in Norway, where I met one young man serving sixteen years for heroin use. Many US states have already begun this process, relaxing mandatory minimums and expanding judicial discretion to divert drug offenders. In 2011 the Global Commission on Drugs, a panel of world leaders including former UN secretary-general Kofi Annan, declared that the "global war on drugs has failed"; the essence of this failure is its focus on punishment, not prevention or treatment. The commission recommended some legalization, and regulation instead of prohibition. We should follow Europe's lead, particularly Germany and the Netherlands, countries I didn't visit because their successes are already so well documented; they focus on minimizing the hazards of drug use and emphasize health care, prevention, treatment, and regulation. And when it comes to the mentally ill, the approach should center on psychiatric hospitals, not prisons. As in the Netherlands, defendants should be dealt with by a multidisciplinary team including a psychiatrist, psychologist, social worker, behavioral therapist, and lawyer or judge.

When other crimes do occur—and we should not distinguish between "violent" and "nonviolent" crimes, since the morality of punishment is profoundly questionable with regard to any sort of wrongdoing—our goal should be to think restoratively. Here the lessons of Rwanda and South Africa are rich. So are the studies of European corrections, where only a small percentage of people convicted are sentenced to prison (6 percent in Germany and 10 percent in the Netherlands). Instead there are fines, mediations, community service, and suspended sentences, akin to probation. The Netherlands, where courts are required to give special reasons whenever a custodial sentence is ordered instead of a fine, uses "transactions"—by which a person who commits a crime pays the treasury or fulfills financial conditions or participates in a training course—and "task penalties," reminiscent of Rwanda's TIG sentences, involving a work order that benefits the community. Here in Norway there's a move toward using electronic monitoring in lieu of prison for all sentences under four months.

After this radical social reform, though, there will still be people who cannot live in a free society because they pose a threat to it. And people whose actions demand that they be removed from the community for a period of time in order to be corrected, and then make reparations. For this latter group we might create an entity that is so unlike a prison as to be called something else entirely—an intervention, perhaps. It will operate in some ways like the prisons of old, as a transitory space that promotes healing; victims can process their pain and assess their needs while offenders, held captive, address what they've done.

In the intervention we can finally confront the self and its poor choices. And therefore in the intervention will live all the programming whose therapeutic value I've witnessed in Uganda, Jamaica, Thailand, Norway, America, Australia, Brazil, South Africa. There will be drama, music, reading and writing, restorative justice seminars—in other words, genuine rehabilitation and "restoration," which, as Professor Christie notes in his book *A Suitable Amount of Crime*, comes from an Old Norse term referring to the rebuilding of a house's foundation. As the Norwegian mantra goes, treat people like humans and they will be human. Family visits and home leave will of course be facilitated and encouraged, and residents given as much personal responsibility and agency as possible. Interventions will be subject to systematic ratings and universal standards. They will be transparent entities, not hidden lands of forgotten people, because we cannot own our institutions without laying eyes on them. As in education, size and staff will matter most; interventions will be small, attracting the sort of superb staff and healthy environment I saw here and in Australia.

"It took a man like [Mandela] to free not only the prisoner but the jailer, too," President Obama declared in his speech at Mandela's funeral. Just as slavery dehumanizes the slave and the master both, a vicious prison system keeps staff and prisoners locked in hell together.

Few people should languish in interventions long; we should follow Norway's lead in keeping sentences short. A 2014 report from the National Research Council on mass incarceration in the United States concluded that more severe sentences do not effectively deter crime; a 2012 Australian report affirmed the same thing. A lot of correction can happen in a relatively little amount of time, after which wrongdoers can begin the process of restitution.

When wrongdoers come home, they will not be subjected to the lifelong torture of being trapped in the prison of their former selves, which is the ultimate denial of humanity. Like Norway and unlike America, we should not provide the public with an easy online system by which past mistakes become permanent scarlet letters; criminal records will be accessible to the justice system, not ordinary citizens. Like Singapore, we will promote hiring of those who've passed through interventions; like New York State we'll offer tax credits to businesses who do so, paying them more than the maximum of $2,400 that New York provides; like some US states we will deny employers the right to ask the criminal-history questions on application forms or in initial interviews. Most important of all, through ad campaigns, marketing, public discourse, and whatever else it takes, we will promote a culture that is not so risk-averse, but rather a climate of forgiveness and community. A culture that truly grasps these words by Russian novelist and former prisoner Alexander Solzhenitsyn: "If only it were all so simple! If only there were evil people somewhere insidiously committing evil deeds, and it were necessary only to separate them from the rest of us and destroy them. But the line dividing good and evil cuts through the heart of every human being. And who is willing to destroy a piece of his own heart?"

This is the ambitious talk I had planned.

But I don't give it. Instead, cowed by the presence of my guru, I offer some bland words about what I've seen in Norway and how unique it is, and how it lived up to many of my expectations.

Professor Christie smiles sweetly, as if to pat me on the head.

"Once I was invited to give a talk at Bastoy, to the staff and prisoners both," he begins, speaking slowly. "It was a beautiful summer day, and the island was looking its finest. The sea, the landscape, the animals—Bastoy resembled the sort of place where everyone would want a summer cottage. After my talk, I turned to the prisoners and I asked them a question. I said, 'If you were offered a home here in Bastoy after you complete your sentence, and you could live here rent-free for life, how many of you would stay?' There was a long pause, and the prisoners looked at each other, looked around the room, looked nervously at the officers. And then, from the back row, came a single cry: 'Never!'

"That is the voice that I hear in my head whenever I dare to think of Norway's prisons as humane. 'Never!' The stigma and the suffering lives here, too. It is harder to pull the blanket off our system because it's prettier, harder to push human rights issues because of our reputation. But this is not a perfect society, either."

I nod. This I concede. And I rattle off some caveats to prove it. Because race is much less of an issue here than almost anywhere else—the majority of Scandinavian prisoners look like the voting majority on the outside—identifying with the prison population is an easier feat. Like everywhere else I've been, prisons here are filled with poor people and drug users. The recidivism rate is in part low because even small crimes like drunk driving or intention to commit crime can land one a prison sentence, and such crimes generally have low reoffending rates. About 30 percent of the current prison population is foreign, mostly from Eastern Europe, and when it comes to them recidivism is indeed a problem, since they tend to return to Norway right after deportation.

At Halden, too, Lasse did apologetically show me the dreary isolation unit, with scratches covering its walls, as eerie as the ones I laid eyes on in Brazil. I know that although one day alone there counts for one and a half days of one's sentence, Norway places no legal limit on the use of solitary. And as for Norway as a whole, its history is hardly spotless. It may never have been a conquering colonizer like many of its European neighbors, but it did make reparations and public apologies for the fact that during World War II it willingly deported more than a third of its Jewish population to death camps.

Feeling more confident, I tell Professor Christie about the pottery class I'd visited at Halden. There I met several prisoners, one of whom seemed no older than nineteen and had three small dots tattooed below his right eye.

"This place is great," he'd said with a haughty chuckle. "The first day I got here I laughed out loud. This is prison? Ha."

The man next to him abruptly looked up from the mask he was carving from clay, an ornate imitation of Edvard Munch's famous *Scream* painting, whose original I'd seen at the National Gallery the day before.

"Really?" he said glumly. "I didn't laugh. I'm still not laughing." Then he went back to molding his *Scream*.

I share this story with Professor Christie. And I tell him about my New York students' first reaction to Otisville, with its rolling green hills and lavish autumn colors. "It's so pretty there," they say, oohing and aahing.

As Wiggo the deckhand had said, prison is prison. No amount of beauty, no flat-screen television, can make up for the profound loneliness, the isolation, the time-freezing effect of a prison stay. I suspect that in fact the young man with the face tattoos who claimed he laughed is, somewhere inside, crying. I'd sensed that he was playing tough, or that he'd bought into the hype: hearing the whole "Halden-is-a-five-star-hotel" routine often enough, he'd started to believe it. And even if this prisoner did indeed laugh, it's a sad statement. Because if prison is better than your life on the outside, what does that say about that life and the society producing it?

"You are right," Professor Christie nods.

I ask him how he feels about Anders Behring Breivik, the Norwegian neo-Nazi who in 2011 bombed government buildings in Oslo, killing eight people, then killed sixty-nine more in a mass shooting at a Labor Party summer camp on the island of Utøya. He represented the biggest-ever test of Norway's justice system.

"He deserved pain delivery"—this is Christie's signature term for prison. He calls it this because, as he writes in *Limits to Pain*, it "sounds like milk delivery": innocuous, natural, normal. "Pain delivery is the concept for what in our time has developed into a calm, efficient, hygienic operation," he writes. "The whole thing has become the delivery of a commodity."

Christie tells me that his country's treatment of the Breivik atrocity made him proud. The trial was handled in a restorative fashion, with every victim, including survivors and families of those murdered, having a direct voice in the courtroom and individually represented, by 174 lawyers. A five-member panel delivered a unanimous sentence of twenty-one years, the maximum for anything less than war crimes or genocide, which adds up to just under one hundred days per murder. Breivik serves his time in a Halden-like setting, where he's taking university classes by correspondence. His incarceration will be no different from anyone else's, its aim being correction. *If* he can be corrected, that is; we know that not everyone can. Surveys show that the public was overwhelmingly happy with the verdict.

"Most of all," Christie says, "there was no hysteria, no cultivating of hate and fear." Instead, the very values that Breivik's deeds looked to demolish—love, acceptance, diversity—were promoted in moving public events. Roses became the symbol of tolerance, left on memorials nationwide, and import tariffs were dropped to make the flowers affordable to all.

As in Rwanda after the genocide, then, tragedy here became an opportunity to build community, not tear it to shreds with vengeance and hate. It sounds like the opposite of post-9/11 America, when public discourse centered on payback and self-centered jingoism. Fear reigned and the government response was war; violence thus bred further violence. Such a response, Angela Davis points out, is a form of emotional abuse of us, the community. She calls it a crime of moral imagination because it asks us to sever ourselves from the suffering of others, thus "killing the moral and emotive dimensions of our citizenship." Why, she asks, "were we so quick to imagine the nation as the limit of human solidarity, precisely at a moment when people all over the world identified with our pain and suffering?"

I ask this about crime in general. What if it became an opportunity not to cultivate an us-versus-them mentality but an us-*and*-them ethos? Not a chance to engender separation from others but a profound reminder of how deeply interconnected we are, such that one person's actions have the capacity to impact so many? This, surely, is utopia.

For the rest of the afternoon, as the snow dances under streetlamps and the other professors one by one take their leave, Professor Christie sits with me and shares his ideas.

"Our job is to create a society in which people can be most wise. To create mechanisms for ordinary people to manage their lives." He speaks against kindergartens—they destroy communitarian spirit by making early childhood education a formal job instead of a joint civic task—and in defense of ghettos and small municipalities, where neighbors can care for, educate, and police each other, where progress happens during village discussions instead of formal meetings and elections. He thinks professors must write for newspapers and other mainstream outlets, and they must write plainly, in order to be understood—"write for your favorite aunt," is how he puts it. He breaks down what's really dangerous about drugs: "the fact that they're considered too dangerous to educate people about." And he describes Norway's annual Meeting in the Mountains, during which incarcerated people, prison officials, and professors come together on a retreat to ski, dialogue, and promote progressive change, in prison and out of it.

Through it all, I marvel at the relentlessly inquisitive mind of this eighty-six-year-old man. He still sees the world with a child's eye, perpetually questioning systems, structures, and ideas that most take for granted. For this he is a true justice hero. I'm suddenly struck by the fact that the opposite of justice is not crime or injustice. It's complacency. Complacency of the sort that made me embark on this prison odyssey to begin with. I realize now that what I was really afraid of when I felt myself get even slightly comfortable in prison was more than just intellectual inertia. What I feared was that I was losing my passion for justice itself.

I think of my students on the outside, at John Jay College. The classes I teach generally revolve around issues connected to race or justice systems, and at the end of the semester, after all those weeks spent questioning two accepted ideological systems, students tend to throw up their hands. "So what's the answer?" they ask. The answer, I tell them, is a question. I'm not trying to be cryptic; the reality is that there is no pat answer to the big questions around race and crime. Humanity is complex and contradictory; any system addressing it must be equally so. Our task is to keep asking questions, to continue unseating dogmas and questioning widely held beliefs. For the past two years, seeing the very same ugly structure in such radically different settings across the globe, from Uganda to Brazil to Australia, has been a call to arms. What sort of vile stagnation is this? How dare humanity be so lazy? I believe in the human capacity to innovate, to imagine, to create. Prisons are a failure of imagination in the most tragic sense of the term.

"I'm not confident that our system is good. We can always do better," Berit Johnsen at the staff academy had said to me. Her words struck a chord. Even in a quasi-utopia, there is work to be done. And in this work lives the very thing I've been searching for—in the *do-better* is justice. As love is an action word, justice is a verb. Justice is a journey. It is never static, never contented, never at ease. Justice is a movement; justice *is* movement.

———

Returning home for the last time, I feel my usual postprison paradox: alienated, alone, and yet, via the lives I'd trespassed on behind bars, supremely connected to others. It's the paradox elucidated by concentration-camp survivor Victor Frankl in his book *Man's*

Search for Meaning: "The more one forgets himself—by giving himself to a cause to serve or another person to love—the more human he is and the more he actualizes himself. What is called self-actualization is not an attainable aim at all, for the simple reason that the more one would strive for it, the more he would miss it. In other words, self-actualization is possible only as a side effect of self-transcendence."

I delve back into the world of prisons on my own shores. Two of my Prison-to-College Pipeline students are still missing in action. They'd come to visit campus when they were released but have lost touch with me since, despite their plans to enroll in college. I don't see their names on the Inmate Locator Web site, which means they—*whew*—haven't gone back inside.

Then I survey the world of prisons I'm trying to keep in touch with. From South Africa, Jonathan sends updates, letting me know that a new cycle of restorative justice workshops has started and that Gerswin, though he is doing well and remembers his conversations with me, is still inside and needs a lot of support.

Santos, too, writes to let me know that the Prison Visiting Project is thriving throughout Rwanda. What he shares about what he and the other youth are learning, visit to visit, tugs on my heart:

Never give up, continue to make our parents to understand that the reconciliation is a one way to build together a lasting peace in our country.

Trusting each other.

Have confidence that we can do it even if it is difficult to restore a relationship destroyed by the Genocide.

Awareness to the people to give forgiveness and to have a culture to ask forgiveness.

Young people should not be extremists but they must be correctable people.

We must not be slave of our bad history.

Having the habit of telling the truth.

Having love.

E-mails from Mara and André in Brazil, Brent in Australia, and Napaporn in Thailand let me know that progressive efforts are still under way there, as well. A package of letters and poems arrives from the prison book club in Norway, which they'd like me to share with my students at Otisville. But it's Uganda that offers the most dramatic developments. Just when I returned from Kampala more than a year ago, APP staff had e-mailed me a scanned letter from Wilson, my former student:

You are dearly missed by your writing class. Thank you for the time you devoted in training us in creative writing. We still write and hopefully someday you shall read a book written by Wilson...Very soon I am finishing my sentence. Greetings to all inmates in the prison where you work and the university students that you teach. Tell them someone loves and prays for you. I pray for the inmates in the prison there to change to better citizens.

The letter was signed "Bafaki Wilson Pastor Boma, President, Creative Writing Club, Kampala Remand Prison." Some days later, at 4:23 a.m., my phone rang: "Unknown," said caller ID.

"Good day to you, Baz!" It was Wilson. I didn't ask how he'd managed to call me from prison, but I did offer words of encouragement: *Six months until freedom.*

Months later, after I'd returned from Brazil, the phone again rang obscenely early. "Baz!" exclaimed Wilson. He was crying. "I am overcome with emotion, Baz. After three years and two months I am free."

He also had a home. In the nick of time, my friend Al—the same friend who was persistently puzzled by my commitment to prisoners—had given Wilson money for a month's rent. And now, after my return from Norway, Al calls to tell me he wants to start a reentry program, connecting incarcerated people to jobs on the outside. The news stuns me to the point of tears. Because it's evidence that change can come person by person, consciousness by consciousness—and not from me, from the foreign *mzungu* agent, but from within.

The news also sums up why I remain a tenacious optimist. My journey has taken me to global hellholes, and being a witness there has changed me irrevocably. It's made me a far better teacher, enabling me to connect the dots and map injustice from one side of the world to another. But it's also fortified my rage and deepened my grave fits of depression. I've witnessed humanity at its worst.

At the same time, from country to country, prison to prison, I've glimpsed humanity at its very best. I've seen the broken systems but also the beautiful people who endure and transcend them, along with the game changers laboring to correct them. Against the dismal backdrop of such evil, heroes shine that much more radiantly. Psychologist Philip Zimbardo writes that, as opposed to Hannah Arendt's banality of evil, we should consider the banality of heroism, which makes "heroism an egalitarian attribute of human nature rather than a rare feature of the elect few."

The banality of heroism is why, when people ask what they can do about the seemingly insurmountable problem of mass incarceration and mass injustice, beyond donating to organizations or showing up at rallies, I offer simple advice: Be conscious. Learn about the problems and the solutions. Then spread the word, to anyone who'll listen—whether it's your friend, your bus driver, the random person you chat with on a street corner. You're an educator if you want to be. And you never know when some small progressive seed you plant in another's mind will sprout and flourish and produce change, just as it did in the case of my friend Al, whom I'd managed to impact without even meaning to, somewhere in the midst of our sightseeing and reggae listening. Changing policy is what will ultimately change reality, yes—but changed policy is a product of changed public consciousness. We all have a hand in that mission.

I hadn't been in Norway very long but still, I noticed on my return that the world had changed slightly for the better in my absence. Three New York colleges agreed to drop questions about past arrests from their admissions procedures. The ACLU received the largest grant in its history and will use it on a campaign to slash incarceration rates. Entering his final months in office, US attorney general Eric Holder, who had months before announced that President Obama would use executive pardon power to release thousands of federal prisoners with drug convictions, made more statements against mass incarceration and called for an expansion of alternatives; former US president Bill Clinton admitted to a group of officials that "a very significant percentage of serious crimes in this country are committed by a very small number" of criminals, but "we took a shotgun to it and just sent everybody to jail for too long." On Election Day in 2014—during which an estimated 5.85 million Americans were unable to vote because of felony convictions—Proposition 47 passed in California, downgrading nonviolent felonies like shoplifting and drug possession to misdemeanors and making up to ten thousand people eligible for early release from prison.

It's enough to make me hopeful that progress in prison reform might continue. Even the right wing has joined the antiprison movement, after all, citing costs as their main rationale. Bill Bennett, Jeb Bush, and Newt Gingrich are among the members of Right On Crime, a national movement of conservatives whose vision of criminal justice reform includes fiscal discipline and cost-effective methods to reduce recidivism while empowering victims. In Republican-controlled Texas, it was projected in 2007 that over 17,000 new prison beds, at a cost of $2 billion, would need to be built by 2012; legislators instead allocated a smaller amount to expand community-based options such as probation, problem-solving courts, and evidence-based drug treatment. Crime dropped by 25 percent and the prison beds were no longer needed.

On these shores, we might begin to imagine that the prison era is on the verge of extinction, and history will place it alongside the stocks and the guillotine as another brutal experiment in punishment that's had its time.

But the reality is that tinkering with the system—a little change here, a bit of reform there—is not likely to produce the "revolution in values" that Martin Luther King called for, in a rousing speech delivered one year to the day before his assassination. History has shown that racist, classist social structures have a way of stubbornly persisting by shape-shifting, just as Jim Crow was reborn when mass incarceration made "felon" the new "colored." An economic argument cannot substitute for a moral one. Doing the right thing for the wrong reasons is not the path to lasting change and greater justice.

And ultimately, the picture is bigger than America is. While we may be starting to slay our demons here in the United States, we have created a monster with tentacles entrenched in communities across the globe: peculiar institutions speaking manifold languages from sea to shining sea. We've exported a bereft system to the world. Such is the manic-depressive nature of prison history, marked by progress and regress, then progress yet again. It's the nature of this work as a whole, too. For every student who begins college in the fall, another is on the verge of being rearrested. March forward, step back.

The key is to keep marching. Justice work is ultimately a grand redundancy, restlessly demanding more of itself: more labor, more movement, more struggle, more victories and losses. And that work is powered by the potent thing I strap on daily, like a life vest, the thing that buoys me and keeps my spirit alive with mission and meaning: hope.

Acknowledgments

Two of the most beautiful words in the world are these: *Thank you.*

It is my honor to dole them out:

To John Jay College of Criminal Justice for supporting both this book and the Prison-to-College Pipeline, every step of the way. To the Office for the Advancement of Research and the English Department for critical travel and research grants, without which I could not have written this book. To wonderful English Department chairs Allison Pease and Valerie Allen. To President Jeremy Travis and Provost Jane Bowers, whose backing and encouragement have been gracious and immense.

To the Prisoner Reentry Institute at John Jay College of Criminal Justice, home to the Prison-to-College Pipeline and a stellar group of activist-scholars whom I'm proud to call colleagues and collaborators-in-justice: Bianca Van Heydoorn, Ann Jacobs, Daonese Johnson-Colon, Krystlelynn Caraballo, and Maja Olesen. To Superintendent Kathleen Gerbing, Deputy Superintendent

Alicia Smith-Roberts, and the staff at Otisville Correctional Facility for making the Prison-to-College Pipeline possible.

To the world-changing prison activists around the globe with whom I've been privileged to collaborate, whose work inspires me daily: Dukuzumuremyi Albert (Santos), Eric Mahoro, Brent Bell, Jocemara Rodrigues da Silva, André Kehdi, Dr. Napaporn, Pastor Jonathan Clayton, Yvonne Lloyd, Carla Gulotta, Brian Steels, Nils Christie, Lasse Andresen, Tom Eberhardt. Likewise, to my brilliant comrades on American shores: Bianca Van Heydoorn, Kirk James, Marlon Peterson, Jeff Aubry, Ali Knight, Debbie Mukamal, Khalil Cumberbatch, Glenn Martin, Vivian Nixon, Soffiyah Elijah, and Todd Clear.

To all of the individuals behind bars in the nine countries I visited, who graciously shared their stories, writing, and spirits with me, and who permitted me to be their student instead of vice versa.

To the organizations who graciously hosted me and/or assisted with access behind bars: the African Prisons Project, Never Again Rwanda, Hope Prison Ministries, the Kamlangji Project, the Yellow Ribbon Project, the Singapore Prison Service, SCORE, Thailand's Ministry of Justice and Office of Justice Affairs, Curtin University, Brazil's Rehabilitation Through Reading program and National Prison Department, and the Norwegian Correctional Service. And to Gary Hill for some critical introductions in this regard.

To the editor par excellence—and sheer force of a human being—that is Judith Gurewich, for standing by this book from the moment she heard of it.

To my indefatigable agent, Sarah Levitt, who persistently believed in the importance of this project and my ability to complete it.

To my editor, Anjali Singh, whose eagle eye and patient hand made this book vastly better than it was.

To my brother Malik Yoba and my sister Beth Skipp, whose love sustains me on a daily basis, whose bond with me runs deeper than biology ever could.

To my brilliant, fierce inspiration of a mentor and mother-sister, Lynda Obst.

To my dear friends who are really my family—my soul brothers and sisters, liming partners, ever-willing shoulders and ears, intellectual sounding boards: Lynn Joseph, Penny Vlagopoulos, Kirk James, Jeffrey OG Ogbar, Jeanille Bonterre, Jackie Simmons, Debbie Sonu, Monika Levy, Helene Sola, Vitoria Setta, Trish Perkins, Tommy Smith, Sanjay Ramanand, Richard Perez, Oscar Michelin, Ornella Schneider, Anya Ayoung-Chee, Natasha Ali, LisaMarie Stewart, Karibi Fubara, Joanne Kehl, Andy Kasrils, Jessie Ben-Ami, Sean Field, Jama Adams, Hank Willis Thomas, Andre Honore, Anand Vaidya, Audrey Moore, Donna Augustin, Carleene Samuels, Daniel Kramer, Edrick Browne, Nathaniel Quinn, Yadi Perez-Hazel, Clinton Hazel, Jonathan Gray, Perry Salzhauer, and Luigi Moxam. And to Keith Sharman for the early reads and ceaseless encouragement.

To my Dreisinger sisters: Tam, Naomi, Riv, Sar. And to my parents, who raised me to never stop asking the most important question of all: *Why?*

Finally, to the islands in the Caribbean—especially Jamaica and Trinidad—which sustain my soul, spirit, and intellect. Thank you for keeping my heart wide open, as it should be.

Bibliography

Introduction

Adler School Institute on Public Safety and Social Justice. *White Paper on Broken Logic: The Over-Reliance on Incarceration in the United States*. Chicago, 2011.

Alexander, Michelle. *The New Jim Crow: Mass Incarceration in the Age of Colorblindness*. New York: New Press, 2012.

American Civil Liberties Union. "Prisoners' Rights." Accessed January 15, 2015. aclu.org/issues/prisoners-rights

Blackmon, Douglas A. *Slavery by Another Name: The Re-Enslavement of Black Americans from the Civil War to World War II*. New York: Doubleday, 2009.

Butler, Paul. *Let's Get Free: A Hip-Hop Theory of Justice*. New York: New Press, 2009.

Clear, Todd R. *Imprisoning Communities: How Mass Incarceration Makes Disadvantaged Neighborhoods Worse*. New York: Oxford University Press, 2007.

Clear, Todd R., and Natasha A. Frost. *The Punishment Imperative: The Rise and Failure of Mass Incarceration in America*. New York: New York University Press, 2014.

Conover, Ted. *Newjack: Guarding Sing Sing*. New York: Doubleday, 2010.

Cusac, Marie-Ann. *Cruel and Unusual: The Culture of Punishment in America*. New Haven: Yale University Press, 2009.

Davis, Angela Y. *Are Prisons Obsolete?* New York: Seven Stories Press, 2003.

_____. *The Prison Industrial Complex*. Audio CD. Oakland, CA: Ak Press, July 1, 2001.

Dilts, Andrew. *Punishment and Inclusion: Race, Membership, and the Limits of American Liberalism*. New York: Fordham University Press, 2014.

Drucker, Ernest. *A Plague of Prisons: The Epidemiology of Mass Incarceration in America*. New York: New Press, 2013.

Garland, David. *The Culture of Control: Crime and Social Order in Contemporary Society*. Chicago: University of Chicago Press, 2002.

_____. *Peculiar Institution: America's Death Penalty in an Age of Abolition*. New York: Harvard University Press, 2010.

_____. *Punishment and Modern Society: A Study in Social Theory*. Chicago: University of Chicago Press, 1993.

Gilmore, Ruth. *Golden Gulag: Prisons, Surplus, Crisis, and Opposition in Globalizing California*. Los Angeles: University of California Press, 2007.

Glazek, Christopher. "Raise the Crime Rate." *n+1*, Winter 2012.

Gonnerman, Jennifer. "Before the Law." *New Yorker*, October 6, 2014.

Gopnik, Adam. "The Caging of America." *New Yorker*, January 30, 2012.

Herivel, Tara, and Paul Wright, eds. *Prison Nation: The Warehousing of America's Poor*. New York: Routledge, 2003.

Human Rights Watch. "Human Rights Watch Daily Brief." April 2, 2015. hrw.org/the-day-in-human-rights

International Centre for Prison Studies. "International Centre for Prison Studies." 1997. Accessed February 11, 2015. prisonstudies.org

International Penal and Penitentiary Foundation. "International Penal and Penitentiary Foundation." Accessed April 5, 2015. international penalandpenitentiaryfoundation.org

Jacobsen, Dennis A. *Doing Justice: Congregations and Community Organizing*. Minneapolis: Fortress Press, 2001.

James, Joy, ed. *States of Confinement: Policing, Detention, and Prisons*. New York: Palgrave Macmillan, 2002.

Kerby, Sophia. "The Top 10 Most Startling Facts About People of Color and Criminal Justice in the United States: A Look at the Racial Disparities Inherent in Our Nation's Criminal-Justice System." *Center for American Progress*. March 13, 2012. Accessed March 20, 2015. americanprogress.org/issues/race/news/2012/03/13/11351 /the-top-10-most-startling-facts-about-people-of-color-and -criminal-justice-in-the-united-states/

Marshall Project. "The Marshall Project." May 3, 2015. Accessed May 3, 2015. themarshallproject.org

Morris, Norval, and David J. Rothman. *The Oxford History of the Prison: The Practice of Punishment in Western Society*. New York: Oxford University Press, 1998.

Moskos, Peter. *In Defense of Flogging*. New York: Basic Books, 2013.

Nagel, Mechthild, and Seth N. Asumah, eds. *Prisons and Punishment: Reconsidering Global Penality*. Trenton, NJ: Africa World Press, 2007.

Penal Reform International. "Penal Reform International." Accessed February 1, 2015. penalreform.org

Perkinson, Robert. *Texas Tough: The Rise of America's Prison Empire*. New York: Henry Holt, 2010.

Place, Vanessa. *The Guilt Project: Rape, Morality, and Law*. New York: Other Press, 2009.

Porter, Eduardo. "In the U.S., Punishment Comes Before the Crimes." *New York Times*, April 29, 2014.

Rideau, Wilbert. "When Prisoners Protest." *New York Times*, July 16, 2013.

Rodriguez, Dylan. *Forced Passages: Imprisoned Radical Intellectuals and the U.S. Prison Regime*. Minneapolis: University of Minnesota Press, 2006.

Roth, Michael P. *Prisons and Prison Systems: A Global Encyclopedia*. Westport, CT: Greenwood, 2006.

Schlosser, Eric. "The Prison-Industrial Complex." *Atlantic*, December 1998.

Sentencing Project. "The Sentencing Project." Accessed April 4, 2015. sentencingproject.org

Shannon, Sarah, and Chris Uggen. "Visualizing Punishment." *Society Pages*, February 1, 2013. Accessed February 1, 2013. thesocietypages .org/papers/visualizing-punishment

Smith, Caleb. *The Prison and the American Imagination*. New Haven: Yale University Press, 2009.

Stageman, David L., Robert Riggs, Jonathan Gordon, and Ethiraj G. Dattatreyan. "Moving the Needle on Justice Reform: A Report on the American Justice Summit 2014" (PDF). John Jay College of Criminal Justice / CUNY Graduate Center. New York: Tina Brown Live Media, 2014.

Sudbury, Julia. *Global Lockdown: Race, Gender, and the Prison-Industrial Complex*. New York: Routledge, 2004.

Thompson, Heather Ann. "Why Mass Incarceration Matters: Rethinking Crisis, Decline, and Transformation in Postwar American History." *Journal of American History* 97, no. 3 (2010): 703–34.

Wehr, Kevin, and Elyshia Aseltine. *Beyond the Prison Industrial Complex: Crime and Incarceration in the 21st Century*. New York: Routledge, 2013.

Wolfers, Justin, David Leonhardt, and Kevin Quealy. "1.5 Million Missing Black Men." *New York Times*, April 5, 2015.

1. Revenge and Reconciliation: Rwanda

Beyond Conviction. DVD produced by Jedd Wider, Todd Wider, and Megan Park, directed by Rachel Libert. Via Buksbazen, 2006.

Boonin, David. *The Problem of Punishment*. New York: Cambridge University Press, 2008.

Gilligan, James. *Violence: Reflections on a National Epidemic*. New York: Vintage Books, 1997.

Golash, Deirdre. *The Case Against Punishment: Retribution, Crime Prevention, and the Law*. New York: New York University Press, 2006.

Gourevitch, Philip. *We Wish to Inform You That Tomorrow We Will Be Killed with Our Families: Stories from Rwanda.* New York: Macmillan, 1999.

Hatzfeld, Jean. *Machete Season: The Killers in Rwanda Speak.* New York: Farrar, Straus and Giroux, 2005.

Minow, Martha. *Between Vengeance and Forgiveness: Facing History After Genocide and Mass Violence.* Boston: Beacon, 1998.

Rwanda. "Kampala Declaration on Prison Conditions in Africa." May 1, 2015. Accessed May 1, 2015. penalreform.org/wp-content/uploads/2013/06/rep-1996-kampala-declaration-en.pdf

Seneca. *Moral and Political Essays.* Edited by J. F Procope, translated by John M. Cooper. New York: Cambridge University Press, 1995.

Staub, Ervin. *The Roots of Evil: The Origins of Genocide and Other Group Violence.* New York: Cambridge University Press, 1992.

Tertsakian, Carina. *Le Château: The Lives of Prisoners in Rwanda.* New York: Arves Books, 2008.

Tutu, Desmond. *No Future Without Forgiveness.* New York: Doubleday, 1999.

Whitworth, Wendy A. *We Survived: Genocide in Rwanda: 28 Personal Testimonies.* New York: Quill Press, 2006.

2. Sorry: South Africa

Arendt, Hannah. *The Human Condition.* 2nd ed. Chicago: University of Chicago Press, 1998.

Drabinski, John E. "Race, Apology, and Ani DiFranco" (blog). December 30, 2013. hutchinscenter.fas.harvard.edu/news/hutchins/john-drabinski-race-apology-and-ani-difranco

Enright, Robert D., and Bruce A. Kittle. "The Meeting of Moral Development and Restorative Justice." *Fordham Urban Law Journal* 7, no. 4 (1999): 337–48.

Gobodo-Madikizela, Pumla. *A Human Being Died that Night: A South African Woman Confronts the Legacy of Apartheid.* New York: Houghton Mifflin Harcourt, 2004.

Griswold, Charles. *Forgiveness: A Philosophical Exploration*. New York: Cambridge University Press, 2007.

Harvard University Department of Sociology. "Boston Reentry Study." January 27, 2014. Accessed April 2015. asca.net/system/assets /attachments/6214/D%20-%20Boston%20Reentry%20Study%20 Summary%20Overview.pdf?1375990136

Kelln, Brad R. C., and John H. Ellard. "An Equity Theory Analysis of the Impact of Forgiveness and Retribution on Transgressor Compliance." *Sage Journal of Personality and Social Psychology* 25 (1999): 864–72.

Lawrence, Ed, and C. R. Snyder. "Forgiving: Coping with Stress: Effective People and Process." *Journal of Family Therapy*, 2001, 50–62.

Loury, Glenn. "A Nation of Jailers." *CATO Unbound: A Journal of Debate*, March 11, 2009. Accessed April 2015. cato-unbound .org/2009/03/11/glenn-loury/nation-jailers

Orcutt, Holly K., Scott M. Pickett, and E. Brooke Pope. "Experiential Avoidance and Forgiveness as Mediators in the Relation Between Traumatic Interpersonal Events and Posttraumatic Stress Disorder Symptoms." *Journal of Social and Clinical Psychology* 24, no. 7 (2005): 1003–29.

Orth, Ulrich, Leo Montada, and Andreas Maercker. "Feelings of Revenge, Retaliation Motive, and Posttraumatic Stress Reactions in Crime Victims." *Journal of Interpersonal Psychology* 21, no. 2 (2006): 229–43.

Plante, Thomas G., and Allen C. Sherman, eds. "Faith and Health: Psychological Perspectives." *Journal of Guilford*, 2015: 107–38.

Reed, Gayle L., and Robert Enright. "The Effects of Forgiveness Therapy on Depression, Anxiety, and Posttraumatic Stress for Women After Spousal Emotional Abuse." *Journal of Consulting and Clinical Psychology* 74, no. 5 (2006): 920–29.

Schwartz, Sunny, and David Boodell. *Dreams from the Monster Factory: A Tale of Prison, Redemption, and One Woman's Fight to Restore Justice to All*. New York: Scribner, 2009.

South Africa. "Restorative Justice." 2014. Accessed January 10, 2015. RestorativeJustice.org

Steinberg, Jonny. *The Number: One Man's Search for Identity in the Cape Underworld and Prison Gangs.* Cape Town: Jonathan Ball, 2004.

Turney, Kristin. *Stress Proliferation Across Generations? Examining the Relationship Between Parental Incarceration and Childhood Health.* Irvine: University of California Press, 2015.

Twersky, Isadore, ed. *A Maimonides Reader.* Library of Jewish Studies. Springfield, MA: Behrman House, 1972.

Walton, Elaine. "Therapeutic Forgiveness: Developing a Model for Empowering Victims of Sexual Abuse." *Clinical Social Work* 33, no. 2 (2005): 193–207.

Wiesenthal, Simon. *The Sunflower: On the Possibilities and Limits of Forgiveness.* New York: Knopf, 2008.

Wilson, Kevin M., Timothy D. Wilson, and Daniel T. Gilbert. "The Paradoxical Consequences of Revenge." *Journal of Personality and Social Psychology* 95, no. 6 (2008): 1316–24.

Worthington, Everett L., Jr. *The Pyramid Model of Forgiveness: Some Interdisciplinary Speculations About Unforgiveness and the Promotion of Forgiveness.* Philadelphia: Templeton Foundation, 1998.

Worthington, Everett L., Jr., Jack W. Berry, and Les Parrott III. "Unforgiveness, Forgiveness, Religion, and Health." *ResearchGate,* 2001: 107–38.

Worthington, Everett L., Jr., et al. "Forgiveness and Justice: A Research Agenda for Social and Personality Psychology." *Journal of Consulting and Clinical Psychology,* 2006: 337–48.

Zehr, Howard. *Changing Lenses: A New Focus for Crime and Justice.* New York: Herald Press, 1990.

———. *The Little Book of Restorative Justice.* Intercourse, NY: Good Books, 2002.

3. The Arts behind Bars: Uganda & Jamaica

Andrinopoulos, Katherine, et al. "Homophobia, Stigma and HIV in Jamaican Prisons." *Culture, Health, and Sexuality: An International Journal for Research, Intervention and Care* 13, no. 2 (2015): 187–200.

Brown, Ian, and Frank Dikotter. *Cultures of Confinement: A History of the Prison in Africa, Asia, and Latin America.* Ithaca, NY: Cornell University Press, 2007.

Freire, Paulo. *Pedagogy of the Oppressed.* 30th Anniversary Edition. New York: Bloomsbury, 2014.

Halperin, Ronnie, Suzanne Kessler, and Dana Braunschweiger. "Rehabilitation Through the Arts: Impact on Participants' Engagement in Educational Programs." *Journal of Correctional Education* 63, no. 1 (2012): 6–23.

Jamaica Constabulary Force. "Jamaica Constabulary Force." March 2012. jcf.gov.jm

Jarjoura, Roger G., and Susan T. Krumholz. "Combining Bibliotherapy and Positive Role Modeling as Alternative to Incarceration." *Journal of Offender Rehabilitation* 28, nos. 1–2 (1998): 127–39.

Kidd, David C., and Emanuele Castano. "Reading Literary Fiction Improves Theory of Mind." *Science,* n.s., 342.6156 (2013): 377–80.

Matshili, Edna. "Jailhouses: Life in Ugandan Prisons." *Consultancy Africa Intelligence.* September 2, 2011. Accessed March 5, 2015. http://consultancyafrica.com/index.php?option=com_con tent&view=article&id=842:jailhouses-life-in-ugandan -prisons&catid=91:rights-in-focus&Itemid=296

Mendonca, Maria. "Prisons, Music, and Rehabilitation Revolution: The Case of Good Vibrations." *Journal of Applied Arts & Health* 1, no. 3 (2010): 295–307.

Prison Arts Coalition. *Prison for Arts Coalition Music.* 2008. Accessed April 5, 2015. theprisonartscoalition.com

Salzman, Mark. *True Notebooks: A Writer's Year at Juvenile Hall.* New York: Vintage Books, 2007.

Sarkin, Jeremy, ed. *Human Rights in African Prisons.* Vol. 10. New York: HSRC Press, 2008.

Schonteich, Martin. "Hidden Cruelties: Prison Conditions in Sub-Saharan Africa." *World Politics Review,* 2015. Accessed April 30, 2015. worldpoliticsreview.com/articles/15366/hidden-cruelties -prison-conditions-in-sub-saharan-africa

Silber, Laya. "Bars Behind Bars: The Impact of a Woman's Choir on Social Harmony." *Journal of Education Research* 7, no. 2 (2005): 251–71.

Song of Redemption. Film produced by Fernando Garcia-Guereta, directed by Amanda Sans Miquel Galofré, 2013.

Soundcheck. "Blending Music with Rehabilitation." February 5, 2010. *WNYC*. Accessed March 10, 2015. soundcheck.wnyc.org/story /43147-blending-music-with-rehabilitation/Feb52010

4. Women and Drama: Thailand

D'Arcy, Anne Jeanne. "Power Points: Battered Women as Authors." In *Anne D'Arcy: Domestic Violence Research Publications*. Oakland: University of California Press, 2008.

Enos, Sandra. *Mothering from the Inside: Parenting in a Women's Prison*. Albany: SUNY Press, 2000.

Kalyanasuta, Kanokpun, and Atchara Suriyawong. "Testimonies of Women Convicted of Drug-Related Offenses: The Criminal Justice System and Community-Based Treatment of Offenders in Thailand." *Resource Material Series* 61 (2002): 265–93.

Kristof, Nicholas. "Serving Life for This?" *New York Times*, November 13, 2013. Accessed January 2014. nytimes.com/2013/11/14/opinion /kristof-serving-life-for-this.html?_r=0

Moller, Lorraine. "Project Slam: Rehabilitation through Theatre at Sing Sing Correctional Facility." *International Journal of the Arts in Society* 5, no. 5 (2011): 1–60.

Napaporn, Havanon, et al. *Lives of Forgotten People: Narratives of Women in Prison*. Office of the Affairs, under the Royal Initiative of HRH Princess Bajrakitiyabha, 2012.

Osler, Mark. "We Need Al Capone Drug Laws." *New York Times*, May 4, 2014.

Richie, Beth. *Arrested Justice: Black Women, Violence, and America's Prison Nation*. New York: NYU Press, 2012.

Sudbury, Julia, ed. *Global Lockdown: Race, Gender, and the Prison-Industrial Complex*. New York: Routledge, 2005.

Talvi, Silja J. A. *Women Behind Bars: The Crisis of Women in the U.S. Prison System.* Emeryville: Seal Press, 2007.

United Nations Economic and Social Council. "United Nations Rules for the Treatment of Women Prisoners and Non-custodial Measures for Women Offenders" (the Bangkok Rules). July 22, 2010. Accessed January 12, 2015. penalreform.org/wp-content /uploads/2013/07/PRI-Short-Guide-Bangkok-Rules-2013 -Web-Final.pdf

Women's Prison Association. April 10, 2015. Accessed April 10, 2015. wpaonline.org

5. Solitary and Supermaxes: Brazil

American Civil Liberties Union. "Alone and Afraid: Children Held in Solitary Confinement and Isolation in Juvenile Detention and Correctional Facilities." New York: American Civil Liberties Union, 2014. aclu.org/files/assets/Alone%20and%20Afraid%20 COMPLETE%20FINAL.pdf

Bazelon, Emily. "The Shame of Solitary Confinement." *New York Times Magazine*, February 19, 2015.

Binelli, Mark. "Inside America's Toughest Federal Prison." *New York Times Magazine*, March 29, 2015.

Briggs, Chad. "Effect of SuperMaximum Security Prisons on Aggregate Levels of Institutional Violence." *Criminology* 41, no. 4 (2003): 1341–76.

Brown, Ian, and Frank Dikotter. *Cultures of Confinement: A History of the Prison in Africa, Asia, and Latin America.* Ithaca, NY: Cornell University Press, 2007.

Davidai, Shai, and Thomas Gilovich. "Building a More Mobile America— One Income Quintile at a Time." *Perspectives on Psychological Science* 10, no. 1 (2015): 60–71.

Dwyer, Jim. "Mentally Ill, and Jailed in Isolation at Riker's Island." *New York Times*, November 19, 2013.

Economist / The Americas. "Race in Brazil: Affirming a Divide." January 28, 2012.

Gawande, Atul. "Hellhole." *New Yorker*, March 30, 2009.

Guenther, Lisa. *Solitary Confinement: Social Death and Its Afterlives*. Minneapolis: University of Minnesota Press, 2013.

Kiernan, Paul. "U.N. Human-Rights Body Expresses Concern Over Brazil's Prisons." *Latin America Wall Street Journal*, January 8, 2014.

Kluger, Jeffrey. "Are Prisons Driving Prisoners Mad?" *Time*, January 26, 2014.

Kraus, Michael W., and Jacinth J. X. Tan. "Americans Overestimate Social Class Mobility." *Journal of Experimental Social Psychology* 58 (2015): 101–11.

Murray, Joseph, et al. "Crime and Violence in Brazil: Systematic Review of Time Trends, Prevalence Rates and Risk Factors." *Aggression and Violent Behavior* 18, no. 5 (2013): 471–83.

Ross, Jeffrey Ian. *The Globalization of Supermax Prisons*. New Brunswick, NJ: Rutgers University Press, 2013.

Salvatore, Ricardo D., and Carlos Aguirre. *The Birth of the Penitentiary in Latin America*. Austin: University of Texas Press, 1996.

Salvatore, Ricardo D., Carlos Aguirre, and Gilbert M. Joseph, eds. *Crime and Punishment in Latin America: Law and Society Since Late Colonial Times*. Durham, NC: Duke University Press, 2001.

Skarbek, David. *The Social Order of the Underworld: How Prison Gangs Govern the American Penal System*. New York: Oxford University Press, 2014.

Wacquant, Loïc. *Punishing the Poor: The Neoliberal Government of Social Insecurity*. Durham, NC: Duke University Press, 2009.

——. "Toward a Dictatorship over the Poor? Notes on the Penalization of Poverty in Brazil." *Journal of Punishment and Society* 5, no. 2 (2003): 197–205.

Waxler, Robert P., and Jean R. Trounstine, eds. *Finding a Voice: The Practice of Changing Lives Through Literature*. Notre Dame, IN: University of Notre Dame Press, 1999.

6. Private Prisons: Australia

American Civil Liberties Union. "Private Prisons." Accessed June 1, 2015. aclu.org/issues/mass-incarceration/privatization-criminal-justice/private-prisons

Bernstein, Nina. "Companies Use Immigration Crackdown to Turn a Profit." *New York Times*, September 28, 2011.

Bogle, Michael. *Convicts: Transportation and Australia.* Historic Houses Trust of New South Wales, 2009.

Bureau of Justice Assistance, U.S. Department of Justice. "Justice Reinvestment Initiative." January 2015. Accessed March 2015. bja.gov/programs/justicereinvestment/index.html

Cantu, Aaron. "4 Disturbing Reasons Private Prisons Are So Powerful." *Salon*, May 3, 2014. salon.com/2014/05/03/4_disturbing_reasons_private_prisons_are_so_powerful_partner/

Goulding, Dot, Guy Hall, and Brian Steels. "Restorative Prisons: Towards Radical Prison Reform." *Current Issues of Criminal Justice* 20, no. 2 (2008): 231–42.

Kirkham, Chris. "How Corporations Are Cashing In on the Worldwide Immigration Crackdown." *Huffington Post*, May 3, 2014.

Mason, Cody. "International Growth Trends in Prison Privatization." *The Sentencing Project*, August 2013. Accessed March 3, 2014. sentencingproject.org/doc/publications/inc_International%20Growth%20Trends%20in%20Prison%20Privatization.pdf

New South Wales Law Reform Commission. "Sentencing—Patterns and Statistics." In *Companion Report.* Sydney: New South Wales Law Reform Commission, 2013.

Schiraldi, Vincent. "Juvenile Crime Is Decreasing—It's Media Coverage That's Soaring." *Los Angeles Times*, November 22, 1999.

Simon, Jonathan. *Governing Through Crime: How the War on Crime Transformed American Democracy and Created a Culture of Fear.* Oxford: Oxford University Press, 2009.

Takei, Carl. "Prisons Are Adopting the Walmart Business Model." *Huffington Post*, September 29, 2014.

7. Reentry: Singapore

Gonnerman, Jennifer. *Life on the Outside: The Prison Odyssey of Elaine Bartlett*. New York: Macmillan, 2005.

Lee Kuan Yew. *From Third World to First: The Singapore Story: 1965–2000*. New York: HarperCollins, 2000.

Low, Donald. "How Not to Relapse." *OZY*, February 1, 2015. Accessed February 11, 2015. ozy.com/acumen/how-not-to-relapse/38931

National Institute for Crime Prevention and the Reintegration of Offenders (NICRO) Web site. Accessed March 28, 2014. nicro .org.za

Pager, Devah, Bruce Western, and Bart Bonikowski. "Discrimination in a Low-Wage Labor Market: A Field Experiment." *Journal of American Sociological Review* 74 (2009): 777–99.

Petersilia, Joan. "Prisoner Reentry: Public Safety and Reintegration Challenges." *Prisoner Journal* 81, no. 3 (2001): 479–529.

_____. *When Prisoners Come Home: Parole and Prisoner Reentry*. New York: Oxford University Press, 2003.

Pieris, Anoma. *Hidden Hands and Divided Landscapes: A Penal History of Singapore's Plural Society*. Honolulu: University of Hawaii Press, 2009.

Prisoner Reentry Institute. "Three-Quarter Houses: The View from the Inside." New York: John Jay College, 2013.

Schmitt, John, and Kris Warner. *Ex-Offenders and the Labor Market*. Washington, DC: Center for Economic and Policy Research, November 2010.

Seiter, Richard P., and Karen R. Kadela. "Prisoner Reentry: What Works, What Does Not, and What Is Promising." *Crime and Delinquency* 49, no. 3 (2003): 360–88.

Singapore. "Ministry of Law: Singapore." 2015. Accessed April 1, 2015. mlaw.gov.sg/content/minlaw/en.html

Stillman, Sarah. "Get Out of Jail Inc." *New Yorker*, June 23, 2014.

Travis, Jeremy. *But They All Come Back: Facing the Challenges of Reentry*. Washington, DC: Urban Institute Press, 2005.

Travis, Jeremy, and Christy Visher, eds. *Prisoner Reentry and Crime in America*. New York: Cambridge University Press, 2005.

Travis, Jeremy, Bruce Western, and Steve Redburn, eds. *The Growth of Incarceration in the United States: Exploring Causes and Consequences*. Washington, DC: National Academies Press, 2014.

Visser, Jaco, Timothy Williams, and Tanzina Vega. "A Plan to Cut Costs and Crime: End Hurdle to Job After Prison." *New York Times*, October 23, 2014.

Winerman, Lea. "Breaking Free from Addiction." *Monitor on Psychology* 44, no. 6 (2013): 30.

8. Justice? Norway

Adams, William L. "Norway Builds the World's Most Humane Prison." *Time*, May 10, 2010.

Christie, Nils. *Limits to Pain: The Role of Punishment in the Penal Policy*. Eugene, OR: Wipf and Stock, 2007.

———. *A Suitable Amount of Crime*. New York: Routledge, 2004.

Davis, Angela Y. *Abolition Democracy: Beyond Empire, Prisons, and Torture*. New York: Seven Stories Press, 2011.

Erlanger, Steven. "Amid Debate on Migrants, Norway Party Comes to Fore." *New York Times*, January 23, 2014.

Fisher, Max. "A Different Justice: Why Anders Breivik Only Got 21 Years for Killing 77 People." *Atlantic*, August 2012. Accessed January 15, 2015. theatlantic.com/international/archive/2012/08/a-different-justice-why-anders-breivik-only-got-21-years-for-killing-77-people/261532/

Frankl, Viktor E., Ilse Lasch, and Harold S. Kushner. *Man's Search for Meaning*. Translated by Ilse Lasch. New York: Beacon, 2006.

James, Erwin. "The Norwegian Prison Where Inmates Are Treated Like People." *Guardian*, February 25, 2013.

Larson, Doran. "Why Scandinavian Prisons Are Superior." *Atlantic*, September 2013.

Lewis, Jim. "Behind Bars...Sort Of." *New York Times*, June 6, 2009.

Mathiesen, Thomas. *The Politics of Abolition*. New York: Routledge, 2015.

Minnesota Department of Corrections. "The Effects of Prison Visitation on Offender Recidivism." St. Paul: Minnesota Department of Corrections, 2011.

New York Times. "Shrinking the Prison Population." Editorial. May 10, 2009.

Parens, Erik. "The Benefits of Binocularity." *New York Times*, September 28, 2014.

Pratt, John, and Anna Eriksson. "Contrasts in Punishment: An Explanation of Anglophone Excess and Nordic Exceptionalism." NY: Routledge, 2013.

_____. "Scandinavian Exceptionalism in an Era of Penal Excess." *British Journal of Criminology* 48, no. 3 (2008): 119–37.

Schenwar, Maya. *Locked Down, Locked Out: Why Prison Doesn't Work and How We Can Do Better*. Oakland: Berrett-Koehler, 2014.

Stevenson, Bryan. *Just Mercy: A Story of Justice and Redemption*. New York: Random House, 2014.

Subramanian, Ram, and Ruth Delaney. *Playbook for Change? States Reconsider Mandatory Sentences*. New York: Vera Institute of Justice, 2014.

Subramanian, Ram, and Alison James. *Sentencing and Prison Practices in Germany and the Netherlands: Implications for the United States*. New York: Vera Institute of Justice, 2013.

Ward, Katie, et al. "Incarceration within American and Nordic Prisons: Comparison of National and International Policies." *International Journal of Research and Practice on Student Engagement*, 2013, 10–50.

▌▌ OTHER PRESS

You might also enjoy these titles from our list:

KAFKA COMES TO AMERICA by Steven T. Wax

A public defender's dedicated struggle to rescue two innocent men from the recent Kafkaesque practices of our vandalized justice system

"In an enthralling, enraging narrative, Wax captures the damage that Guantánamo has done to America's reputation abroad, and shows how the legal fights on behalf of detainees might restore it." —*The New Yorker*

THE FAITHFUL SCRIBE by Shahan Mufti

A journalist explores his family's history to reveal the hybrid cultural and political landscape of Pakistan, the world's first Islamic democracy

"*The Faithful Scribe* is an impassioned and insightful look into the heart of a troubled but vital country. This is a history of Pakistan from the pen of a keen observer, whose own story represents Pakistan's past and whose vision reflects its hope for the future."
—Vali Nasr, *New York Times* best-selling author of *The Dispensable Nation: American Foreign Policy in Retreat*

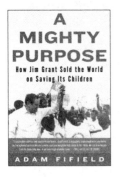

A MIGHTY PURPOSE by Adam Fifield

The inspiring story of how the iconoclastic humanitarian Jim Grant succeeded in saving the lives of tens of millions of children through his extraordinary ability to win over world leaders

"Adam Fifield's entertaining biography of the little-recognized Grant shows that entrepreneurs can appear in the most unpromising environments…Grant was the right man in the right place at the right time."
—*Wall Street Journal*